Welcome to the Trans Canada Trail in
Southern British Columbia

The Trans Canada Trail, when completed, will be the longest and most spectacular shared use trail in the world. It will provide a sensational recreational, tourist and educational amenity for all to enjoy. Hikers, cyclists, horseback riders, cross-country skiers and snowmobilers (where appropriate) can all explore this fantastic national trail.

This book describes what is surely going to be the most spectacular section of the Trans Canada Trail, the route through British Columbia. The trail has been designed as a multi-use route for all to enjoy. By using a combination of historical railway beds, various road systems and both new and established trail systems, it is possible to follow the route from Victoria through to the Alberta border. Stretching over 1,750 kilometres across southern B.C., the diversity of terrain is incredible and the scenery is breathtaking.

Detailed maps have been combined with route descriptions to allow you to follow the Trans Canada Trail in separate sections. For day trips and shorter extended trips, these section breaks will help you pick and choose the pieces of trail you wish to explore. For the long distance traveller, the section breakdowns make planning even easier. Other essential planning tools such as access points, camping and picnic locations, points of interest and highlights are all well documented throughout the guidebook.

The Trans Canada Trail: The British Columbia Route has also been designed with the armchair traveller in mind. A variety of pictures and interesting editorial comments have been added throughout the book to make it an enjoyable read. The very nature of the Trans Canada Trail is to learn more about your community. We have followed this trend by adding a variety of interesting facts pertaining to the route from historical notes to geographical points of interest.

Whether you are looking for a short day hike, a country bike ride or a long distance adventure, the *Trans Canada Trail: The British Columbia Route* will surely become your planning and travelling essential.

Special thank you to our corporate sponsors:

www.coastmag.com

BC Gas
Naturally
Resourceful.

BRITISH COLUMBIA TOURS.COM

D0761577

Mussio Ventures Ltd.

DIRECTORS
Russell Mussio
Wesley Mussio
Penny-Stainton Mussio

COVER DESIGN & LAYOUT
Farnaz Faghihi

SALES & MARKETING
Shawn Caswell
Jason Marleau

WRITERS
Jason Marleau
Russell Mussio

CANADIAN CATALOGUING IN

PUBLICATION DATA

Marleau, Jason, 1972-

Mussio Ventures & Trails BC present Trans
Canada Trail: the British Columbia route: a
detailed reference guide of the route across
southern British Columbia.

Includes index.
ISBN 1-894556-15-1

1. Trans Canada–Guidebooks. 2. British
Columbia–Guidebooks. 3. Trails–British
Columbia–Guidebooks. I. Mussio, Russell,
1969- II. Title. IV. Title: Trans Canada
Trail: the British Columbia route.

GV199.44.C22B74664 2001   917.1104'4

C2001-901189-X

Published by:

232 Anthony Court
New Westminster, B.C. V3L 5T5
P. 1-604-438-3474   F. 1-604-438-3470
E-mail: info@backroadmapbooks.com
www.**backroadmapbooks**.com

Acknowledgement

This book could not have been created without the hard work
and dedication of the Mussio Ventures Ltd. staff, Shawn
Caswell, Trevor Daxon, Farnaz Faghihi, Brett Firth, Dale Tober
and Jennifer White. Without their hard work and support, this
comprehensive trail guidebook would never have been completed as accurately as it was. We would also like to give a
special thank you to Leon Lebrun for his tireless effort to help
make this book and the Trans Canada Trail in Southwestern
BC a reality.

In addition there are many Trails BC volunteers and helpful
individuals who contributed invaluable information along the
route. They all deserve special mention:

Bill Archibald, Don Barnett, Donna Bishop, Rod Brown, Sue
Burnham, John Butterworth, Les Carter, Gillian Cooper, Dean
Corkill, Bob Dupee, Joan Field, Heather Gordon, Steve
Graham, Hanne Heintz, Dave Hignell, Jeanette Klein, Richie
Mann, Raymond Maslek, Lance Mitchell, Chris Moslin, Sergio
Mussio, Arlene Ridge, Ron Sherk, Murphy Skewchuck, Al
Skucas, Jim Stolth.

Most of all we would like to Nancy Mussio, Wesley Mussio,
Penny Stainton-Mussio and Heather K. Smith. Their patience
and support helped us during the many hours spent working on,
researching and writing the *Trans Canada Trail, the British Columbia Route* guidebook.

Disclaimer

Mussio Ventures Ltd. and Trails BC do not warrant that the
roads, trails, trestles, bridges or tunnels in this guidebook are
completely accurate. Also, Mussio Ventures Ltd. and Trails
BC do not warrant that the various roads, trestles, bridges or
tunnels in this guidebook can be walked, run, biked or rode.
Therefore, please be careful when using this or any source to
plan and carry out your outdoor recreation activity.

Please note that travelling on roads and trails is inherently
dangerous and without limiting the generality of the forego-
ing, you may encounter poor road or trail conditions, unexpected traffic, poor visibility and low or no road /trail maintenance. Please use extreme caution when travelling logging
roads and trails.

Please adhere to all signs and respect private property, especially as it relates to private railgrades owned by CN or CPR
and/or privately owned land. It is your responsibility to know
when and where road and trail closures and restrictions apply.

Table of Contents

Foreword 4
Message from the President 5
Volunteers 6
Things You Should Know 7-16
   Geography 7
   Weather / Climate 7-10
   Trail Etiquette 11
   Hazard 11-12
   Animals 13-14
   Insects 14
   Water 14-15
   Camping 15
   Service Providers 16
Helpful Hints 17-19
   Equipment 17
   Travel Distances 17-18
   Remote Biking / Hiking 18
   First-Aid / Emergency 18-19
   Winter Travel 19
How to Use This Book 20
Map Legend 21
Southern BC's Route Map 22
Vancouver Island Region 23-72
   Victoria 25-29
   Langford 30-35
   Shawnigan Lake 36-39
   Kinsol Trestle 40-42
   Cowichan Valley 43-49
   Chemainus 50-54
   Ladysmith 55-57
   Extention 58-60
   Nanaimo 61-64
   Saanich Peninsula/
   Swarts Bay 65-70
Southwestern BC Region 74-161
   West Vancouver 76-82
   North Vancouver 83-87
   Vancouver 88-94
   Burnaby 95-99
   Port Moody 100-103
   Coquitlam 104-109
   Maple Ridge 110-115
   Mission 116-119
   Abbotsford 120-125
   Cultus Lake 126-130
   Chilliwack River Valley 131-134
   Chilliwack Lake 135-139
   Silver Hope Valley 140-142
   Hope 143-147
   Coquihalla River 148-149
   Iago Station/
   Coquihalla Summit 150-153
   Coldwater River 154-157

Brookmere 158-160
Okanagan Region 162-230
   Brookmere 164-165
   Otter Valley 166-169
   Tulameen 170-173
   Princeton 174-178
   Erris Station 179-181
   Osprey Lake 182-185
   Trout Lake 186-188
   Summerland 189-191
   Penticton 192-196
   Chute Lake 197-201
   Myra Canyon 202-207
   Moculloch 208-210
   Arlington Lake 211-213
   Beaverdell 214-217
   West Kettle Valley 218-220
   Rock Creek 221-225
   Midway 226-228
Boundary Region 230-249
   Midway 232-233
   Greenwood 234-237
   Grand Forks 238-242
   Christina Lake 243-248
West Kootenay Region 250-273
   Rossland 252-258
   Trail 259-264
   Pend D'Oreille River 265-268
   Kootenay Summit 269-272
Rocky Mountains Region 274-330
   Kootenay Summit 276
   Upper Summit Creek/
   Summit Creek 277-279
   Creston Valley 280-282
   Creston 283-284
   Kid Creek 285-287
   Moyie River 288-289
   Moyie Lake 290-291
   Lumberton 292-294
   Cranbrook 295-299
   Fort Steele 300-302
   Bull River 303-304
   Jaffray 305-307
   Elko 308-311
   Fernie 312-315
   Hosmer 316-317
   Sparwood 318-320
   Highway3/Elkford 321-323
   Quarry Creek/ Elk River/
   Elk Pass 324-329

Index 332-334

Foreword

The Trans Canada Trail has long been a dream of many Canadians across the country. It is only now, after years of time and dedication that the Trans Canada Trail is beginning to reach a completed state in several parts of the country. The first province to officially complete their portion of the Trans Canada Trail was Prince Edward Island. As other provinces follow suit, the longest complete land-based trail in the world will become a reality.

Over the past few years with the growing publicity of the national trail initiative, the reality of the Trans Canada Trail has finally hit the communities across Canada and British Columbia. In British Columbia, the trail has been welcomed with open arms, especially in most rural areas of the province where the tourism dollar is a hot commodity and an important fabric of the local economies. National publicity has also created a surprisingly early demand for information on the vast trail network.

Over the past few years, outdoor recreation groups, such as Trails BC, have been inundated with e-mails and telephone calls requesting information on the Trans Canada Trail. With this need in hand Trails BC began the initial idea of creating a trail guide for the province. Trails BC later approached the independent outdoor publishing company, Mussio Ventures Ltd. to help create the project. Soon after, a partnership was formed to produce and publish Canada's first Trans Canada Trail guide. Proceeds from the sales of this book will go toward the establishment and maintenance of the trail in B.C.

From the initial research stage to the press, the combined efforts of Trails BC and Mussio Ventures Ltd. have literally helped shape the Trans Canada Trail in British Columbia. In the beginning, there were vast stretches of the province that had yet to be mapped or even considered for the Trans Canada Trail. Through perseverance and hard work, volunteers and research staff created a complete trail from the shore of the Pacific in Victoria to the Elk Pass in the Rocky Mountains. Some of this route is still in the planning stage so it is important to check locally, with Trails BC or **www.backroadmapbooks.com** for updates.

Trans Canada Trail: the British Columbia Route is the first complete publication on the Trans Canada Trail in British Columbia. All of us here at Mussio Ventures Ltd. and Trails BC hope you will indulge yourself in exploring this trail book. We have had some remarkable adventures in creating this guide and we hope it can help you plan some fantastic outdoor adventures that lifelong memories are made from.

Message From the Trails BC President

On behalf of Trails BC, I would like to thank Mussio Ventures Ltd. for creating this excellent guidebook to the Trans Canada Trail in British Columbia. It will be a valuable resource for everyone who visits or helps build the Trail.

The Trans Canada Trail is a work in progress. It began as a mere dream, and has now progressed to the point where a real route on the ground can be followed almost the whole way across BC. As more and more communities along the route realize the value of the Trans Canada Trail, we expect it to become an increasingly important part of their lives, and to be better and better developed and maintained. We look forward to the day when the Trans Canada Trail stands out everywhere as a clearly recognized, high quality amenity for the citizens of Canada.

The Trans Canada Trail has been made possible by the countless hours spent by many dedicated volunteers both in BC and across Canada. They have raised and donated the funds to build the Trail, searched for the best route, negotiated with land owners and managers for permission for the public to use the route, and have then gone out with their tools and "elbow grease" to clear trail, build bridges, install culverts and put up signs. The efforts of those individual volunteers have been greatly assisted by national corporate donors including Jeep, Canada Trust, McLean's Magazine, Canadian Geographic, Navitrak, and Tetra Pak. In communities all along the Trail, local businesses have donated key building materials and equipment. In 2000, The BC government declared the Trans Canada Trail its major Millennium project, created a special team to help build the Trail, and has continued invaluable support in virtually every aspect of its development.

Some sections of the Trans Canada Trail, such as the old Kettle Valley Railwail are well established, and used by thousands of visitors each year. Other sections, such as the route from Salmo to Creston, still need much concentrated effort. The Trans Canada Trail is not a one-time project. It is intended to endure for as long as Canada exists. It will always need the care of people who believe in it.

Trails BC is a non-profit society formed to coordinate and assist the volunteers building the Trans Canada Trail across BC. We welcome the participation of all who would like to be involved in this exciting venture – as trail builders, as stewards of the completed trail, or as donors of the resources needed to build and look after the Trail. If you would like to help, or to find out about the local volunteer group nearest to you, please contact the Trails BC office at:

Email: trailsbc@trailsbc.ca
Phone: (604) 737-3188 - Fax: (604) 738-7175

Happy trails to you!

Les Carter President, Trails BC

5

A special thanks to all the Volunteers who helped make the trail possible.

For more information on volunteering for the trail visit:

http://www.trailsbc.ca/

Things to Know

Geography

British Columbia is the third largest province in Canada with a landmass of 952,264 square kilometres. The province is blessed with varied geographical characteristics including the large mountains and temperate rainforest that are the stereotype of B.C. However, the province is also home to many other unique geographical landforms including desert terrain. The Trans Canada Trail travels through the southern portion of the province, creating the opportunity to experience this vast array of geographical conditions.

Vancouver Island is made up of mainly rolling mountains usually covered by thick vegetation. Although there are elevation gains along the Island section of the trail, the majority of the climb is from Victoria to the Shawnigan Lake area. The Lower Mainland lies along the Fraser Valley and makes up a good portion of the lower elevation areas along the Trans Canada Trail. High mountain peaks surround the Fraser Valley and the trail climbs as it approaches the Coquihalla Mountain Pass of the Coast Mountains.

On the east side of the Coquihalla Pass lies the Okanagan Valley, which is typified by rolling mountain terrain rather than high elevation mountains. Since much of the precipitation falls on the west side of the Coast Mountains, the Okanagan is the home of many semi-arid geographical forms. As the Trans Canada Trail leaves the Okanagan Valley towards the Purcell Mountains, areas such as Creston lie in almost mini temperate climates. Once on the east side of the Purcell Mountains, near Cranbrook, the arid mountain effect takes place again.

Finally, the Trans Canada Trail travels through perhaps the most significant geographical landmass in North America, the Rocky Mountains. Along the Elk Valley many mountain peaks lie in the range of 2,500 m-3,000 m (8,202 ft-9,842 ft) above sea level, making the Rockies a monumental geographical experience.

Weather / Climate

With the dramatic change in geography from Victoria to the Rocky Mountains, British Columbia also boasts significantly different weather conditions from region to region. Along the Trans Canada Trail, these differences can be even more dramatic due to elevation changes along the route.

In essence, as you climb into the higher elevated terrain, you should expect varied weather patterns based on the time of year. The mountainous terrain of the province affects weather systems quite dramatically. For example, along the Coquihalla Pass, a weather system that was raining heavily on the Lower Mainland hours before could create sudden snow squalls in a matter of minutes even during summer months.

The weather patterns have been generally outlined for the six different regions below:

Vancouver Island
Vancouver Island lies along the temperate zone of the Pacific Ocean, characterized by large amounts of precipitation throughout the year and a very mild climate. From Victoria to Nanaimo, you can expect rain throughout the spring and fall period with very little snow during the winter. If you are looking for a section of the trail to do in the colder months of the year, the Island section is the best alternative. Along the Island, the Trans Canada Trail does traverse some steep grades; however, the climate change due to the elevation change is not often significant.

January	Average Temperature	Average Precipitation
Victoria	3.1 °C/37.6 °F	137.7cm/5.4in
Nanaimo	3.2 °C/37.8 °F	166.8cm/6.6in

July	Average Temperature	Average Precipitation
Victoria	16.3 °C/61.3 °F	16.9cm/0.7in
Nanaimo	18.0 °C/64.4 °F	24.0cm/0.9in

Lower Mainland
From Vancouver to Hope there is very little elevation gain compared to some portions of the trail. The Trans Canada Trail traverses lower elevations much of the way; however there are a few exceptions, such as the alternate route over Sumas Mountain Park. In general, the climate that can be expected in this region is similar to Vancouver Island, as the region is quite temperate. Although much of the land has been cleared to make way for agriculture and development, less than two centuries ago the climate in this region supported one of the most lavish temperate rainforest ecosystems in North America.

January	Average Temperature	Average Precipitation
Vancouver	2.7 °C/36.9 °F	145.7mm/5.7in
Hope	2.4 °C/36.3 °F	204.3mm/8.0in

July	Average Temperature	Average Precipitation
Vancouver	17.3 °C/63.1 °F	31.3mm/1.2in

Hope   18.0 °C/64.4 °F   51.6mm/2.0in

Okanagan
The Okanagan is one of the most arid climates in Canada. In fact, the area between Osoyoos and Oliver, which is south of Penticton, is regarded as the only real desert region in Canada. In this region, you can expect very hot summer days at times with cool nights, while the winter can be quite chilly. The main mountain pass entering the Okanagan is the Coquihalla. This pass is prone to crazy weather throughout the year, so be sure to be prepared for virtually anything when out on the trail.

January	Average Temperature	Average Precipitation
Princeton	-8.2 °C/17.2 °F	47.8mm/1.9in
Penticton	-2.5 °C/27.5 °F	29.1mm/1.1in

July	Average Temperature	Average Precipitation
Princeton	17.2 °C/63.0 °F	25.7mm/1.0in
Penticton	20.1 °C/68.2 °F	23.9mm/0.9in

Boundary
The Boundary region marks a transition stage from the arid, even desert type climate of the Okanagan to the more temperate nature of the West Kootenays. Grand Forks is the prime example of this transition, as the grassy field terrain lies more to the west of the city while the temperate valley leading to Christina Lake lies to the east. The main geographical challenge in this section is the Dewdney Trail/Old Cascade Highway. The high elevation nature of this section of the trail can create unexpected mountain weather conditions along this stretch of the route.

January	Average Temperature	Average Precipitation
Grand Forks	-6.7 °C/19.9 °F	47.4mm/1.9in

July	Average Temperature	Average Precipitation
Grand Forks	20.5 °C/68.9 °F	28.1mm/1.1in

West Kootenay
This region is typified mainly by lush forests, which thrive on the generally increased amount of annual precipitation in the region. One word of caution is that the Trans Canada Trail traverses some mountainous terrain in this region, including from the mountain town of Rossland to the highest pass along the route, the Kootenay Pass. The Kootenay Pass is well known for its unpredictable weather and it is not uncommon for it to snow during July or September. When proceeding over the pass, be sure to be prepared for mountain weather.

January	Average Temperature	Average Precipitation
Trail	-3.2 °C/26.2 °F	50.1mm/2.0in

July	Average Temperature	Average Precipitation
Trail	19.9 °C/67.8 °F	26.0mm/1.0in

Note: Trail data is based on nearby reports from Castlegar, BC and Northport, Washington.

Rocky Mountains

The town of Creston marks the beginning of the Rocky Mountain section of the Trans Canada Trail through BC. The Creston Valley is an agricultural region that is known to have the mildest climate in the interior other than the Okanagan. As the trail climbs out of the valley towards Cranbrook, the climate changes to a more arid character with lower amounts of precipitation. The Kootenay River Valley can get hot during the summer, but it is still much cooler on average compared to the Okanagan. As the Trans Canada Trail travels into the Rockies past Fernie, you should begin to expect cooler weather patterns coupled with marginal mountain weather patterns. Since the trail travels through the Elk Valley, the chance of unpredictable weather is less compared to high elevations but is much more unpredictable compared to lower elevations.

January	Average Temperature	Average Precipitation
Creston	-5.0 °C/23.0 °F	58.9mm/2.3in
Cranbrook	-8.3 C/17.1 F	23.3mm/0.9in
Fernie	-7.9 C/17.8 F	31.4mm/1.2in

July	Average Temperature	Average Precipitation
Creston	18.7 °C/65.7 °F	23.7mm/0.9in
Cranbrook	18.2 C/64.8 F	32.8mm/1.3in
Fernie	16.6 C/61.9 F	35.1mm/1.4in

Note: Creston data is based on Porthill, Idaho. Fernie precipitation data is based on reports of nearby Eureka, Montana.

Trail Etiquette

Along any trail system, including the Trans Canada Trail, there is a code of etiquette. The code has evolved to ensure safety and limit environmental impact along the route in order for all users to enjoy it in the same state as you did. In general, the recommended rules of the route for trail travel is summed up by the following:

1) Travel only on marked routes especially on farmland/ranchland.
2) Respect private property and the privacy of nearby residents.
3) Take only pictures and nothing else from the area.
4) Leave no trace of your travels and carry out all garbage.
5) Camp at designated campsites only.

When on the trail, the general rule is that horses always have the right-of-way. Hikers yield to horses and bikers yield to everyone. When on a bike it is often easy to forget about other travellers along the trail. Since the Trans Canada Trail is a multi-use trail, bikers have to be aware of other users and anticipate where others may be when travelling along the trail. When passing hikers, be sure to let your presence be known by a call or bell, then slow down or even walk your bike, ensuring safe passage. If everyone follows these simple guidelines, everyone will be able to enjoy the Trans Canada Trail safely.

Hazards

Private Property

Large portions of the Trans Canada Trail system travel near or through private property. Many private property owners have graciously offered use of their lands to help complete this fantastic trail; therefore, it is essential to respect property owner's wishes. Trails BC has gone to great lengths to contact all private owners along the route and hopefully, there will be no problems; however, situations do change. If you do encounter an unexpected problem with a property owner along the trail, simply abide by their wishes and report the incident to Trails BC. Trails BC can then contact the owner and solve any concerns or find an alternate route around the problem area.

Tunnels

Much of the Trans Canada Trail through southern British Columbia follows old railbeds. One of the largest such sections is the abandoned Kettle Valley Railway. Most of the railbed has been converted to trail including portions with old rail tunnels. There has been extensive research on all of the tunnels that are noted as passable in this guidebook; however there are tunnels that are off or along the route that may look inviting to explore. We do not condone tunnel exploring, as deactivated tunnels have been deactivated for a reason and could be very dangerous.

When travelling through all tunnels it is common practice to carry a flashlight or headlamp, as some tunnels are so long that lighting in the tunnel can be a major problem. It is also recommended that bikers walk through all tunnels due to low visibility, avoiding a collision with another passer by or more commonly hitting of rock debris along the tunnel floor. One last hazard that you may encounter in tunnels along the route are cattle. Near ranching areas, cattle sometimes will group in tunnels to find shade or solace from inclement weather.

Bridges/Trestles

Trestles and bridges make up some of the most spectacular scenery and experiences along the Trans Canada Trail. All bridges and trestles are generally safe for travel as outlined and many have been refurbished strictly for the enjoyment of Trans Canada Trail users. However, over time conditions can change and a judgement call may have to be made if you feel safe to travel across. Be sure to abide by all posted signs, as a wash outs or landslides can create unsafe conditions. A highly recommended practice for bikers is to dismount and walk along trestles, especially trestles without railings.

Wash Outs/Landslides

Wash outs and landslides are a regular occurrence in British Columbia and must be adapted to when encountered. Annually, it is almost guaranteed that portions of the trail will be damaged by a wash out or landslide. If you happen upon a new landslide or wash out, be sure to contact Trails BC to report the site to ensure speedy repair or posting of the problem for other users.

Road Crossings

Along many parts of the trail, especially in the urban sections of the Trans Canada Trail, it is impossible to avoid road and highway crossings. Be sure to have a clear view of oncoming traffic and use extra caution when crossing busy highways. Hopefully, in the future, busy crossing will be limited and perhaps traffics lights or alternate routes around the crossing will be added.

Animals

Bears

Other than in urban areas, bears can be encountered along the entire Trans Canada Trail in British Columbia. Black bears and grizzly bears are two types of bears that can be found along the trail. Black bears can be found throughout the entire rural stretches of the trail, while grizzly bears are found predominantly in the region from the Okanagan to the Rocky Mountains. While an encounter with any bear is rare, encountering a grizzly is very rare since the animal frequents remote alpine areas much of the year.

Although the possibility of a bear encounter may seem intimidating, it must be remembered that bears are inherently extremely shy animals and are rarely aggressive to humans. In reality, you have a better chance at being struck by lightning than being attacked by a bear. This does not mean that you should disregard the animal completely. The best way to avoid an encounter is to make your presence known by making noise. While on a bike or when hiking, ringing a bell or singing can alert the animal and if they hear you, it is almost certain they will run away. Be alert in prime areas, such as near rivers or berry patches, while also looking for signs such as hair on trees (used for scratching) or bear scat (feces). It is this type of awareness that will help avoid the confrontation well before it even happens.

When camping in bear country it is essential that you keep a clean campsite free of garbage. Be sure to hang the food pack with all the scented items between two trees well away from the ground and the tree trunks. If a bear does travel to your site, it will soon realize that there is nothing there to get at and move on.

Cougars

Over the past few years, cougar attacks have been in the news. The large feline has always been known to attack the odd dog and cat but rarely bother humans. The Trans Canada Trail passes through large tracts of cougar territory, although the threat that this animal poses is minimal, especially when travelling in groups. Attacks are extremely rare and are often a case of mistaken identity.

Cattle

A popular animal that is encountered along the Trans Canada Trail are cattle. There are large sections of the trail that travel next to or through ranch land, with cattle free to roam the area. Although cattle are virtually harmless, be sure to not to bother the animals, as they are important and private livestock. A marquee of cattle country that you may want to keep an eye open for is the cattle guard. Cattle guards can be found across sections of the Trans Canada Trail in a number of areas. To avoid injury, be sure to dismount off your bike when crossing any cattle guard.

Snakes

Rattlesnakes can still be found from the Naramata area south to Osoyoos in British Columbia. Rattlers are encountered occasionally along the Kettle Valley Railway bed and can be easily avoided. The snake has very poor sight and hearing, making it imperative that you avoid approaching the creature at close range.

Insects

The two main biting insects that travellers should be prepared for are mosquitoes and ticks. In general, the mosquito population is not a dramatic hindrance as it is in other parts of the country. Basically, expect mosquitoes in late spring/early summer, dissipating gradually through the summer months. By the late summer/fall, most of BC is relatively mosquito free, although this may not be true at higher elevations. Since the season is a microcosm of the season at lower elevations, the situation may be significantly different at the higher elevation level. To ward off mosquitoes it is best to cover you body by wearing pants and a long sleeve shirt. There are also a variety of natural and not so natural deterrent sprays available on the market.

Ticks are perhaps a larger irritant than mosquitoes, as they often find their way up pant legs and into shirts and begin burrowing into the skin. Ticks are found more prevalently in the spring and are best avoided by tucking in your shirt and pants to hinder their travel. The sprays mentioned above can also be effective in warding off this tiny critter.

Water

Even though British Columbia's hundreds of kilometres of cool clear streams, rivers and lakes may look like pure, untouched sources, the fact of the matter is many of Southern BC's water sources contain the organism Giardia. Giardia causes the sickness better known as 'beaver fever', and can be contracted by drinking a contaminated water source. Although the common thought is that animals contaminate water sources, it is actually most often contaminated by human excrement during the ever increasing use of the backcountry. To avoid Giardia there are three recommended things you can do to backcountry water:

1) Use a water filter pump.
2) Boil all water for minimum of ten minutes.
3) Use iodine tablets.

The best and most preferred method is to spend the hundred dollars or so on a filter, as boiling water is a nuisance and iodine tablets taste horrible.

Camping Opportunities

The Trans Canada Trail in British Columbia basically offers four options if you plan to camp. Provincial parks, forestry recreation sites, private campgrounds and Crown land or wilderness camping all have their own benefits and attractions.

1. Provincial Park Campgrounds range from well-developed to rustic campsites. They are well kept camping areas that usually have a host on site. Picnic tables, fire rings and wood, water and washrooms of varying degrees are always offered. They are often open from May through October with a nightly fee over $10/night. Discover Camping (1-800-689-9025 or 1-604-689-9025 in Greater Vancouver, **www.discovercamping.ca**) allows you to find out more information or reserve certain provincial park campgrounds.
2. Forestry Recreation Sites also range from well-developed to rustic campsites. The larger, more popular sites have a host on-site from May through October and charge a $10 fee ($5 is you have an annual pass). The smaller, more rustic sites have a nightly fee of $8 or an annual fee of $27 and are user maintained with very basic facilities. Regardless of which type of site you visit, one should expect a wilderness type camping area. Picnic tables, fire rings and an outhouse or two may or may not be available. Camping is permitted year-round.
3. Private Campgrounds range in quality and price. They are usually a little more expensive but offer a lot more amenities such as hot water. We have tried to list a few of the camping and/or better accommodation options at the back of each region. Please try to support these sponsors of the *Trans Canada Trail: The British Columbia Route* guidebook.
4. Crown land or wilderness camping is the only free option. Although this type of camping can be fun, one has to be totally self-sufficient and be prepared for all sorts of unexpected things. Please ensure you practice no-trace camping and do not trespass on private property.

Service Providers

At the end of each region, you will find added information on contacts in the region for things like accommodations, repairs, etc. These sponsors have taken the opportunity to financially support the Trans Canada Trail guidebook initiative and are recommended stops along the trail. These sponsors will help make planning your trip all the easier. Simply flip to the back of the region to find what you need to help complete your trip along the way.

The organization, British Columbia Tours, has quickly become one of BC's most dynamic eco-tour based organizers in the province. Whether you are a first time trail traveller, or have years of experience, British Columbia Tours offers a variety of services that may indeed help your trip run a little smoother. The company has established an in depth website for tour planning and also offers a toll free phone service helping visitors plan outdoor vacation adventures. In addition to a planning service, British Columbia Tours now offers fully guided mountain biking tours throughout the Okanagan, specializing in the spectacular Myra Canyon portion of the Trans Canada Trail. Other guided services include alpine fly-fishing, golfing vacations and guided wine tours. For all your travel needs be sure to visit **www.britishcolumbiatours.com** or call toll free **1-800-797-6335.**

Pricing Information :

1 Day Mountain Biking Tours :
-   Myra Canyon Bike Tour
-   Big White To Kelowna Bike Tour
$ 30 Per Person / You provide your own bike
$ 50 Per Person / Mountain Bike Included
Multi-Day Mountain Biking Tours
-   Kettle Valley Railway Tour (18 Trestles, 2 Tunnels, Overnight in rustic log cabins)
-   Big White to Kelowna Tour (Stopping for remote fishing along the way)
$ 160 Per Person / Per day (Includes food and accommodation)
Guided Alpine Fishing
-   Over 30 fabulous lakes within 1 hour of Kelowna
$150-$200 Per Person.

Helpful Hints

Equipment

The equipment required for a trip along the Trans Canada Trail will vary from trip to trip and depends on which activity you choose to do. If travelling on a bike be sure your group travels with the basic tools needed to make emergency repairs to your bike. This should definitely include a tire repair kit and pump.

For all travellers, the basic essential is proper outerwear and footwear. Be sure to dress in layers, in order to enable you to peel off or add clothing as needed to adjust your comfort level. When travelling over high elevation terrain this is extra important, as sudden weather changes can quickly put a damper on your outdoor fun. Footwear is often overlooked by novice trippers, although once you have experienced improper footwear along a day of hiking or biking, you are sure never to make that mistake again. Many hikers prefer boot type footwear to increase ankle support and reduce the chance of an ankle injury. Bikers should have properly fitted shoes that do not slip easily from the pedal confine, yet will allow you to get your foot out in the case of a fall.

Most experienced travellers have preferences and some established items that they take along on trips, however, we have compiled a basic checklist to help planning of your trip. The checklist is based on the premise that a portion of your route will be travelling through some rustic terrain:

Day Trip Necessities	Long Distance Additional Necessities
- Matches/lighter	- Tent
- Camera & film	- Extra clothing
- Flashlight and/or headlamp	- Lantern and/or candles
- Bug spray/sunscreen	- Water purifier
- First-aid kit (including iodine tablets)	- Sleeping bags
- Bush money (toilet paper) and trowel	- Tarp
- Raingear and/or wind gear	- Biodegradable soap, towel and other items
- Guidebook/map(s)	- Garbage bags
- Compass	- Rope
- Bell/whistle	- Sleeping pad or air mattress
- Multi purpose knife	- Lightweight camping stove
- Extra socks	- Fuel
- Food	- Cooking gear (pots, plates, cups and utensils)
- Water (bottles or skins)	- Extra batteries for flashlight and/or headlamp
- Backpack and/or fanny pack	- Lightweight collapsible saw

Travel Distances

Estimating the distance that you can cover along the Trans Canada Trail is a challenging endeavour because there are many variables that play a role in determining your rate of travel. The main factors include your experience, physical well being, weather and the terrain travelled. With this in mind, we have created a very basic framework of travel times to be used for basic planning purposes only. The daily averages below are based on continuous travel for 5 day stretches with 8 hour days (6 hours of actual travel):

Hiker

Lightweight pack, sleeping and eating in a facility each night   25km (15.5mi)
20kg (44lb) pack, tenting, filtering water, cooking meals   15km (9.3mi)

Biker (Based on mountain bikes)
Riding light with small pack, emergency supplies and water   60km (37.3mi)
20kg (44lb) in panniers, tenting, filtering water, cooking meals   40km (24.8mi)

Horseback Rider
Travelling light with minimum rations with tent and sleeping bag   25km (15.5mi)
Travelling with pack horse carrying full equipment, food and feed   20km (12.4mi)

Remote Biking / Hiking
Along several stretches of the Trans Canada Trail in British Columbia, the terrain can be very remote making travel to urban development or the nearest home challenging in case of an emergency. If you plan to travel through these remote sections of the route it is imperative that you leave a detailed itinerary with friends or family and check in on a regular basis to ensure your safety. In case of a problem, it may take a person days to find help. In the event that the emergency is so serious that you are stuck in the wilderness or lost, if you fail to check in, a search and rescue party will be sent out to find you.

First-Aid/ Emergency
On any trip, especially long distance trips, all travellers in your group should have a basic understanding of first aid. Although injury is rare, literally anything can happen out there from a heart attack, a sprained ankle, or simply heat stroke. Your group should be prepared for all situations and have a first-aid kit available. Depending on the remoteness and length of your trip, you can adjust the necessities required to carry on your first-aid kit. Two of the most common injuries obtained while biking or hiking are heat exhaustion, heat stroke and hypothermia.

Heat Exhaustion and Heat Stroke

Almost everyone has experienced the effects of heat exhaustion at one time or another. Heat exhaustion is created by salt and water deprivation while in the hot sun. Heat stroke is a potentially serious condition disabling the body's ability to regulate its core temperature. Both of these conditions can be easily avoided by drinking plenty of water along the trail and knowing your limits. If you feel lightvheaded or weak you may be suffering from heat exhaustion. Quickly find some shade to take a break, eat a little and drink plenty of water.

Hypothermia

The over cooling of the core temperature of your body causes hypothermia. This can be caused at any time of the year, especially when travelling in changing climatic regions such as along mountain passes. Generally cold temperatures, wetness or even wind chill can cause hypothermia. Wetness is perhaps one of the most underestimated causes of hypothermia. During the spring and early summer months, near freezing mountain runoff water can cause hypothermia. Deceivingly, the air temperature may be 15 °C in the area but if you are immersed in runoff water for less than a minute, hypothermia can set in.

Be sure to be aware of the factors and dress in layers in order to remove or add clothing as required for comfort. Symptoms include dizziness, lack of co-ordination, slow pace, difficulty in speaking and uncontrollable shivering. To treat hypothermia proceed with the following three basic steps:

1) Prevent additional loss of body heat (add clothing, blankets, etc.).
2) Use external heat sources to warm the victim (ie, fire, embrace).
3) Supply hot fluids and food.

If the victim is wet, remove all wet clothing and put on a dry outfit. If condition persists, seek medical attention.

Winter Travel

Winter travel along the Trans Canada Trail is an excellent option to avoid the mid-winter blues. On Vancouver Island and Southwestern BC, travel along the trail is usually snow free; however, obviously much cooler than during the summer months. For interior travel along the Trans Canada Trail, cross-country skiing and snowshoeing is a very good alternative as large tracts of the trail are relatively flat, making for ideal winter travel conditions. Another interesting travel option along the trail is snowmobiles. Snowmobiles are to be the only motorized mode of travel permitted along the trail and can be a great way to see the backcountry during the winter.

How to Use This Book

The Trans Canada Trail Guide: The British Columbia Route is divided into six different regions for your planning convenience. Within each region there is the complete set of maps required to follow the trail along with written text on the entire route. The six regions for the Trans Canada Trail: The British Columbia Route area:

1) Vancouver Island
2) Southwestern BC
3) Okanagan
4) Boundary
5) West Kootenay
6) Rocky Mountains

Maps

Each region is complete with colour 1:100,000 scale maps that lie on a north south plain unless specified. The urban areas around Victoria, Nanaimo and Vancouver have larger scale 1:50,000 scale maps to provide more detail.

Each map throughout the book is named according to a main focal point along that portion of the trail, such as a town or geographical feature. This makes for quick and easy map referencing when glancing at sections throughout the book.

In accordance with the map key, each map offers recreational symbols marking various activities such as campsites or other trail systems. The actual official Trans Canada Trail route is highlighted with a dark red hue, while side routes or potential future routes are marked with a lighter red hue making for quick and easy trail identification.

Text

The text portion of the guidebook describes all the primary aspects needed to help travel along a certain section of the Trans Canada Trail. As you may notice on the maps, there are numbered points along the route, which co-ordinate with the text portion in the book. For example, on the map of Victoria the section from point 3-4 is marked as the Galloping Goose Trail portion of the Trans Canada Trail. To read the detailed description of this part of the Trans Canada Trail, simply flip to section 3-4 in the text portion of the book. Each region is divided into several individual sections, helping break up the complete route making for both easier long distance and day trip planning.

Trans Canada Map Legend

Scale:

1cm = 1km   1:100,000
1cm = 0.5km   1:50,000

(1) Trail break points

1cm = 1km

Main TCT Route
Alternate/Future Route

Line Definition:

Highway ....
Main Road ....
City road ....
Logging road....................
Forestry spur road ....
Trail / Old Road ....
Route (Undeveloped Trail) ....
Ferry Route ....
Transmission line ....
Oil/gas Pipeline ....
Railway ....

Trail activities:

Hiking...............................
Cycling..............................
Horseback Riding.....................
Cross Country Skiing ....
Snowmobiling ....

Recreational Activities:

Anchorage...........................
Boat Launch.........................
Campsite / Limited Facilities ....
Campsite / Trailer Park ....
Picnic Area/ Rest Area.................
Paddling (canoe-kayak) ....
Golf Course..........................
Swimming ....
Beach ....

Miscellaneous:

Airport / Airstrip ....
Ferry.......................................
Forestry Lookout, water tank ....
Gate..
Highways ....
Trans-Canada Hwy...........................
Interchange ....
Microwave Tower ....
Mine Site (abandoned) ....
Parking ....
Point of Interest, Historical feature............
Town, Village, Railway Station ....
Travel Information ....
Viewpoint, Lookout ....
Waterfall ....
Customs/border crossing......................
Hospital ....
School / remote hut ....
Trans Canada Trail Pavilion...................

Land Designation:

Urban Area ....

Indian Reserve ....

Provincial Park ....

City Park/ Wilderness Area ....

Dept. of Nat Defense (DND)/
Restricted Area ....

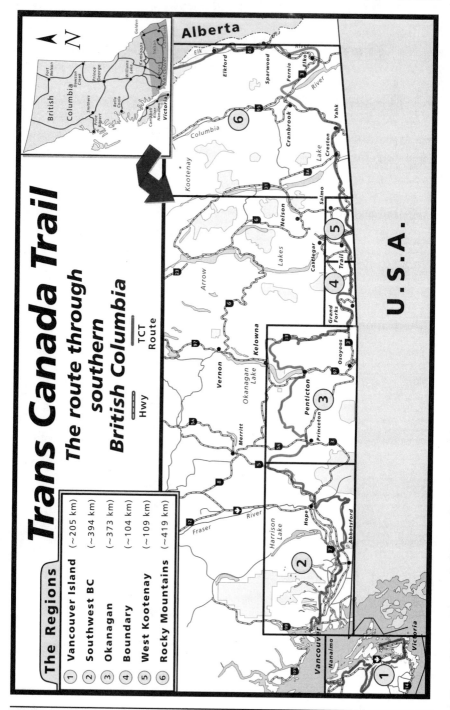

Trans Canada Trail

The route through southern British Columbia

TCT Route

Hwy

The Regions

1. Vancouver Island (~205 km)
2. Southwest BC (~394 km)
3. Okanagan (~373 km)
4. Boundary (~104 km)
5. West Kootenay (~109 km)
6. Rocky Mountains (~419 km)

Vancouver Island

The Trans Canada Trail through much of Vancouver Island has been established along several existing trail systems and similar to most of the province, along old abandoned railbeds. Perhaps one of the most notable features of the Island section is 'Mile Zero', which lies along the Pacific Ocean south of the city of Victoria. Through Victoria the trail follows established road routes and trail systems such as the Galloping Goose Trail. Heading north the route travels through old growth forest sections past the infamous Malahat eventually meeting up with an old railbed south of Shawnigan Lake. From Shawnigan Lake, the route traverses some of the most spectacular terrain along the entire Trans Canada Trail as it traverses along the Cowichan River Valley and back. From the city of Duncan north to Nanaimo, the route traverses along mainly semi-rural roads with scenic ocean views before entering the more wilderness section south of Nanaimo. The Island Region ends at the Departure Bay Ferry Terminal in Nanaimo. Along the Saanich Peninsula, a side route follows a combination of an old railbed, roads and trails to link travellers to the Swartz Bay Ferry Terminal.

Both hikers and bikers can easily share the majority of the Trans Canada Trail along Vancouver Island. Other than a few tight trail areas south of Nanaimo, there really is no reason why bikers cannot follow the same route as hikers throughout the entire trail. One drawback of the Island route for horseback riders are the large stretches of highway and paved road travel. Also, the highly developed areas around Victoria, Chemainus and Nanaimo are not suitable for horseback use. The temperate climate on the Island restricts cross-country skiing and there is virtually no chance to explore the route on snowmobile.

Currently, one of the main problem points along the Island portion of the Trans Canada Trail is the area from Victoria to the Malahat. In this section, the route follows the side of the highway through a steep gorge. Coupled with the lack of space along the highway and the often heavy traffic flow, this section can be unnerving, especially to hikers. An alternate route has been established along the Saanich Peninsula to Brentwood Bay, then across the ferry to Mill Bay just north of Malahat. Although much of the trail is well developed on Vancouver Island, there is a portion of trail from just north of Ladysmith to just south of Nanaimo that is currently under construction. We have provided an interim route to use until the planned route is completed. For up-to-date information on these proposed changes and/or any other developments along the Island contact Trails BC or visit **www.backroadmapbooks.com**.

Along the sections from Victoria to Shawnigan Lake, the route traverses through mainly urban areas, with help always nearby. This also holds true for the section from Lake Cowichan to Ladysmith. The most remote portions of the route on the Island are from Shawnigan Lake to Lake Cowichan and along the planned route from just north of Ladysmith to just south of Nanaimo. These wilderness sections are truly a highlight of the Island route.

Vancouver Island

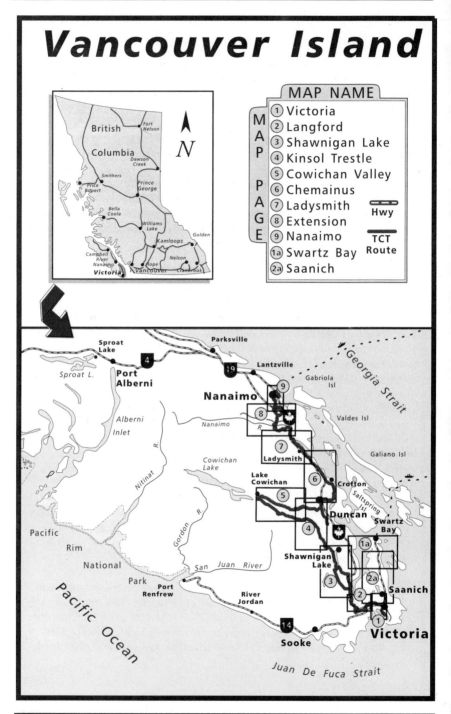

MAP NAME / MAP PAGE

1. Victoria
2. Langford
3. Shawnigan Lake
4. Kinsol Trestle
5. Cowichan Valley
6. Chemainus
7. Ladysmith
8. Extension
9. Nanaimo
1a. Swartz Bay
2a. Saanich

Hwy
TCT Route

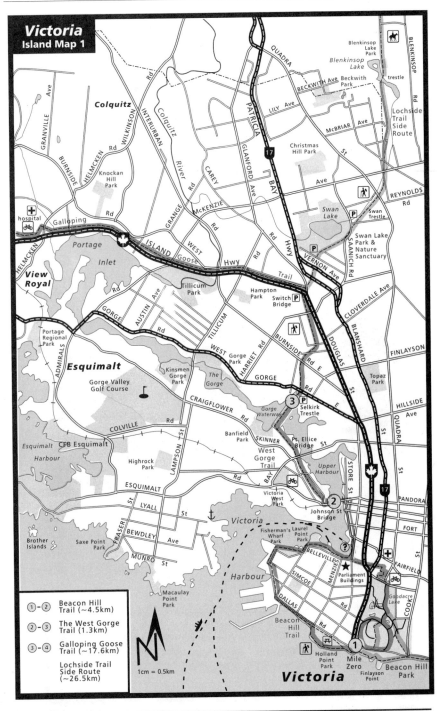

Victoria
Island Map 1

Colquitz

View Royal

Esquimalt

Lochside Trail Side Route

Swan Lake Park & Nature Sanctuary

Victoria

Victoria Harbour

Beacon Hill Park

Parliament Buildings

Victoria

①—② Beacon Hill Trail (~4.5km)

②—③ The West Gorge Trail (1.3km)

③—④ Galloping Goose Trail (~17.6km)

Lochside Trail Side Route (~26.5km)

1cm = 0.5km

Vancouver Island Map 1: Victoria

Vancouver Island Section 1-2
4.5 km
Beacon Hill Trail
At the edge of the majestic city of Victoria lies a large plaque signifying the beginning of this great national trail stretching across Canada. The 'Mile Zero' plaque lies in an open area of Beacon Hill Park in the southern end of Victoria. The scenic backdrop of the Strait of Juan de Fuca in the Pacific Ocean makes the perfect beginning to what is surely the most scenic portion of the Trans Canada Trail, the British Columbia Route.

Mile 0   J. Marleau

The curious thing about 'Mile Zero' is that it stands alone, without a trail to or from it. Despite this, it is definitely a suitable starting point to the B.C. section of the Trans Canada Trail.

For visitors that would like to explore the Pacific oceanfront near 'Mile Zero', there are a few moderate trails just south of the plaque and across Dallas Road. These trails lead down to the shoreline where you will find great views and photo opportunities of the cliffs and harbour areas of southern Victoria and Vancouver Island.

The most scenic walking route from 'Mile Zero' is a waterfront route that travels from 'Mile Zero' to the Johnson Street Bridge in the heart of Victoria. It is a pleasant walking route but cyclists may prefer to avoid the crowds and take the more direct route north through Beacon Hill Park.

From 'Mile Zero' you cross Dallas Road to a paved trail that leads to the Fonyo Beach Trails named after Steve Fonyo, the courageous one-legged runner who completed a run across Canada to raise funds for cancer research. The Fonyo Trails eventually lead back to Dallas Road where the route follows a number of different roads along the Victoria Harbour Front all the way to the British Columbia Parliament Buildings. From Dallas Road the waterfront route follows Erie Street, St. Lawrence Street, Kingston Street, Montreal Street and finally Belleville Street where the route passes the Parliament Buildings.

The Fairmont Empress   J. Marleau

From Belleville Street you will find yourself immersed in the essence of Victoria and it is best to follow Government Street north from there. Government Street will lead along the historic James Bay and eventually to Wharf Street. Following Wharf Street north will take you through a portion of Victoria's downtown and eventually to the Johnson Street Bridge.

For added scenic value, it is possible to travel on the paved paths in the Fisherman's Wharf area. This is a popular path with walkers, joggers and even in-line skaters. The route follows the harbour front most of the way to the Johnson Street Bridge.

The preferred cycling route, follows the many interconnecting trails that travel through Beacon Hill Park. Although no trail leads from the Mile Zero sign, the trails are easy to find and follow. Many of these trails are paved and there are plenty of benches to stop and enjoy this lovely urban park. At the north end of the park, you will need to cross Blanshard and Douglas Streets on Belleville Road. Continue west to the Parliament Buildings and then follow Government and then Wharf Streets north to the Johnson Street Bridge.

Seawall and Parliment Buildings   J. Marleau

Vancouver Island Section 2-3

1.3 km

The West Gorge Trail

The Trans Canada Trail route crosses the Johnson Street Bridge and the Upper Victoria Harbour, which is referred to as the Gorge Waterway. On the west side of the Gorge, an old railway has been converted to trail. For travellers interested in following the whole Trans Canada Trail route in Canada, you will find many such areas.

Selkirk Trestle   *L. Lebrun*

The immediate area along the western side of the Gorge is part of a transition of an old industrial harbour area. The surrounding scrub brush is slowly reclaiming the area and returning it to a more natural state. After crossing under the Port Ellice Bridge, you will see the Selkirk Trestle. The 300 m long trestle is a definite highlight of the route as it crosses the Gorge Waterway.

A biker alternative to this route is to follow the Johnson Street Bridge to Tyee Road. Tyee Road will take you all the way to Arthur Currie Lane (unmarked), which leads down to the Selkirk Trestle and the start of the Galloping Goose Trail.

The city of Victoria is one of British Columbia's oldest centres and was first established as a Hudson's Bay Company Fort in 1843. The fort was originally to be named Fort Comosak and then Fort Albert, although Fort Victoria was the overwhelming choice and was finalized on June 10, 1843. By 1862, a mere 19 years later, the area had grown significantly and Fort Victoria was incorporated as a city of the British Empire. The city would then become the capital of British Columbia in 1868; three years before British Columbia entered Confederation of the Dominion of Canada.

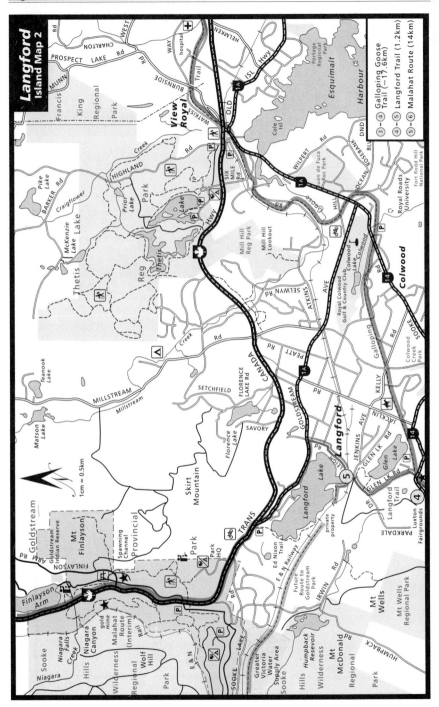

Vancouver Island Maps 2: Langford

Vancouver Island Section 3-4
~17.6 km
The Galloping Goose Trail

The Selkirk Trestle marks the beginning of the Galloping Goose Trail. Greater Victoria's historic railgrade has been converted into an extremely popular regional park and trail. At the southern end of the trestle, you will see a Trans Canada Trail Pavilion displaying the hundreds of donors to this section of the Trans Canada Trail. Along the way to the Luxton Fairgrounds in Langford, there are several different areas to access this popular trail system.

Galloping Goose Trail

J. Marleau

On the north side of the trestle the area is dominated by views of the harbour, the surrounding homes and industrial area. Continuing north you will cross over six urban roads including the busy Gorge and Burnside Roads before approaching the Switch Bridge. The Switch Bridge is a 100 m bridge that spans across the Trans Canada Highway.

At the north side of this bridge, the first official side route of the Trans Canada Trail continues north towards Swartz Bay. Formerly known as the Lochside Trail, this side route is now complete and includes impressive features such as the newly restored Blenkinsop Trestle. The multi-use trail links numerous parks, recreational facilities and neighbourhoods. In future years, there will be many of these side routes accessing the Trans Canada Trail.

The Trans Canada/Galloping Goose Trail continues from the north end of the Switch Bridge and parallels the highway over 6 km to Watkins Road (see Map 2). Along the way to Watkins Road, the paved trail crosses over the Wilkinson Road and Interurban Road bridges as well as an underpass under Helmken Road. The bridges and underpass make life for trail travellers much easier as the busy roads can be passed by without the anxiety of a high traffic crossing.

The route follows the Galloping Goose on the east side of Watkins Road and across the Trans Canada Highway to Atkins Road. Once at Atkins Road, the trail takes on a different character as it begins to follow an old railbed from here. The trail also travels through a more rural setting providing the tranquility of a semi-urban escape.

Galloping Goose Trail   J. Heighton

Along the railbed from Atkins Road, the Trans Canada/ Galloping Goose Trail traverses over the Colwood Delta. The delta is a massive gravel formation that was created over 12,000 years ago by glacial runoff from near Langford Lake. Most of the towns of Langford and Colwood are built upon this big gravel heap that can be over 90 metres in depth.

Along the old railway, the Trans Canada/Galloping Goose Trail crosses several streets while on its way towards the Luxton Fairgrounds. The more notable roads include the Sooke Highway and Jacklin Road. The trail eventually passes near Glen Lake before the intersection of the Sooke Highway and Glen Lake Road. At the intersection, the Trans Canada Trail travels north along Glen Lake Road.

The Galloping Goose Trail was officially established in 1989. It is a multi-use trail system that spans some 57 km from the heart of Victoria all the way to the historic site of Leechtown. The trail was laid out along the old railbed of the Canadian National Railway, which had originally established the connecting route from Sooke to Victoria in the early 1900's. The name "Galloping Goose" was adopted from the nickname the raucous gas powered rail cars adopted during their tenure as passenger cars along the route.

Vancouver Island Section 4-5

1.2 km
Langford Route

South of the town of Langford, a great route follows Glen Lake Road north from the Luxton Fairgrounds all the way to Langford Lake. Most of the trail is set along the west side of the road, travelling next to homes and a quiet community.

A short trail connects Glen Lake Road with Leigh Road. This trail offers a more secluded setting and crosses the E & N Railway.

Vancouver Island Section 5-6

14 km
Malahat Route

Beginning at the E & N Railway crossing, we have created an interim route for those wishing to follow the Trans Canada Trail route north to Nanaimo. This is not an ideal route and is not recommended for hikers and especially equestrian riders. For this reason, a scenic alternative route will be described at the end of this

For the angler at heart, there is a well established side route at the west end of Leigh Road. This short trail leads to the southern shore of Langford Lake, a surprisingly good trout fishery found in the heart of Langford. In the future, it is hoped to link this side route with the trails at the west end of Langford Lake. A trail system will skirt the E & N Railway before meeting up with the peaceful trail network of Goldstream Provincial Park.

region.

From the railway crossing, follow Leigh Road east to a gravel pathway on the east side of the road. This trail is known locally as the Leigh Trail. There are a few trail markers along the route to help you stay on the trail. The trail passes through a residential area and eventually intersects with Goldstream Avenue. Along Goldstream Avenue, the trail travels west approximately 1.6 km to the Trans Canada Highway.

The trip along Goldstream Avenue is generally easy, although the vehicle traffic is more noticeable compared to the side roads that lead up to the secondary highway. There is a decent shoulder along much of the road; however, there are a few tight sections along the way that should be passed with caution. Along a good portion of the route, you will find nice views of Langford Lake to the south.

Along the Trans Canada Highway, the route becomes quite challenging and should be travelled

Leigh Trail   J. Marleau

with due caution. The route travels north on the shoulder of the highway through Goldstream Provincial Park to the community of Malahat. There are a number of precarious sections along this stretch and hazards include heavy vehicle traffic, tight shoulders in sec-

View North of Goldstream   J. Marleau

tions and a moderate to difficult climb. In fact, this section of the highway climbs almost 275 m (900 feet) from Langford Lake towards the infamous Malahat Summit. Hikers should try to travel on the outside of the highway barrier whenever possible. Although there are various states of footing available, it is much better than walking next to the traffic.

Although this section offers its challenges, it also offers spectacular scenery as it winds its way through Goldstream Provincial Park and stands of old growth forest. It is highly recommended to stop at the park, especially when the salmon are spawning in the fall. In addition to a beautiful campground, day-trippers will find plenty of picnic tables available, along with barbecues and washrooms. If you plan on camping, resevations are highly recommended. Call or visit Discover Camping at 1-800-689-9025 or www.discovercamping.ca.

Before heading along this portion of the trail, be sure to check with Trails BC or www.backroadmapbooks.com for a possible alternate route. The proposed Trans Canada Trail route in this section was initially planned to skirt the west side of the Warwick Range along a powerline right-of-way. The route is temporarily re-routed because the proposed plan would have brought the trail right through an important Victoria watershed area. In the future, it is hoped that the Trans Canada Trail will be able to find an alternate route through this scenic backcountry.

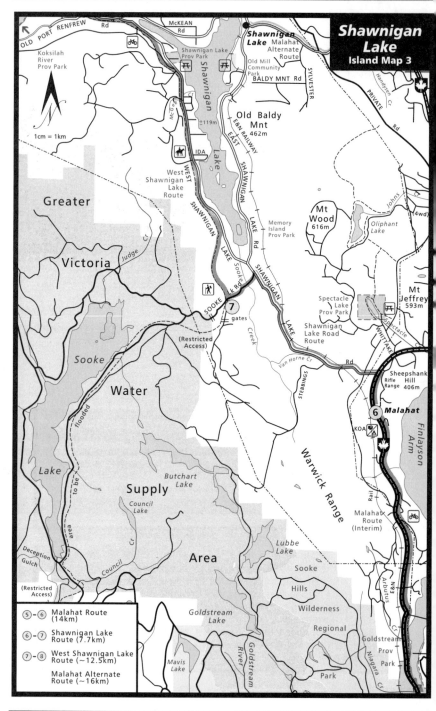

Shawnigan Lake
Island Map 3

1cm = 1km

Malahat Route (14km) — 5 - 6
Shawnigan Lake Route (7.7km) — 6 - 7
West Shawnigan Lake Route (~12.5km) — 7 - 8
Malahat Alternate Route (~16km)

Vancouver Island Map 3: Shawnigan Lake

Vancouver Island Section 6-7

7.7 km
Shawnigan Lake Road Route

Around the commu-
nity of Malahat, the
trek along the Trans
Canada Highway be-
comes easier due
mainly to larger
shoulders on the
highway. Just north
of Malahat, the Trans
Canada Trail route
turns west onto
Shawnigan Lake
Road. The road is
paved and travels
through a mix of ru-
ral settlement and
forested areas. The
route follows the road
for approximately 6
km before heading
southwest onto
Sooke Lake Road.

The gravel Sooke
Lake Road leads to
the trailhead of the
old abandoned rail-
way. The road winds
up a gradual grade to
the trailhead, which can be easily spotted on the north side of the road. There is
a small parking area available at the trailhead as well as a trail sign.

Big Cedar   J. Marleau

The Canadian Northern Pacific Railway, which is now the Canadian National Railway, established this railway in 1911 to connect Victoria with Port Alberni. Up until the mid 1980's, it served as a key link between the markets in Victoria and the timberlands of the north. Highlights along the 50 km route from south of Shawnigan Lake to Lake Cowichan include four major trestle crossings. Many of the sites throughout this section still use the old mileage markers denoting the number of miles on the CNR line to Victoria. By the time of printing both the Marie Canyon (Mile 66.2) and Holt Creek Trestles (Mile 59.7) will be restored. The 70.2 trestle is scheduled for completion by the fall of 2001. The Kinsol Trestle still remains as a formidable obstacle along this section of the Trans Canada Trail route.

Vancouver Island Section 7-8

~12.5 km
West Shawnigan Lake Route

Beginning at the trailhead off Sooke Lake Road, the Trans Canada Trail begins its path into some more remote areas. This is a fairly remote 50 km stretch that will introduce you to some of the wild terrain that makes British Columbia such a beautiful place to live and/or visit. Animals, abrupt changes in the weather and limited access to civilization are just some of the things to be prepared for.

The old railbed makes the perfect trail for all users and offers some fine views of Shawnigan Lake

Shawnigan Lake   J. Marleau

along the way. The trail crosses the McGee Trestle, an alternate access point, and offers fine views of Shawnigan Lake. Eventually, you will cross the Old Port Renfrew Road and it is recommended to continue north to the spectacular Kinsol Trestle (Mile 51). Although the trestle is currently closed, it is well worth the effort to visit the new viewing platform.

The Kinsol Trestle was originally erected in 1921 and remains the largest curved span wood trestle in the British Commonwealth. The original trestle was made out of local timber to cross the Koksilah River and still stands despite the ravages of time. The remains of the old Kinsol Mine, Kinsol Sawmill and the village of Kinsol rest nearby.

Equestrian riders and hikers who chose the alternate route from Victoria will rejoin the main Trans Canada Trail route at the Old Port Renfrew Road. Follow this main road west a short distance to the infamous Burnt Bridge (the trail shown on the south side of the river actually crosses private property and should be avoided).

The town of Shawnigan Lake is easily accessed off the Old Port Renfrew Road. Full facilities including all forms of accommodation are available in this popular recreational area.

At Burnt Bridge an imposing gate must be negotiated. Continue north on what is now a forest road for about 1.5 km and follow the trail (marked by a red arrow) east. Despite the signs, the trail does rejoin the old railgrade northeast of the Kinsol Trestle. This short 2.5 km section of trail is quite rough with sections of stairs and is not recommended for cyclists. Unfortunately, there is no easy alternative for cyclists at this time.

Camping is certainly possible in this area. On the south side of Burnt Bridge, informal campsites are found scattered in the woods. On the north side of the river, about 150 meters down the trail is an area suitable for camping. The location is much more quiet than the Koksilah River Provincial Park on the south side of the river.

Before heading out on this section of the trail, it is recommended to inquire with Trails BC or locally about the condition of the Kinsol Trestle. In any event, the trip from Sooke Lake Road is a fantastic day trip. If the trestle is washed out, it is possible to rejoin the Trans Canada Trail route northwest of the Kinsol Trestle. South of Duncan, look for the Koksilah Road to the west. This road crosses the river and joins Riverside Road, which eventually loops close to the old railgrade.

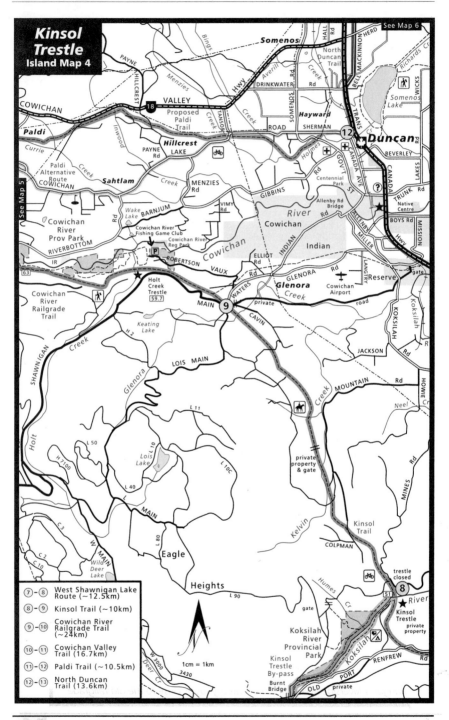

Kinsol Trestle
Island Map 4

⑦-⑧	West Shawnigan Lake Route (~12.5km)	
⑧-⑨	Kinsol Trail (~10km)	
⑨-⑩	Cowichan River Railgrade Trail (~24km)	
⑩-⑪	Cowichan Valley Trail (16.7km)	
⑪-⑫	Paldi Trail (~10.5km)	
⑫-⑬	North Duncan Trail (13.6km)	

1cm = 1km
3430

Vancouver Island Map 4: Kinsol Trestle

Vancouver Island Section 8-9

~10 km
Kinsol Trail

The Trans Canada Trail route from the Kinsol Trestle northwest to Lake Cowichan offers an even more remote wilderness experience. The old railbed travels through a forested area, crossing a few creeks and logging roads. The old railbed eventually intersects Waters Road just south of the village of Glenora.

There is little grade along this section of the trail and the trek is quite easy, although there is one potential problem you may encounter along the way. A portion of the railgrade was purchased some time ago by the Trans Canada Pipeline and may be fenced off. At the time of printing of this book, there were ongoing discussions on

Kinsol Trestle Luco

how to remedy this obstacle. One of the many ideas that are being considered is adding gates at the fenced in points. Be sure to check locally or with Trails BC on the condition of the area before heading out.

Camping is possible along this stretch of the Trans Canada Trail route. Near the Kinsol Trestle you will find a private, full service campground. For a more rustic (no facilities) experience, you will find signs of camping at nearby Koksilah River Provincial Park. Please respect the environment and practice no trace camping by packing out what you pack in.

For supplies like food and refreshments, it is a short trek to the village of Glenora once you reach the intersection of Waters Road. The town can be found approximately 1.5-2 km east of the trail intersection.

Cowichan Trail   J. Marleau

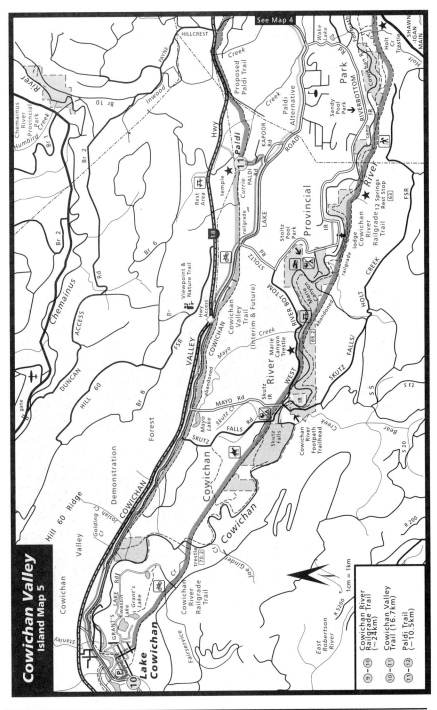

See Map 4

HILLCREST

Wake Lake

Cowichan Park

Holt Cr Trestle

SHAWN- IGAN MAIN

PAYNE

Inwood

Creek

Proposed Paldi Trail

Paldi Alternative

Creek

RIVERBOTTOM

Sandy Pool Park

Camp

Chemainus River

Humbird Creek

Chemainus Provincial Park

Br 10

Br 1

River

KAPOOR Rd

Paldi

PALDI Rd

Currie

temple

Paldi

Hwy

Provincial

River

Cowichan River Railgrade +2 Springs Rest Stop 63

FSR

Br 2

Rest Area

railgrade

LAKE

STOLTZ

Stoltz Pool Park

railgrade lodge

IR

HOLT

Chemainus Rd

ACCESS

Viewpoint & Nature Trail

Br

Rd

Park

STOLTZ Rd

Provincial

Canyon

abandoned

CREEK

Br 2

Br 6

Hwy Access

Cowichan VALLEY Trail (Interim & Future)

Mayo

Creek

RIVER BOTTOM

WEST

Marie Canyon Trestle

66.2

SKUTZ FALLS

S 5

S F2

DUNCAN

HILL 60

Br 8

abandoned

COWICHAN

Mayo Rd

Skutz IR

River

IR

SKUTZ

Bear

FSR

Mayo Lake

Skutz Cr Rd

MAYO Rd

FALLS

SKUTZ

Cowichan River Footpath Trailhead

Creek

S 20

Forest

Demonstration

COWICHAN

Skutz Falls

R 200

Hill 60 Ridge

Valley

(Golding Cr)

(Josiah Cr)

Cowichan

Cowichan

Cowichan

East Robertson River

gate

Stanley

Kwassun Lake

GRANT'S LAKE Rd

Grant's Lake

trestle

70.2

(of Grinder Cr)

R 5200

1cm = 1km

Fairservice

Cowichan River Railgrade Trail

Lake Cowichan

Cowichan

10

P

Cowichan Valley
Island Map 5

9 – 10 = Cowichan River Railgrade Trail (~24km)

10 – 11 = Cowichan Valley Trail (16.7km)

11 – 12 = Paldi Trail (~10.5km)

Vancouver Island Map 5: Cowichan Valley

Vancouver Island Section 9-10

~24 km

Cowichan River Railgrade Trail

The old railbed trail travelling west from Waters Road is truly magnificent. The trail travels through some dense forest sections as it meanders its way through the Cowichan Valley en route to the town of Lake Cowichan. Along the way, the trail crosses several impressive trestles and passes through portions of the Cowichan River Provincial Park. Highlights include the Holt Creek Trestle (Mile 59.7), 12 Springs Rest Stop (Mile 63), Marie Canyon Trestle (Mile 66.2), Skutz Falls and the 70.2 Trestle. Picnic tables and rest areas can be found at 12 Springs as well as a few different park locations. For day-trippers, Marie Canyon, Skutz Falls and the Cowichan River Fish & Game Club parking area also make ideal access points. Camping is offered at Skutz Falls and Stoltz Pool of the Cowichan River Provincial Park during the spring and summer.

Cowichan River   J. Marleau

The Holt Creek Trestle was formerly called the Sutton Creek Trestle. The impressive 73 m (240 ft) trestle has recently been refurbished, although the majority of the structure dates back to 1937.

Hikers may wish to take advantage of the nearby Cowichan River Footpath. The 20 km path stretches from Robertson Road in the east to Skutz Falls in the west and takes about 7 hours one way to walk. The path intersects the old railbed and the Trans Canada Trail in several locations. The unique flora and fauna, patches of old growth forest and the spectacular river views are some of the highlights of this beautiful trail.

Kayaker   J. Marleau

Cowichan River Provincial Park is a fascinating provincial park that offers a number of great sights and outdoor recreation opportunities including:
Heritage Park – boat launch and fishing.
Marie Canyon – spectacular views of the 2 km long canyon, picnic areas, short trails, and fishing.
Sandy Pool – beach area, short trail, boat launch.
Skutz Falls – camping and picnic area, trails, fish ladders, fishing, swimming and a great area for kayaking or whitewater rafting.
Stoltz Pool – camping and picnic area, short trails, swimming, fishing, easy kayaking/tubing and a boat launch.

One of the truly magnificent sections of the entire Trans Canada Trail is the Marie Canyon. The newly refurbished trestle serves as a key historical link in the old railway and is a genuine must see. The 90-metre bridge deck towers above the river and offers a breathtaking view of the canyon. Take the opportunity on the trestle to view the rushing Cowichan River below. Also, be sure to look up as eagles can sometimes be spotted overhead.

The Cowichan River is a world-renowned sport fishing destination. Resident rainbow trout and brown trout can be found throughout the year. The infamous steelhead fishery reaches its peak during the winter run (from December to April). During the fall months literally thousands of salmon travel up the river from the Pacific Ocean in search of their native spawning grounds. The best place to view this event is at the fish ladder found just west of the Marie Canyon off the south side of Riverbottom Road. There is a well marked parking area and a short trail down to the river. Be sure to be aware of bears, as the salmon run often attract them.

From the Marie Canyon Trestle, the trail winds its way along the abandoned railbed and intersects West Riverbottom Road, Mayo Road and Skutz Falls Road before the long trek into Lake Cowichan. Along the way to Lake Cowichan, the 70.2 Trestle crossing of the Cowichan River will form a barrier until the fall of 2001 (the anticipated completion date for upgrading).

The last leg of this long stretch of the Trans Canada Trail

Marie Canyon Trestle   J. Marleau

route takes you from the beautiful forest sprawl of the Cowichan Valley into the town of Lake Cowichan. The route follows the old railbed past quaint Grant's and Kwassin Lakes and through the heart of Lake Cowichan. Along the way, the route crosses a number of different streets, including Cowichan Avenue before meeting Wellington Road. Follow Wellington Road west all the way to its end and the junction with South Shore Road. Head east along South Shore Road trekking through the scenic small downtown corridor and over the Cowichan River. After the bridge crossing, the route meets up with Cowichan Lake Road a short distance down South Shore Road. Heading east, Cowichan Lake Road takes the Trans Canada Trail back through the Cowichan Valley towards Duncan.

The town of Lake Cowichan and surrounding area offer all of the supplies and accommodations needed to make an enjoyable stay. Camping options range from forestry recreation sites to provincial parks and private campgrounds. For those looking for a roof over their head, there are resorts, motels and quaint bed and breakfast locations to choose from.

The local economy of Lake Cowichan has relied mainly on the forest industry; however, with the growing popularity of the spectacular natural attractions in the region, tourism has quickly become an economic mainstay. Along South Shore Road, there are very picturesque views of the confluence between the Cowichan River and Lake Cowichan. The rolling mountain hills above the town also make for a scenic photo opportunity. While in town, be sure to visit the small park and museum available along the waterside.

Cowichan Lake is a popular spot for angling, boating, swimming and many other outdoor pastimes. The name of the lake is derived from the native word 'Kaatza', meaning big lake. For an exciting off the beaten path tour, there is a maintained road around the big lake spanning over 75km in distance. Along the lake loop, there are a number of fantastic forest recreation campsites available as well as boat access areas to the lake. If you have the time and energy, you can continue west past the lake towards the island coast and Carmanah Provincial Park, which is home to some of the largest spruce trees in the world.

Vancouver Island Section 10-11

16.7 km
Cowichan Valley Trail
Along South Shore Road, the trail crosses the Cowichan River in the north end of the town of Lake Cowichan. Eventually, you will come upon the Old Cowichan Lake Road. The Trans Canada Trail currently follows the road east over 16 km all the way to the settlement of Paldi. The paved road is not very busy providing a safe route for both bikers and hikers. The trail travels through second growth forest and passes a number of rural homes. Along the way, you will also pass by Skutz Falls Road, Mayo Road and Stoltz Road before meeting Kapoor Road. Follow Kapoor Road north for a mere 100 m to the intersection with Paldi Road. The Paldi Road travels north to the settlement of Paldi, the

Cowichan River   Sahtlam Lodge

site of a small East Indian settlement. Just before you enter the settlement, you will cross an old railgrade.

An off-road alternative is being negotiated in the section between Lake Cowichan and Paldi. The abandoned CP Railbed runs parallel to the Old Cowichan Lake Road and is the prefect alternative for the Trans Canada Trail route in the valley. Before heading along this portion of the trail, be sure to check locally, with Trails BC or www.backroadmapbooks.com for the status on the old railbed.

The town has plenty to offer; including accommodation, food, entertainment, some equipment and it is definitely worth the time to explore. Many of the downtown sidewalks are made up of boardwalks, which definitely add lustre to the character of the town.

Chemainus Mural   *J. Marleau*

 The first European settlers arrived in the Chemainus Valley in late 1850's. These original settlements near the town of Chemainus are among the oldest European settlements on Vancouver Island. The town's first major economic influx came from the construction of a small sawmill in 1862. Chemainus became an established mill town for over 100 years until in 1983 when the town's main mill closed and marked the end of an era. With the glooming economic despair of a main economic provider lost, the local residents heroically developed a plan to attract outside business. The town transformed itself into one of the most splendid seaside towns on Vancouver Island and today has become one of the most popular tourist destinations on Vancouver Island. One of the main attractions of the town is the dozens of hand painted murals that are found on business walls throughout the town. The town has literally transformed itself into one of the most magnificent outdoor art galleries in North America.

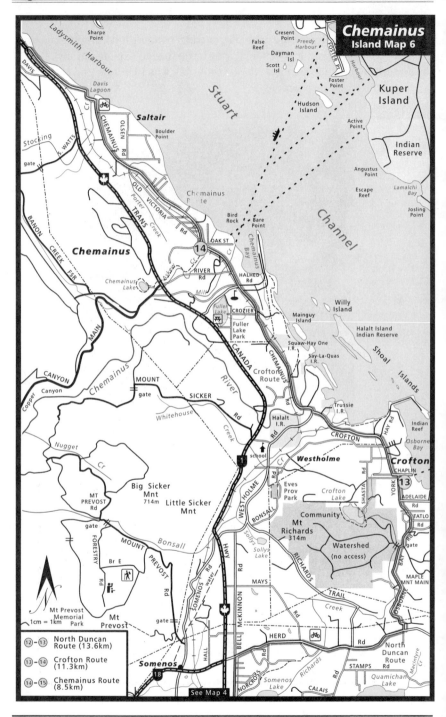

Chemainus
Island Map 6

Ladysmith Harbour
Sharpe Point
DAVIS
Davis Lagoon
OLSEN Rd
Saltair
Boulder Point
Stocking
gate
S. WATTS
CHEMAINUS
Porter Creek
OLD VICTORIA Rd
TRANS
BANON CREEK FSR
Chemainus
Chemainus Route
Bird Rock
OAK ST
14
Chemainus Lake
Willow Cr
RIVER Rd
HALHED Rd
Mill
Fuller Lake
CROZIER
Fuller Lake Park
CANYON
MAIN
Copper Canyon
Chemainus
MOUNT
gate
SICKER
Whitehouse
River Rd
CANADA
Rd
Crofton Route
CHEMAINUS
Rd
Squaw-Hay One I.R.
Say-La-Quas I.R.
Nugget Cr
Big Sicker Mnt 714m
Little Sicker Mnt
Creek
Halalt I.R.
Trussie I.R.
CROFTON
MT PREVOST Rd
gate
Bonsall
1
school
Cr
Westholme
Eves Prov Park
Crofton Lake
SHASTA Rd
HAY Rd
Indian Reef
Crofton
CHAPLIN
13
YORK
ADELAIDE Rd
TATLO Rd
FORESTRY
Br E
MOUNT PREVOST Rd
WEST HOLME Rd
BONSALL Rd
Sollys Lake
Community
Mt Richards 314m
Watershed (no access)
RICHARDS Rd
MAPLE MNT MAIN
gate
BAY Rd
OSBORNE
Mt Prevost Memorial Park
1cm = 1km
Mt Prevost
HALL Rd
SOMENOS water Rd
BELL McKINNON Rd
MAYS Rd
Sollys Rd
TRAIL Creek
North Duncan Route Rd
NORCROSS Rd
HERD Rd
STAMPS Rd
Quamichan Lake
Macintyre Cr
Somenos
18
Somenos Lake
CALAIS Rd
Richards Rd

Stuart
Channel
Crescent Point
False Reef
Dayman Isl
Scott Isl
Preedy Harbour
FOSTER FT
Harbour
Foster Point
Kuper Island
Hudson Island
Active Point
Angustus Point
Escape Reef
Lamalchi Bay
Josling Point
Indian Reserve
Bare Point
Chemainus Bay
Willy Island
Mainguy Island
Halalt Island Indian Reserve
Shoal Islands
Osborne Bay

(12)–(13) **North Duncan Route (13.6km)**
(13)–(14) **Crofton Route (11.3km)**
(14)–(15) **Chemainus Route (8.5km)**

See Map 4

Vancouver Island Map 6: Chemainus

Vancouver Island Section 1 13

13.6 km
North Duncan Route

Travelling north from the city of Duncan the Trans Canada Trail makes a short jaunt next to the Trans Canada Highway once again. Along the highway, it is recommended to travel on the west side of the road and cross at the Bell-Mackinnon/Drinkwater Road junction some 1.3 km north of Sherman Road.

Ocean View   J. Marleau

After crossing the highway, the route follows Bell-Mackinnon Road approximately 1.7 km to Herd Road. The trip along Herd Road is quite scenic with views of rolling fields and distant rolling hills. Herd Road is not very busy with traffic and is a decent hike or bike. At the junction of Osborne Bay Road, the Trans Canada Trail continues north to the town of Crofton.

The scenery along Osborne Bay Road is quite pleasant as you will pass the odd home and a few comforting treed areas. While entering the town of Crofton, Osborne Bay Road changes to York Avenue. The town of Crofton is quite small, although it can provide for the basic needs of hungry and weary travellers. The town's economy is predominantly based on the forest industry, as there are a number of loading docks and a mill within the town. The main attraction of the

Vancouver Island Map 7: Ladysmith

Vancouver Island Section 15-16
8.9 km
Ladysmith Route

From the intersection of the Chemainus Road and the Trans Canada Highway, The Trans Canada Trail travels across the highway to Davis Road and then east on Dogwood Drive. Dogwood Drive takes you through a small semi-wooded valley mixed with residential homes. Well within the town of Ladysmith, the trail eventually reaches the intersection of Dogwood Drive and Methuen Street. Follow Methuen Street south to its end. From the end of the street there is a new paved trail found just off the south end of the road.

TransferBeach Park at Dusk   *J. Marleau*

The paved trail is quite short and traverses underneath the highway via a tunnel. At the other side of the tunnel, you will find Transfer Beach Park next to Ladysmith Harbour.

From Transfer Beach Park, the Trans Canada Trail route is a bit tricky to follow. From the tunnel, the trail follows Transfer Beach Boulevard to an old railway line trail that is very difficult to spot. Along the boulevard, as it is beginning to leave the park, a trail can be spotted off the north side of the road. As of March 2000 the trail is marked with an about a half metre stick jutting from the ground with some scarce marking tape. One hint on finding the trail is that if you find yourself past

One of the points of interest at Paldi is the historic Indian temple that can be found in the west end of the settlement. To find the temple, follow Paldi Road north past the railgrade crossing to Bischan Road. The temple is about 200 m west down Bischan Road.

Vancouver Island Section 11-12

~10.5 km

Proposed Paldi Trail

From Paldi Road, the old railbed is barely noticeable and can be easily missed if you are not paying attention. Since this route alternative has not been officially designated as the Trans Canada Trail, there are no signs in the area. Further, it may be necessary to re-route along one of the many rural roads in the area. The railgrade is in decent shape east of Paldi providing an easy to moderate trip all the way to the city of Duncan.

Artisian Village   J. Marleau

Along the way, the old railgrade crosses the Old Cowichan Lake Road before heading through a wooded area leading into a residential area. The route parallels Sherman Road east to the Trans Canada Highway, where the route begins to head north.

Please note that this section of the Trans Canada Trail stretches from Map 5 back to Map 4.

The settlement of Duncan was originally incorporated in 1912 and is known as the "city of Totems". Beginning in 1985, the city helped co-ordinate local native carvers to construct dozens of totems poles throughout the city. Today, the city is home to over 80 magnificent totem poles and is a fascinating attraction. Most of the poles have been carved by residents of the local Cowichan Tribes and is an impressive display of native culture and an ancient heritage art form. Enquire locally at the travel information centre or the Cowichan Native Village for information on guided interpretive tours of the totems.

Vancouver Island Section 14-15

8.5 km

Chemainus Route

Chemainus Road is the main road through the town of Chemainus and is part of the Trans Canada Trail route north out of the town of Chemainus. The route north of the town is generally easy, although can be busy with traffic at times. Along the way, there are a number of great views offered of Ladysmith Harbour, Stuart Channel and the Gulf Islands beyond. Chemainus Road eventually intersects the Trans Canada Highway 8.5 km later.

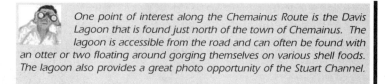

One point of interest along the Chemainus Route is the Davis Lagoon that is found just north of the town of Chemainus. The lagoon is accessible from the road and can often be found with an otter or two floating around gorging themselves on various shell foods. The lagoon also provides a great photo opportunity of the Stuart Channel.

Mural   J. Marleau

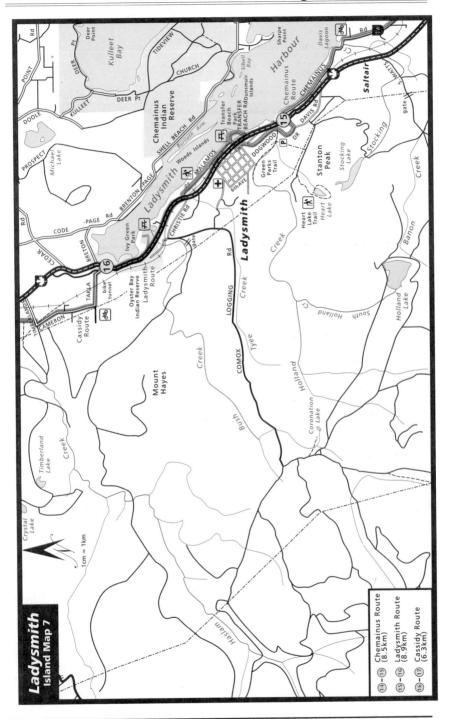

Ladysmith
Island Map 7

Crystal Lake

1cm = 1km

Chemainus Route (8.5km)
Ladysmith Route (8.9km)
Cassidy Route (6.3km)

small town is that it offers some of the first views of the Stuart Channel of the Pacific Ocean.

Before leaving the town of Crofton, you will reach the end of York Avenue. From here, the Trans Canada Trail route travels north a short way along Chaplin Street and quickly to Crofton Road.

There is no shortage of areas to pick up supplies or to rest in the urban areas of south Vancouver Island. From Duncan north to Ladysmith you will be traveling through both rural and urban areas. There are a host of bed and breakfast locations, motels and even private campgrounds to stop at.

Crofton's original inhabitants were a small band of pioneer homesteaders who arrived sometime in the late 1800's. The area remained basically undisturbed until 1902 when a copper smelter was built at the townsite to process ore that was being mined at nearby Mount Sicker. The smelter was the base of building much of the town, although quickly outlived its use to the mining company and was closed. The town suffered economically until 1957, when B.C. Forest Products built the pulp and paper mill, which makes up much of the current day economy of the area.

Vancouver Island Section 13-14
11.3 km
Crofton Route

Just as you begin north along the Crofton Road, you will notice the industry that supports the area. Crofton Road passes by a mill and a few industrial buildings before the Trans Canada Trail route reaches a set of active rail tracks. Shortly after the rail crossing, the route comes to a junction with Chemainus Road. The Trans Canada Trail route follows Chemainus Road north approximately 7 km to the ocean side town of Chemainus. Chemainus Road has its share of traffic, although is definitely not as busy as the Trans Canada Highway. The road slowly leads into town with a gradual increase of homes and businesses resident along the route.

Chemainus is a beautifully quaint island town and has become a favourite get-away for many mainland residents. The town is stretched out between the main road and the ocean and provides a number of superb views of Chemainus Bay.

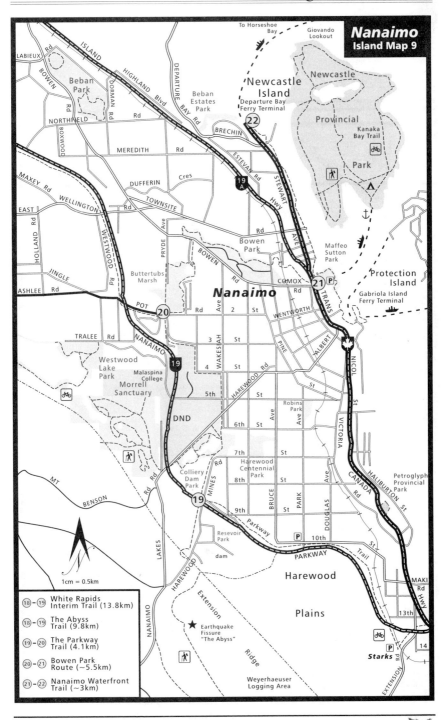

Nanaimo
Island Map 9

To Horseshoe Bay

Giovando Lookout

Newcastle Island

Newcastle

Departure Bay Ferry Terminal

Provincial

Kanaka Bay Trail

Park

LABIEUX Rd

ISLAND HIGHLAND

BOWEN Rd

Beban Park

DORMAN Rd

NORTHFIELD

BOXWOOD

Rd

DEPARTURE BAY Rd

Beban Estates Park

BRECHIN

MEREDITH Rd

MAXEY Rd

WELLINGTON

DUFFERIN Cres

TOWNSITE

Rd

ESTEVAN Rd

STEWART AVE

19 A

Rd

Bowen Park

EAST HOLLAND Rd

WESTWOOD Rd

PRYDE Ave

COLLIERY BOWEN Rd

Maffeo Sutton Park

JINGLE

Buttertubs Marsh

Nanaimo

COMOX

Rd

21 P

Protection Island

Gabriola Island Ferry Terminal

ASHLEE Rd

POT

20

Rd Ave 2 St

WENTWORTH

TRANS

NICOL St

TRALEE Rd

NANAIMO

19

3 WAKESIAH St

PINE Rd

ALBERT

Westwood Lake Park

Malaspina College

4 St

HAREWOOD Rd

St

VICTORIA

HALIBURTON St

Morrell Sanctuary

5th St

Robins Park Ave

Petroglyph Provincial Park

DND

6th St

CANADA Rd

MT BENSON

7th St

Harewood Centennial Park

Colliery Dam Park

MINES Rd

8th St

BRUCE St

PARK Ave

DOUGLAS Ave

St

19

9th St

Parkway

MAKI Rd

Resevoir Park

dam

10th P

PARKWAY

Trail

13th

LAKES Rd

HAREWOOD Rd

NANAIMO Rd

Extension

★ Earthquake Fissure "The Abyss"

Harewood

Plains

Starks Rd

P

14

EXTENSION HWY

Ridge

Weyerhaeuser Logging Area

1cm = 0.5km

18 – 19 White Rapids Interim Trail (13.8km)

18 – 19 The Abyss Trail (9.8km)

19 – 20 The Parkway Trail (4.1km)

20 – 21 Bowen Park Route (~5.5km)

21 – 22 Nanaimo Waterfront Trail (~3km)

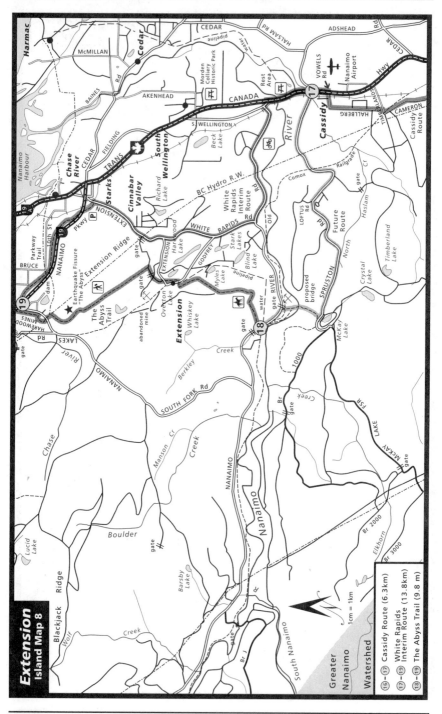

Extension
Island Map 8

Greater Nanaimo Watershed

16 – 17 Cassidy Route (6.3km)
17 – 19 White Rapids Interim Route (13.8km)
18 – 19 The Abyss Trail (9.8 m)

1cm = 1km

Vancouver Island Maps 8: Extension

Vancouver Island Section 17-19

13.8 km

White Rapids Interim Route

There are grand plans for this section of the Trans Canada Trail route, which are well underway, although are currently incomplete. Hopefully, in the near future, the bridge over the Nanaimo River will be established and the more remote route will be opened. Meanwhile, we will provide a 14 km interim route that is still very scenic and is a pleasure to travel.

The White Rapids interim route starts from the junction of the Trans Canada Highway and Spruston Road. Travel north along the highway to Nanaimo River Road. The highway is usually quite busy, although once you reach Nanaimo River Road the traffic diminishes considerably and the trip becomes much more enjoyable. Nanaimo River Road is a paved route that traverses a second growth forest where some old Douglas fir trees can still be spotted from the road. Follow Nanaimo Road to White Rapids Road, where the interim route heads north. More adventurous travellers may want to pick up the water pipeline route described below.

Parkway Trail   *J. Marleau*

Continuing north along White Rapids Road takes you past the odd home, field and forest area. White Rapids Road eventually leads to Extension Road and the urban community of Cinnabar Valley. Just as Extension Road approaches the Island Highway, it passes the trailhead of the Parkway Trail. The Parkway Trail is a paved trail that traverses along the north side of the Island Highway west all the way to Harwood Mines Road and the connection with the Abyss Trail.

Vancouver Island Section 21-22
~3 km
Nanaimo Waterfront Trail

From the mouth of the Millstone River, the Trans Canada Trail route follows the Nanaimo Waterfront Trail north to Departure Bay. The route is well marked with Trans Canada Trail signs as it treks along the waterfront area. Along the trail, there are many opportunities to snap a photo of the harbour area and Newcastle Island Channel. Across the channel lies Newcastle Island, which is protected in its entirety as a provincial park. If you have time, the park is a fantastic place to visit and offers a multitude of trails and camping opportunities. There is one last view of the channel before the trail veers further inland back towards the Trans

Nanaimo's name is derived from the first native Coast Salish people known as 'Sneneymexw' or 'great and mighty people'.

Newcastle Island is named after the British mining city of Newcastle and was home to coal mining from the 1850's to the early 1900's. After the end of mining on the island, the island soon became a regular getaway to local Vancouver Island residents and passing boaters. Today, the island is protected for its historical and natural relevance as Newcastle Provincial Park. The park offers an endless array of outdoor recreation opportunities, including hiking, biking, camping, swimming and fishing. Near the island ferry terminal on the south side of the island, a visitor centre welcomes ferry passengers. During the summer months, informative tours are operated by the park staff for all visitors to enjoy.

To reach Newcastle Provincial Park, visitors can travel on a paddlewheel ferry, which leaves from Maffeo Sutton Park. The ferry terminal can be found by following an established city trail, which can be picked up near the junction of the Millstream River and the Trans Canada Highway. It is about a 300 m trek to the ferry terminal from the highway crossing.

Canada Highway and eventually to Departure Bay. The ferry at Departure Bay travels to Horseshoe Bay in North Vancouver.

the log display that is readily noticeable, you have gone too far.

Once you find the old railbed trail, the route is generally easy to follow and follows the old rail line through a mix of forest cover and scrub all the way to Melamos Road. At the old rail/road junction, the Trans Canada Trail route follows the newly paved road back to the Trans Canada Highway. At the intersection, the Trans Canada Trail follows the highway north past Ivy Green Park to Takala Road.

Both Transfer Beach Park and Ivy Green Park are ideal locations to stop for lunch or a needed rest stop. Flush toilets are offered throughout the summer season. For those travellers interested in stopping for the night, there are full facilities found in Ladysmith including motels and bed and breakfast locations. Camping is restricted to private campgrounds in this area of the Island.

The town of Ladysmyth lies on the 49th parallel and is named after the old British Empire town Ladysmith, which is located in South Africa. As the story goes, in 1899 in the South African town of Ladysmith, a large garrison of British troops was under siege by the Boers during the Boer war. The garrison held out for some eleven months before relief arrived. As a result, it became a heralded story throughout the British Empire. B.C.'s Ladysmith received its name after James Dunsmuir, founder of the B.C. town, named the British Columbian town in memory and delight of the British success in South Africa.

Vancouver Island Section 16-17

6.3 km

Cassidy Route

Takla Road is found off the west side of the Trans Canada Highway and is the continuation of the Trans Canada Trail. The route offers some solace from the busy highway and is a roughly paved route. From Takla Road, the route follows Cameron Road north to Timberland Road. After a very quick jaunt east along Timberland Road, the Trans Canada Trail picks up by following Hallberg Road north to Vowels Road. Follow Vowels Road east back to the highway, where the trail follows the highway north for a very short trek to Spruston Road.

Please note that this section of the Trans Canada Trail stretches from Map 7 to Map 8.

Vancouver Island Map 9: Nanaimo

Vancouver Island Section 19-20
4.1 km
South Nanaimo Trail

The route through this part of Nanaimo is well marked with Trans Canada Trail signs and should be quite easy to follow. At the junction of the Nanaimo Parkway and Harewood Mines Road, you can find the Trans Canada Trail/Parkway Trail hidden in the forest on the west side of the road. The trail parallels Harewood Mines Road north through the forest cover to Lower Lake and eventually to a crossing of the Chase River. After the crossing of the river, the trail begins its trek through the urban streets of Nanaimo as it traverses along Wakesiah Avenue north to 4th Street. Passing through the Malaspina College campus, the trail then travels west along 4th Street and veers north to the junction of 3rd Street. The Trans

Welcome to Nanaimo Sign   J. Marleau

Canada Trail route then follows 3rd Street all the way to Jingle Pot Road.

Vancouver Island Section 20-21

~5.5 km
Bowen Park Route

Once at the junction of Jingle Pot Road, the Trans Canada Trail follows Jingle Pot Road about 300 m east to the 18-hectare Buttertubs Marsh Park. The trail veers north through the marsh before reaching Buttertubs Drive. The route traverses along the east side of Buttertubs Drive before entering the scenic Bowen Park.

Nanaimo Boardwalk   R. Brown

Following the Millstone River, the trail travels through the picturesque park setting as it heads east towards the Nanaimo waterfront. The Trans Canada Trail leaves the park as it crosses a set of train tracks, although the route continues to follow the river all the way to the junction of the Trans Canada Highway near the Nanaimo waterfront. Trans Canada Trail signs are well placed throughout this area and it should be easy to follow the route.

The 36-hectare Bowen Park is the perfect setting for a picnic or rest stop as there are a number of amenities available in the park, including washrooms and covered picnic shelters. Throughout the year, Bowen Park also offers a number of facilities including a swimming pool, tennis courts, petting zoo and an interpretive nature centre for all visitors to enjoy. Besides the Trans Canada Trail, there are a number of interconnecting trails that wind their way through the park that are all decent alternates to the main trail. The park flora is comprised of a mix of forest cover, which includes mature stands of maple, hemlock, fir and cedar trees. While traveling through the park, visitors often spot various animal species such as deer, otter, beaver and a wide variety of birds. Some sights of interest in the park include a number of totem poles, a small waterfall and a fish ladder on the Millstone River.

In the near future, there are plans for the Trans Canada Trail to follow Spruston Road. Spruston Road is found off the west side of the Trans Canada Highway and is a winding paved road. The route will follow the road for approximately 9 km to near McKay Lake, where it is planned to cut a trail north. The trail is to trek through some heavy forest cover as it meanders down to the Nanaimo River. Plans for a bridge are in the works to lead the trail across the river, where the route will then travel northwest along the river to a crossing of Nanaimo River Road.

Vancouver Island Section 18-19
9.8 km
The Abyss Trail

This trail north of Nanaimo River Road is currently passable although not officially signed. In addition to offering a pleasant off-road route, it also passes by an interesting geographic site.

From the paved road, a water pipeline route heads north to a crossing of Godfrey Road. Just north of Godfrey Road, the Trans Canada Trail joins an existing trail named the 'Abyss Trail'. The Abyss Trail traverses some very picturesque forest cover

The Abyss   R. Brown

and over a magnificent rock fissure, which is part of the earthquake fault line of the lower Nanaimo area. The trail eventually connects with the well established Parkway Trail near Harewood Mines Road south of Nanaimo.

The Abyss is a unique 90+ m (300+ foot) fissure cut deep into a rocky area south of Nanaimo. It is actually part of an earthquake fault line. The 'Abyss' is a very fascinating element of geography. If you drop a small rock in the fissure, you can literally hear it fall out of earshot as it bounces down back and forth off the deep tight rock slit.

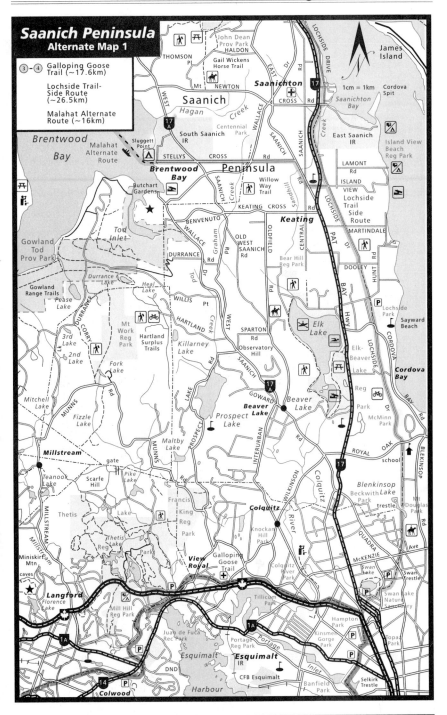

Saanich Peninsula
Alternate Map 1

③-④ Galloping Goose Trail (~17.6km)

Lochside Trail-Side Route (~26.5km)

Malahat Alternate Route (~16km)

1cm = 1km

John Dean Prov Park HALDON
THOMSON PL
Gail Wickens Horse Trail
Mt NEWTON
Saanichton
17 A
CROSS Rd
James Island
Cordova Spit
Saanichton Bay

Saanich
Hagan Creek
17 A
South Saanich IR
Centennial Park
WALLACE
CROSS
SAANICH
Rd
East Saanich IR
Island View Beach Reg Park

Brentwood Bay
Malahat Alternate Route
Sluggett Point
STELLYS CROSS
Brentwood Bay
Butchart Gardens
Saanich Creek
Peninsula
Willow Way Trail
KEATING CROSS
Rd
Keating
LAMONT Rd
ISLAND VIEW
Lochside Trail Side Route
MARTINDALE

Tod Inlet
BENVENUTO
WALLACE
Graham Rd
OLD WEST SAANICH Rd
OLDFIELD
CENTRAL
Bear Hill Reg Park
PAT BAY Hwy
DOOLEY
HUNT Rd

Gowland Tod Prov Park
DURRANCE
Tod Dr
Durrance Lake
Heal Lake
WILLIS Pt
Lochside Park
Sayward Beach

Gowland Range Trails
Pease Lake
CORRY Rd
Mt Work Reg Park
Hartland Surplus Trails
HARTLAND
Killarney Lake
WEST SAANICH
SPARTON Rd
Observatory Hill
Elk Lake
Elk-Beaver Lake
Cordova Bay

3rd Lake
2nd Lake
Fork Lake
MUNNS Rd
LAKE
PROSPECT
GOWARD
Rd
17
Beaver Lake
Reg Park
McMinn Park
CORDOVA BAY

Mitchell Lake
Fizzle Lake
Millstream
Teanook Lake
Scarfe Hill
gate
Pike Lake
Maltby Lake
Prospect Lake
INTERURBAN
Colquitz
ROYAL
17
OAK
school
BLENKINSOP
Blenkinsop Lake
Beckwith Park
Mt Douglas Park
trestle

MILLSTREAM
Thetis Lake
Francis King Reg Park
Thetis Reg Lake Park
Colquitz
Knockan Hill Park
Colquitz River
WILKINSON
QUADRA
McKENZIE Ave

Miniskirt Mtn
caves
Langford
Florence Lake
Galloping Goose Trail
View Royal
Colquitz river Park
Swan Lake
Swan Trestle
Swan Lake Nature Sanctuary

1A
Mill Hill Reg Park
Tillicum Park
Hampton Park
Topaz

1A
Juan de Fuca Rec Park
Portage Reg Park
Kinsmen Gorge Park

14
Colwood
DND
CFB Esquimalt
Esquimalt
IR
Portage Inlet
Banfield Park
Selkirk Trestle

Esquimalt Harbour

Vancouver Island Alternate Maps 1/2: Saanich Peninsula/Swartz Bay

~26.5 km
Lochside Trail Side Route

For travellers wishing to access the Trans Canada Trail from the southern mainland ferry route, a fabulous side route has been established. This route, called the Lochside Trail Side Route, takes travellers south from the Swartz Bay Ferry terminal towards Victoria. The route travels through a rural environment dominated by rolling farmland, woodlands and fantastic ocean views. You will eventually

Walkers on Lochside Trail   J. Marleau

join the Galloping Goose Trail at the Switch Bridge.
From the ferry terminal take Lands End Road east to Curteis Road and head south. The route heads south along Curteis Road all the way to McDonald Park Road. The park offers little more than a campsite for road weary travellers.

After about 2 km along McDonald Road, the route connects to a paved trail that parallels the Pat Bay Highway (Hwy 17). The trail travels along the perimeter of the community of Sidney to Ocean Road. Follow Ocean Road to Fifth Street, where the route heads south towards Tulista Park. Tulista Park is a quaint ocean side community park that is a fine place for a rest stop or lunch.

The Lochside Trail Side Route continues south from the park along Lochside Drive, which is easily picked up off Fifth Street. The route follows Lochside Drive south along scenic Bazan Bay. This stretch of the route travels along the cliffs of the bay and is a real treat for travellers. In the distance, you can usually spot a number of vessels and several leisure boats during the summer.

Lochside Drive eventually intersects Cross Road. The trail follows Cross Road west for a short jaunt to the trailhead of the Lochside Trail. The Lochside Trail is an established green space trail that is well maintained and was once designated for road expansion. The trail is well marked, easy to follow and often sports a loose gravel surface, making for smooth travel.

Mural   L. Lebrun

The trail travels between urban development and offers a picturesque route cutting through various woodlands of the Saanich Peninsula. This portion of the route crosses over a number of main streets including Island View Road and Martendale Road before reaching Lochside Park and the intersection with Cordova Bay Road.

At Cordova Bay Road, the Lochside Trail Side Route crosses the road and continues south again along Lochside Drive. This section of the route passes through a quiet urban area offering views of Cordova Bay from time to time. After McMinn Park, Lochside Drive soon meets up with Royal Oak Road, marking a resurgence of the more rustic section of the Lochside Trail. Across Royal Oak Road, the route follows the Lochside Trail again, amidst urban development, but within its own secluded environment. The trail meets Belkinshop Lake and crosses over the trestle leading to the intersection with Cedar Hill Cross Road.

The route continues over the Cedar Hill Cross Road and McKenzie Drive before meeting a paved section of the route. This developed section heads southwest over Quadra and Saanich Roads before reaching the lovely green space surrounding Swan Lake. From the south end of Swan Lake Park, the Lochside Trail Side Route travels over two trestles then under Vernon Avenue and Blanshard Street before meeting the Switch Bridge and the Galloping Goose Trail. The Galloping Goose Trail can now be used to head south into the heart of Victoria or by heading west, bypassing the main portion of the city.

~ 16 km
Malahat Alternate Route

One of the main downfalls of the main Trans Canada Trail route north from Victoria is that the interim route travels along the Trans Canada Highway (Highway 1). Along this highway portion of the route, the trail is squeezed between the high mountain walls through a small canyon, making for uncomfortable travel next to the busy highway. Until a better route is chosen, Trans Canada Trail travellers may wish to follow this alternate route.

Lochside Trail Bikers   J. Marleau

To bypass the Malahat Route, the alternate route is to take the Brentwood Bay Ferry from the Saanich Peninsula to Mill Bay, just north of Malahat. To reach the Brentwood Bay Ferry follow the Lochside Trail Side Route north from the Switch Bridge. This dynamic trail system eventually joins Island View Road. The alternate route then follows a series of rural roads that can be busy with vehicle traffic.

Follow Island View Road west over the Pat Bay Highway (Hwy 17) to East Saanich Road. Travel north along East Saanich Road to Stelly's Cross Road. Follow Stelly's Cross Road west towards Brentwood Bay. Near Brentwood Bay, take Peden Lane south off Stelly's Cross Road. Peden Land leads to Verdier Avenue and to the Brentwood Bay Ferry Terminal.

After a relaxing, half hour ferry ride the Malahat Alternate Route continues south of Mill Bay. Follow Mill Bay Road north to the quaint little Island town. Along this section of the route, you will be rewarded with fantastic views of the Saanich Inlet and the Saanich Peninsula to the east. The inlet is a popular spot for boaters and is a prime recreation area for divers and anglers alike.

From Mill Bay Road, the alternate route follows Deloume Road for about 0.2 km to the Trans Canada Highway. The route crosses over the highway at the traffic light and follows the highway north for about 0.5 km. Look for the Shawnigan Lake Mill Bay Road heading west. This busy rural road leads to the tiny town of Shawnigan Lake. From here, continue around the northern tip of the big lake and follow the main road as it turns into the Old Port Renfrew Road. On the west side of the lake, you will rejoin the main Trans Canada Trail route. Look for the old railbed.

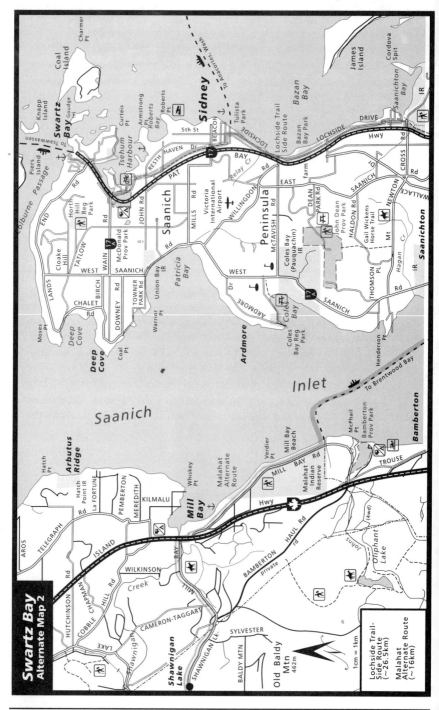

Swartz Bay
Alternate Map 2

Lochside Trail-
Side Route
(~26.5km)

Malahat
Alternate Route
(~16km)

1cm = 1km

VANCOUVER ISLAND SERVICE PROVIDERS

Accommodations

HI-Victoria

Located in Downtown Victoria. Main Attractions within walking distance.

516 Yates Street
Victoria, BC, V8W 1K8
(250) 385-4511
1-888-883-0099
www.hihostels.bc.ca

Malahat Bungalows Motel

Cottages, fireplaces, kitchens, hot tubs, pool, picnic tables, laundry in wooded setting.

300 Trans Canada Hwy
Malahat, BC, V0R 2L0
(250) 478-3011
1-800-665-8066
www.malahatbungalows.com

Sahtlam Lodge

Secluded cabins, woodburning fires, duvets, robes. 16 km from Duncan.

5720 Riverbottom Rd. West
Duncan, BC, V9L 6H9
(250) 748-7738
www.sahtlamlodge.com

The Doctor's Inn

An old roomy house right in the town of Lake Cowichan. 4 bedrooms.

98 Comiaken Ave.
Lake Cowichan, BC, V0R 2G0
1-877-749-4203
www.islandnet.com/doctorsinn

Supplies & Services

Cycle BC.ca Rentals

BC's largest selection of motorcycles, scooters, & bicycles at guaranteed "Best Prices & Service".

747 Douglas St. & 950 Wharf St.
Victoria, BC, V8X 2B4
1-866-380-2453
www.cyclebc.ca

Vancouver Island Canoe & Kayak Centre

Canoes and kayaks for rent, sale, guided tours, lessons and repairs.

575 Pembroke Street
Victoria, BC, V8T 1H3
(250) 361-9365
www.canoeandkayakcentre.com

The Community Farm Store

Full service grocery, organic foods, produce, bakery & more.

3633 Glenora Road
Duncan, BC
(250) 748-6227
nichwell@island.net

Sports Rent

Victoria's best sport rental.
Bicycles, camping gear, skies & more.

611 Discovery St.
Victoria, BC, V8T 5G4
(250) 385-7368

www.sportsrentbc.com

Tours and Guides

BC Ferries Key Link in Trans Canada Trail

One of the most interesting and unique things about the Trans Canada Trail in British Columbia is that BC Ferries service is actually part of the official Trans Canada Trail route. The main route is the trip from Nanaimo on Vancouver Island to Horseshoe Bay on the mainland. The trip from Tsawwassen on the mainland to Swartz Bay on Vancouver Island accesses the first official side route from the main Trans Canada Trail. The ferry system is a relaxing way to further experience the dynamic nature of British Columbia and BC's Trans Canada Trail. The ferry rides are very comfortable, with all the creature comforts, including cafeterias, outdoor viewing platforms and even arcades.

Visitors can also take advantage of BC Ferries' impressive service to other regions of the province. Full service is available to a variety of fabulous BC destinations including the Gulf Islands and Sunshine Coast, plus mid and north coasts ports of call by way of the Discovery Coast Passage, Inside Passage and Queen Charlotte Islands Routes. If you have the time, any one of these side trips can provide the thrill of a lifetime. Through a combination of short ferry travels and road and trail trekking, this part of BC is a favourite among visitors and residents alike.

For more information on BC Ferries or for fares, schedules and maps visit their website at **www.bcferries.com.**

To speak with a Passenger Service Agent, access recorded information or make reservations on the Northern or Tsawwassen-Southern Gulf Islands routes:
(250) 386-3431 - In Victoria, or long distance from outside British Columbia.
1-888-BC FERRY (1-888-223-3779) - In British Columbia, outside the Victoria dialing area.

For vehicle reservations on Vancouver-Vancouver Island routes:
1-888-724-5223 toll free from anywhere in British Columbia.
(604) 444-2890 from outside the province.

Southwestern British Columbia

Creating the Trans Canada Trail through Southwestern BC was truly a remarkable feat. It is the most populated portion of the province and a number of municipalities, governments and private owners consulted to create the trail in this region are staggering. Pieces of the route follow the footsteps of the historical Centennial Trail, while others make use of the diverse road and dike systems throughout the region. New trail systems have been added to join the sections into one of the most diverse routes you will find in the world.

The temperate climate limits the type of travellers to predominately summer users in the western portion of the region. Perhaps east of Chilliwack and especially north of Hope, cross-country skiers and occasionally snowmobilers will be able to follow the sections of the route that are established. Equestrian riders will be able to follow most of the route starting east of Coquitlam on the North PoCo trail. There is also a separate equestrian route to follow in Maple Ridge. Hikers and cyclists will find a couple of different sections where the terrain requires a separate cycling route. These areas are found on both the West Vancouver and Abbotsford maps. Hikers will also want to note that the interim route along the Coquihalla Highway, north of Hope, is not open to walkers. As always, it is recommended to check locally, with Trails BC or visit **www.backroadmapbooks.com** for updates on the route.

Perhaps the most convenient things about this region is the easy access to the route. Trans Canada Trail signs are in place along most of the western section of the route so it is relatively easy to find and follow. Day-trippers will also find that there are several different access points that are easily accessible by public transport. The West Coast Express can be used to access stretches of the trail as far out as Mission and the Matsqui Trail.

Most of the western part of the region travels through an urban or semi-rural setting. Although civilization is close at hand, it is important to note that finding the right service or supplier can be tricky. Accommodations and camping areas are readily available if you know where to look. For your planning convenience, we have tried to note camping and picnic areas along the route.

In the eastern section of this region, the Trans Canada Trail travels through vast stretches of wilderness terrain. In addition to possible encounters with wildlife, abrupt weather changes are possible, especially along the route near the Coquihalla Summit. If you come prepared for wilderness travel, the backcountry scenery is a truly rewarding experience.

Southwestern British Columbia

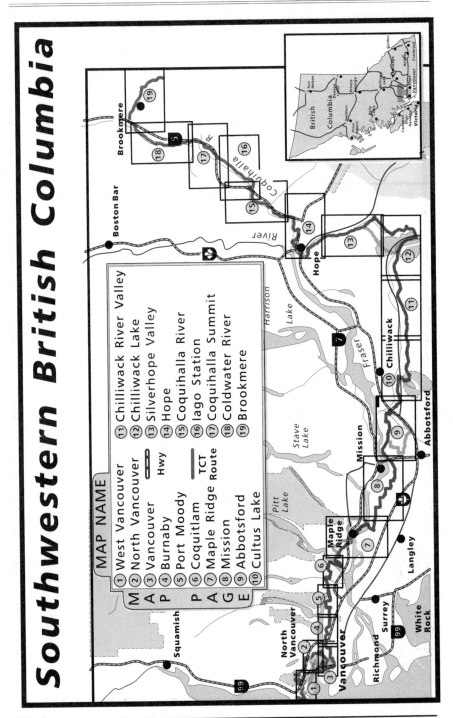

MAP NAME

M 1 West Vancouver
A 2 North Vancouver
P 3 Vancouver
P 4 Burnaby
P 5 Port Moody
A 6 Coquitlam
G 7 Maple Ridge
E 8 Mission
9 Abbotsford
10 Cultus Lake

11 Chilliwack River Valley
12 Chilliwack Lake
13 Silverhope Valley
14 Hope
15 Coquihalla River
16 Iago Station
17 Coquihalla Summit
18 Coldwater River
19 Brookmere

Hwy

TCT Route

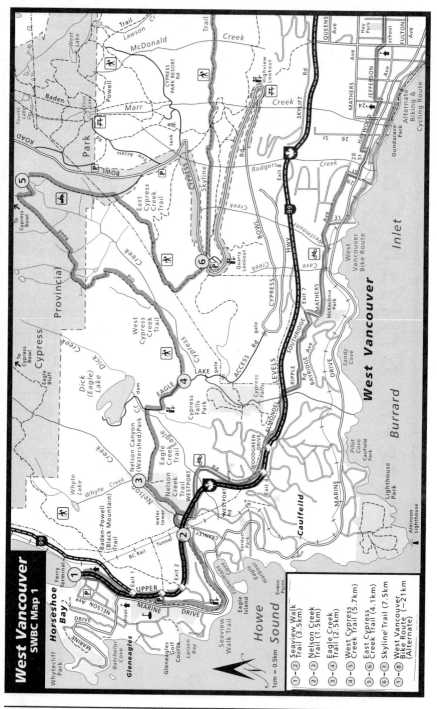

West Vancouver
SWBC Map 1

1cm = 0.5km

1 – 2 Seaview Walk Trail (3.5km)
2 – 3 Nelson Creek Trail (1.5km)
3 – 4 Eagle Creek Trail (2.5km)
4 – 5 West Cypress Creek Trail (5.7km)
5 – 6 East Cypress Creek Trail (4.1km)
6 – 7 Skyline Trail (7.5km)
1 – 8 West Vancouver Bike Route (~21km) (Alternate)

Southwestern BC Map 1: West Vancouver

Southwestern BC Section 1-2

3.5 km

Seaview Walk Trail

Horseshoe Bay marks the beginning of the Trans Canada Trail on British Columbia's mainland. There a few different options to the Trans Canada Trail route through West and North Vancouver. We will start with the main route, which is only recommended for those who are walking. We have described an alternative route for bikers later in this book.

Fisherman's Cove   R. Mussio

At the ferry terminal, construction has forced a short detour around Keith Road. The detour takes the traveller up Bay Street to Royal Avenue. From Royal, follow Chatham Street to a set of stairs, which climbs to Marine Drive. The Trans Canada Trail crosses Marine Drive and proceeds south to the entrance to the Gleneagles Golf Course. Across Marine Drive from the golf course entrance, lies the beginning of the signed Seaview Walk Trail.

The trailhead to the 2 km Seaview Walk Trail lies on the east side of Marine Drive, be careful crossing the road. The Seaview Walk is a popular West Vancouver trail that follows an old rail grade to a vantage point with a park bench overlooking Fisherman's Cove and Eagle Island. Continuing along the Seaview Walk, the trail will start to descend towards Nelson Creek.

Horseshoe Bay is a quaint little village that was once a notorious fishing community. In addition to a scenic ocean front shopping area, there is a nice park complete with picnic tables and washrooms.

Southwestern BC Section 2-3

1.5 km
Nelson Creek Trail

As you begin to hear the distant rumble of traffic, you will see the all too familiar Trans Canada Trail signs pointing you north away from the Seaview Walk. This new trail system takes you up the west side of Nelson Creek on a rather ingenious route. The trail travels over the BC Rail Tunnel entrance up some stairs and under the impressive Upper Levels Highway Bridge. The forested trail switchbacks up to the old highway bridge, which crosses over the creek to the Nelson Canyon Watershed. A toilet can be found at the edge of the highway, approximately 50 feet west of the bridge.

At the water tank, a sign informs walkers to continue north and up the access road. This is the start of the hiking trail to Capilano Regional Park requiring one to be in good physical condition and well prepared. The biking route continues southeast and back under the Trans Canada Highway Bridge.

At the top of the access road, hikers will find another water tank. Here the Trans Canada Trail route continues on a new trail found on the east side of the tank. This newly cut trail leads through a magnificent forested area before spilling out on a service road.

> There are a few intimidating signs in this area. One signals the possibility of encountering bears. This is a common problem on the whole Trans Canada Trail route throughout British Columbia. Please take precautions when in wilderness areas. We recommend attaching a bear bell to your hiking gear.
>
> Other signs are posted forbidding trespassing in the watershed. Please respect the fragile watershed area and do not stray off the trail.

Southwestern BC Section 3-4

2.5 km
Eagle Creek Trail

Follow the service road for a short distance to the top of a hill. At the top of the hill, there is an opening in the forest on your left, which is the beginning of a trail to the Eagle Lake Access Road. The trail travels through a mixed coastal forest setting all the way to an access road to the Eagle Lake Reservoir. The Trans Canada Trail follows the access road south until it meets the West Cypress Creek Trail.

Be sure to keep your eyes open to the right along the access road. En route to the West Cypress Trail there is a short turn-off that veers off to the right. This branch leads to a short trail and a great view of the Georgia Strait.

Southwestern BC Section 4-5

5.7 km
West Cypress Creek Trail

At the gate on the Eagle Lake Access Road, the West Cypress Creek Trail branches northeast on a fire access road that is surrounded by thick brush. The road climbs sharply towards Cypress Provincial Park. In fact you will gain over 450 m (1,510 ft) in elevation but you will be rewarded with the occasional view of Burrard Inlet and Vancouver far below. When the route dips toward Cypress Creek you will find a bridge that allows you to cross the creek to the next section of the Trans Canada Trail route.

At the top of the West Cypress Creek Trail travellers can choose to continue up to the Cypress Bowl Ski Area. This area makes a popular summer and winter retreat for residents of Vancouver. There are virtually unlimited trails to explore; from short day forested trails to rugged alpine trek the sky is the limit. In winter everyone from downhill ski enthusiasts to cross-country skiers and snowshoers can be found in the area.

At the Cypress Bowl parking area, explorers can find the signs marking the Baden Powell Trail. If you continue east, the popular forested trail will link you back to the Skyline Trail on the Trans Canada Trail route just west of Brothers Creek.

Southwestern BC Section 5-6

4.1 km
East Cypress Creek Trail

The Trans Canada Trail route continues on the east side of Cypress Creek after crossing the bridge. The East Cypress Creek Trail follows another utility access road through a heavily forested area. The route is very easy to follow but there is one branch road that can lead you astray. This fork in the road is found about 1 km from the footbridge. Take the right fork.

Continuing southeast, you will soon be following under a small powerline that eventually leads past a British Properties gate. Just past the gate, the trail meets up with the Cypress Bowl Road and the start of the Skyline Trail. Just south of the junction of Cypress Bowl Road, there is a fantastic lookout found at an old quarry just off the Cypress Bowl Road. This viewpoint offers a splendid view of Vancouver from an elevation of 620 m (2,030 ft).

Hidden trails branch off the access roads in this area and are part of the infamous North Shore Mountain Biking Trails. These are extreme trails that are difficult to walk let alone ride. There are teeter-totters, vertical drops, log crossings and many other ingenious gimmicks. There are also several lookouts found along the powerline.

Southwestern BC Section 6-7

7.5 km
Skyline Trail

At the crossing of the Trans Canada Trail route over Cypress Bowl Road to the Skyline Trail, there is a small parking lot and pit toilets available for visitors. The Skyline Trail is a moderate hiking trail that travels east about 7.5km all the way to the Cleveland Dam in the Capilano River Regional Park. The trail traverses over half a dozen prominent creeks as well as a few suburban roads before reaching the park. Along the route, the Skyline Trail also passes by several superb viewpoints, which include lush ravine areas and a few majestic waterfalls found along creek areas. Please take care when travelling this section when it is wet. There are a number of tricky footing areas along stairways and bridges that can be quite slippery when wet.

Skyline Trail   R. Mussio

> *In the forested areas next to the Skyline Trail several branch trails can be found. Two of the more famous routes include the Baden Powell Trail and the Brothers Creek Trail. Both of these moderate trails are well marked and take you through impressive stands of second growth forest and vestiges of past logging operations.*

Southwestern BC Section 1-8

~21 km

Cycling Trail

For cyclists the Trans Canada Trail route offers a secondary interim route from the Horseshoe Bay Ferry to Capilano River Park and the Cleveland Dam. Currently this cycling route follows mainly quiet city roads. An off-road route will be determined at a future date.

Beginning at the Horseshoe Bay Ferry Terminal, the Trans Canada Trail cycling route follows the Trans Canada Highway east to Exit #4. This is a very busy, noisy highway that has the added bonus of a short stiff climb. At the exit, cross over the highway along the bridge and take the first right onto Woodgreen Drive.

From Woodgreen Drive, the route follows several different roads all the way to Taylor Way. These roads do not see much in the way of traffic but there are tight or blind corners and virtually no shoulder to ride on. Although you will be following several different roads, commuter cycling signs and the TCT logo are well displayed along the route. If you pay attention to the signs, you should have no problems following the route.

As you begin on Woodgreen Drive, north of the rumble of the Trans Canada Highway, the cycling route skirts past a few rock bluffs on its way to Woodcrest Road and then to Almondel Road. From Almondel Road the route starts to lose elevation as you traverse under the highway before connecting with Ripple Road. From Ripple Road, the route quickly follows Westwood Road to Southridge Road and to a short dirt trail. The 60m dirt trail connects Southridge Road on the west to Mathers Avenue to the east. The trail follows Mathers Avenue for a while to 29th Street. The route takes 29th Street south to the busy Marine Drive. The section from Almondel Road to Marine Drive takes you past many beautiful homes and even offers you the occasional glimpse of Burrard Inlet. This section is also mostly all downhill. Be sure to have your brakes in good working order.

From Marine Drive you will hook up with 28th, which leads up to Haywood Avenue. The route travels east along Haywood Avenue to a short uphill jaunt on 24th Street and then continues east along Jefferson Avenue. From Jefferson

Avenue, the route heads past Pauline Johnson School along Inglewood Avenue. The route travels uphill again on the busier 15th Street and then east on Kings Avenue before heading south along Burley Drive. From Burley Drive, the route takes Inglewood Avenue east again to Taylor Way. This section of the Trans Canada Trail cycling route is a little more demanding on the legs. The route also takes you past several more nice homes and a couple small parks.

At Taylor Way, the cycling route becomes somewhat more challenging. Not only will you gain a lot of elevation but the roads are a little busier. The climb is rewarded with nice vantage points, more beautiful homes to admire and a fabulous park section to ride in.

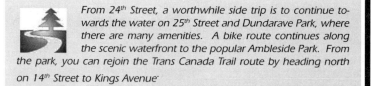

From 24th Street, a worthwhile side trip is to continue towards the water on 25th Street and Dundarave Park, where there are many amenities. A bike route continues along the scenic waterfront to the popular Ambleside Park. From the park, you can rejoin the Trans Canada Trail route by heading north on 14th Street to Kings Avenue

From Taylor Way the Trans Canada Trail cycling route climbs north to Stevens Drive. Once again you will cross under the Trans Canada Highway to a beautiful boulevard. The trees on this boulevard create a magnificent display in spring when they blossom. The cycling route continues up along Stevens Drive, past the Capilano Golf Club and to Deep Dene Road. There is a short turn onto Deep Dene Road before the route then follows Glenmore Drive north. Eventually, you will notice a cycling right-of-way on the east side of Glenmore Drive. This is the beginning of the path that leads to the Cleveland Dam and where cyclists and walkers come together again.

The path leads into the forested Capilano River Regional Park and climbs along a wide swath. Short branch trails (walking only) lead east to fabulous viewpoints of the river and the dam. The cycling route again branches from the walking route before crossing the dam and hooking up with Capilano Park Road on the east side of the dam. The Trans Canada Trail cycling route follows Capilano Park Road south to the busier Capilano Road, rejoining the walkers near Edgemont Boulevard and the start of the Edgemont Trail.

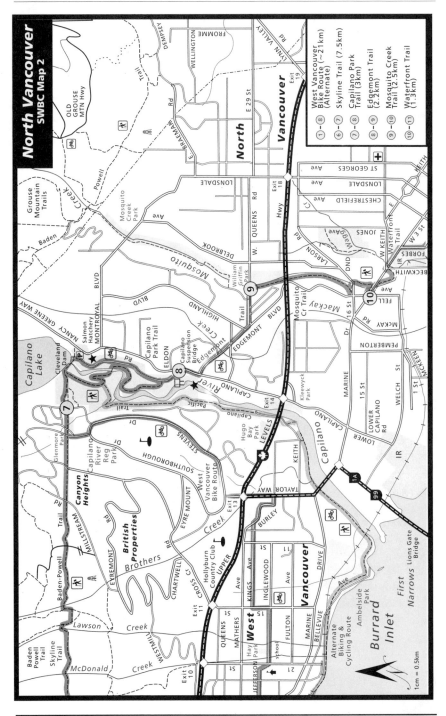

North Vancouver
SWBC Map 2

West Vancouver Bike Route (~21km) ①–⑧ (Alternate)
Skyline Trail (7.5km) ⑥–⑦
Capilano Park Trail (3km) ⑦–⑧
Edgemont Trail (3km) ⑧–⑨
Mosquito Creek Trail (2.5km) ⑨–⑩
Waterfront Trail (1.3km) ⑩–⑪

1cm = 0.5km

Southwestern BC Map 2: North Vancouver

Southwestern BC Section 7-8

3 km '

Capilano Regional Park Trail

Continuing from where the Skyline Trail meets the Capilano River Regional Park, the Trans Canada Trail route enters the beautifully wooded park. The trail winds downstream along a broad path next to the deep river canyon. Side trails lead to the scenic Cleveland Dam as well as some fine canyon and river views. Please be careful if you venture off the main path as these trails are not well maintained.

Eventually you will cross the river at the salmon hatchery. This is an interesting place to stop and you can even view a fish ladder in action. From the salmon hatchery, the Trans Canada Trail route follows a path past the entrance to the world famous Capilano Suspension Bridge. This busy area is found south of the intersection of Capilano Road and Edgemont Boulevard.

Cleveland Dam   R. Mussio

The Capilano Suspension Bridge is one of the highlights of the Vancouver area. A man named George Mackay originally constructed the bridge in 1888. Mackay built the bridge in order to cross to the other side of the steep canyon from his cabin. Today, the reconstructed bridge recaptures the rustic essence of Mackay's first bridge. The suspension bridge sits some 70 m (230 ft) above the Capilano River nestled within a spectacular canyon. The bridge is 137 m (450 ft) in length and sways and creaks as it is crossed, making for a hair raising but exhilarating experience.

Southwestern BC Section 8-9

2.2 km

Edgemont Trail

The Edgemont Trail is the beginning of the transition from the semi-wilderness route to an urban route. Both cyclists and pedestrians can follow this route.

The Trans Canada Trail route skirts the busy Edgemont Boulevard through Edgemont Village and turns east onto West Queens Road. Travelling east along West Queens Road, the route leads to William Griffin Park Recreation Centre along Mosquito Creek.

Southwestern BC Section 9-10

2.5 km

Mosquito Creek Trail

Parking is available at the William Griffin Park and Recreation Centre where you will find the trailhead to the Mosquito Creek Trail. The Trans Canada Trail follows the Mosquito Creek Trail south towards the Trans Canada Highway. The trail traverses along the peaceful creek side, eventually leading under the highway and continues south to 16th Street.

Cross 16th Street at the traffic lights (three in all) at Fell Avenue and 16th Street. After the crossing, the route continues east to a crossing of Mosquito Creek. The trail then follows the east side of the creek south to another traffic light crossing at the intersection of Fell Avenue and Marine Drive.

Along the Mosquito Creek Trail, there are a number of spawning channels that have been created to help enhance salmon spawning success. During the fall, spawning salmon can be viewed along the trail.

Southwestern BC Section 10-11

1.3 km
Waterfront Trail

On the south side of Marine Drive the Trans Canada Trail begins to follow a route called the Waterfront Trail, which leads down to the Burrard Inlet waterfront. The trail begins by following Marine Drive to another crossing of the Mosquito Creek, then travels south along the creek before connecting with Beckwith Avenue. The route follows Beckwith Avenue east towards 2nd Street and finally to 3rd Street. After a short jaunt along 3rd Street, the trail follows Forbes Street south over Esplanade Avenue and into Waterfront Park. The route continues east to Longsdale Quay Public Market and the Seabus Terminal. The Seabus Terminal marks the end of the Trans Canada Trail on the North Shore.

Mission Reserve Heritage Site   L. Lebrun

Along with a multitude of educational programmes available at the Mission Reserve Heritage Site, Xaytem lies on a native archaeological heritage site. Ongoing research at the site has helped provided conclusive evidence of the presence of early natives in the region. This fascinating Interpretive Centre also offers visitors the chance to explore the history of the Sto:lo, locally settled early indigenous peoples, and learn about the science of archaeology. The centre is open year round. For more information call 1-604-820-9725.

Waterfront Park is small city park that is found just before the Seabus Terminal. Interpretive signs are posted throughout the park, which provide information on the harbour area and its history.

For an alternate adventure, the Royal Hudson BC Rail train can be picked up off First Street. For a modest fee, the train takes passengers past Whistler and Squamish to the interior of British Columbia. The train offers a scenic ocean and mountainous journey. Many passengers take the train in the early morning up to Whistler for the day and return in the evening. The walk to the train station is just over 2 km from the Trans Canada Trail route near Beckwith Avenue.

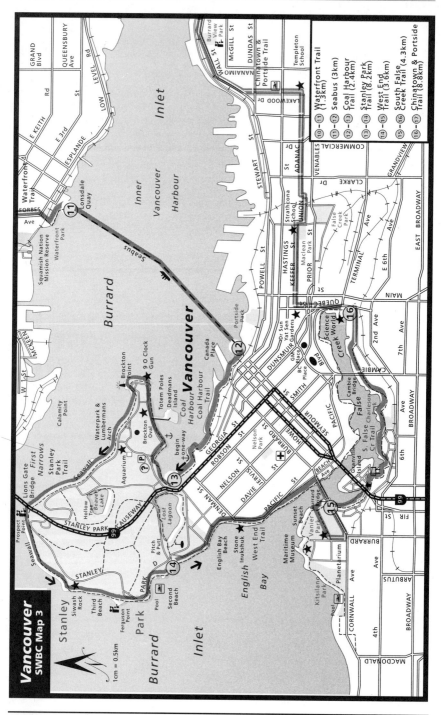

Vancouver
SWBC Map 3

1cm = 0.5km

10–11 Waterfront Trail (1.3km)
11–12 Seabus (3km)
12–13 Coal Harbour Trail (2.4km)
13–14 Stanley Park Trail (8.2km)
14–15 West End Trail (3.6km)
15–16 South False Creek Trail (4.3km)
16–17 Chinatown & Portside Trail (8.8km)

Southwestern BC Map 3: Vancouver

Southwestern BC Section 11-12

3 km
Seabus

The Seabus crosses the Burrard Inlet from the North shore to Vancouver every 15 or 30 minutes. The trip takes approximately 20 minutes and offers a first hand view of the busy Vancouver seaport and skyline. The cost of the Seabus varies on the time of day but ranges from \$1.75-\$2.50. It can be quite crowded, especially during rush hours.

Southwestern BC Section 12-13

2.4 km
Coal Harbour Trail

S. Burnham

From the Seabus terminal, the Trans Canada Trail route follows a new Vancouver pathway known as the Coal Harbour Trail. Turn right when you exit the station and head west past Canada Place down the hill to Coal Harbour. The paved pathway skirts newly built condominiums and a recreation centre, where washrooms and a cafe are found. Continue along the path past more waterfront development to Devonian Harbour Park, which hosts interesting sculptures and offers a great harbour view. The paved path eventually connects with the Stanley Park Trail near the tunnel leading to Lost Lagoon.

Southwestern BC Section 13-14

8.2 km
Stanley Park Trail

Stanley Park is another world famous destination found in the city of Vancouver. The park and Seawall Route host millions of visitors each year. The scenic route begins at the Lost Lagoon crossover and travels past Burrard Inlet, Lions Gate Bridge, Prospect Point and Third Beach. The paved trail provides great city and mountain views, access to forested trails and beaches as well as several unique and interesting points to explore. The Vancouver Aquarium, Totem Park, lighthouses and sculptures are just a few of the highlights of the route. Restrooms and concession stands can be found off the seawall path. The Stanley Park Trail ends at Second Beach where it connects with the West End Trail.

Siwash Rock   S. Burnham

One important item to note is that wheeled travellers (cyclists and in-line skaters) must travel in a counter clockwise direction (from Coal Harbour to English Bay). This one-way routing has been done to limit collision incidents, as well as to create a smooth flow along the often busy seawall. The Stanley Park Trail is also wheelchair accessible.

Those travelling east to west will need to access the one-way Seawall Trail. This can be done by following the path from 2nd Beach, past Lost Logoon, to Coal Harbour.

An interesting side trip can be accessed from Second Beach to the north side of the Lost Lagoon. The route follows the Stanley Park Bridal Path through stands of giant Douglas fir and Cedar trees. From the Bridal Path, there are also several separate park trails that can be explored that take you through the heart of Stanley Park.

Deadman's Island is so named because it was once a burial ground for both the Squamish and Musqueam First Nations People. It was also used for burial purposes by immigrants during the smallpox epidemic in the early 1890's. Today the island is the site of the HMCS Discovery Naval Reserve Base.

This 407 hectare (1,000 acre) park was established in 1887 by the city of Vancouver and was originally leased to the city by the Federal Government for an annual fee of $1.00. The world famous park is home to some of the largest cedar trees in the region and is the preservation site for several original native totem poles. The main trail found through the park is the Seawall, which traverses the perimeter of the park providing excellent views of the Burrard Inlet and English Bay.

The Lions Gate Bridge is the oldest standing bridge in the Lower Mainland. Constructed in the late 1930's, the bridge was opened for use as a toll bridge in 1939. Unbeknownst to many, the bridge was not originally met with enthusiasm by local residents. In fact, the first bridge referendum in 1927 was lost with a strong 'no bridge' vote. Thanks to the heavy lobbying of the provincial and federal government by local businessman A.J. Taylor, the bridge became an eventual reality. With the financial backing of the multi millionaire and father of Guinness beer, Sir Arthur Guinness of Britain, it was difficult for the governments to pass up such a major development that would be needed in the future. The city of Vancouver eventually purchased the bridge in 1963 and soon after eliminated the need for toll fares. Ironically, today Vancouver finds itself in a similar situation as the city ponders the construction of another crossing.

Southwestern BC Section 14-15

3.6 km
West End Trail

The West End Trail is Vancouver's western extension of the Seawall. The route heads south from Second Beach towards the Burrard Street Bridge. The trail passes several great natural viewpoints providing photo perfect sights of the majestic English Bay. The trail also passes by English Bay and Sunset Beaches. Due to the proximity of Downtown Vancouver, this area is a popular retreat and can be very busy, especially on sunny days.

At the Aquatic Centre, the Seawall ends and The Trans Canada Trail route turns up Thurlow Street to cross False Creek on the western sidewalk of the historic Burrard Bridge. The Trans Canada Trail route leads into Vanier Park, where you will find the beginning of the South False Creek Trail.

An alternate crossing of False Creek is to take the Aquabus from Sunset Beach to the Maritime Museum near Vanier Park. An established trail travels east from the museum that will quickly connect with the Trans Canada Trail near the Burrard Bridge.

 From the Burrard Bridge, a side trip can be taken along the shoreline of English Bay through Kitsilano Park to the UBC Campus. Along with the UBC campus, the Museum of Anthropology, Pacific Spirit Park and infamous Wreck Beach are interesting attractions that are worth visiting.

Southwestern BC Section 15-16

4.3 km
South False Creek Trail

On the west end of the Burrard Bridge turn right on Chestnut Street and right again on the roadway leading to the Planetarium and the College of Music. This road heads towards the waterfront and the heart of Vanier Park. Here one can enjoy one of the many park benches or visit the Maritime Museum and the Planetarium.

Continue past the College of Music and turn right at the marina. Make your way east through the marina and rejoin the Seawall Walk, which will take you to the entrance of Granville Island. The Island is definitely worth exploring with food, beverages, some fantastic shopping and even washrooms close by.

Shortly after crossing the road to Granville Island and the pond you will see the familiar looking Trans Canada Trail Pavilion. The route continues on the Seawall on the south side of False Creek. The area offers several benches and a variety of businesses that cater to the young and vibrant owners in this posh False Creek condominium area. The views include the former site of Expo 86 (now called Yaletown), Cambie Street Bridge and Science World.

The Trans Canada Trail route continues east and passes under the Cambie Street Bridge, where it enters a rather dingy looking industrial area. This area is slated to build a self sustaining neighbourhood and a new waterfront trail. In the meantime, a temporary path follows 1st Avenue to Ontario Street. Turn north at the end of False Creek along the marked bicycle path and meet up with the impressive mirror ball known as Science World. Washrooms and snacks are available at the southwest side of the building.

Despite being only 77 ha in size, False Creek forms the heart of the city of Vancouver. It's shoreline is highly developed and the waterbody is heavily used by recreational boaters.

Southwestern BC Section 16-17

8.8 km
Chinatown & Portside Trail

From Science World continue north on Quebec Street, past the intersection and under the Sky Train and the Georgia Viaduct to Keefer Street. The Trans Canada Trail route follows Keefer Street and the well signed Adanac Bike Route east past the produce and meat markets of Chinatown. Several other interesting stores are found in the immediate area, while the popular Dr. Sun Yat Sen Gardens can be found at the beginning of Keefer Street.

Continue east past the Strathcona Community Centre, where washrooms are available, to Maclean Park. At Maclean Park the trail takes a short trek south along Hawks Avenue to the junction of Union Street. The route then follows Union Street east to a short jog north along Vernon Drive to Adanac Street.

The Strathcona District is one of the oldest communities in Vancouver. Many of the original homes still remain. The Trans Canada Trail also skirts by Strathcona School, which is the oldest in the city.

The route along Adanac (Canada spelled backwards) begins a gradual climb through an industrial area to Woodland Park, where washrooms can be found. Next up is Commercial Drive. This is the hub of the Italian Community and it is certainly worth exploring the few blocks south of the route.

Continue east and up the hill along Adanac. You will pass Victoria Drive before reaching Templeton School. The school has interesting mosaics of provincial birds and even built a plaza specifically for the Trans Canada Trail.

At Lakewood Drive, the route heads north from the Adanac Bike Route past more East End residences. Cross Hastings and Dundas Streets to the end of Lakewood, where a short park trail leads you to Wall Street.

The Trans Canada Trail route follows the scenic Wall Street east past Burrard View Park and then Dusty Greenwell Park and its large grain elevator. At the end of Wall Street a path leads to McGill Street. Turn left and take the east side of the overpass down to Commissioner Street. You will eventually come to a dock that allows people an upclose view of the harbour area.

Cross over the railway tracks leading into New Brighton Park. During the summer this park comes alive with a pool and concession stand with washrooms. The route through the park is unmarked.

Pedestrians can follow the east sidewalk to a stairway, which leads to a new seawall, while cyclists should follow the east sidewalk to the overpass ramp. The seawall path heads east towards the Cascadia Grain Elevators and to another crossing under the railway tracks. The path connects with Bridgeway Street and follows Bridgeway to a sharp turn south to Skeena Road.

For now, the route then follows Skeena Road through an underpass. Turn right at the crosswalk just past the underpass and take the path going north to Bates Park. The park offers stunning views of Vancouver, Burrard Inlet and the North Shore.

If time permits, it is highly recommended to take a side trip to Burrard View Park. A short route leads up to a great viewpoint that provides a picturesque view of the busy Inner Harbour of Burrard Inlet.

This confusing section will be replaced by a path over the railway tunnel connecting Bridgeway Street with Boundary Road. For now take the route through Bates Park and turn left at the trail at the end of Boundary Road. Boundary Road marks the end of the Vancouver portion of the Trans Canada Trail.

The Haida Native people first settled the beautiful region of Vancouver. The first European visitor to the region was Spanish pilot, Jose Maria Narvez, who discovered the mouth of the Fraser River in 1791. One year later, Captain George Vancouver explored the area intensely in search of the fabled "Northwest Passage". In the early 1800's settlement began along the Fraser River as routes to the east and Hudson Bay began to become more known. With the establishment of various outpost forts such as Fort Langley, settlement prospects were further enhanced and the region grew significantly.

If you were to imagine Vancouver in the late 1800's, the city was literally log cabins amid giant cedar and fir trees. By 1898, Vancouver established its first newspaper, the "Daily Province" and in 1908, the University of British Columbia was founded. Today, more than 1.5 million people live in and around the city of Vancouver and the city has firmly established itself as one of the leading commercial centres of Canada. The Port of Vancouver welcomes ships from over ninety countries, making it one of the busiest ports on the Pacific Ocean.

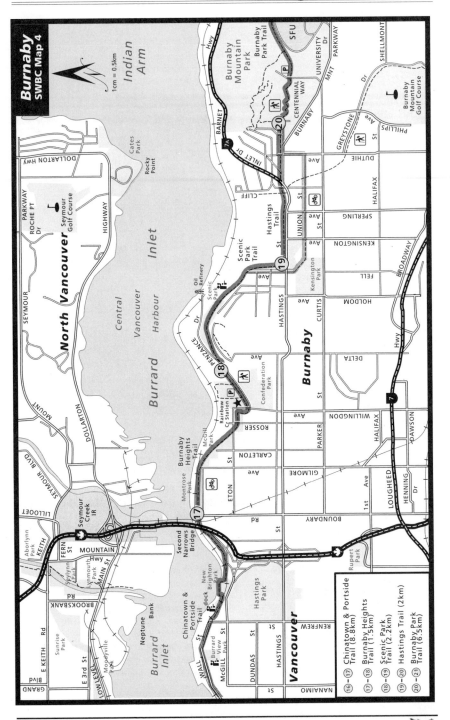

Burnaby
SWBC Map 4

1cm = 0.5km

Trails:

16 – 17 Chinatown & Portside Trail (8.8km)
17 – 18 Burnaby Heights Trail (1.5km)
18 – 19 Scenic Park Trail (2.2km)
19 – 20 Hastings Trail (2km)
20 – 21 Burnaby Park Trail (6.5km)

Southwestern BC Map 4: Burnaby

Southwestern BC Section 17-18

1.5 km
Burnaby Heights Trail

At Boundary Road near the Burrard Inlet shore, the Trans Canada Trail route travels along what is known as the Burnaby Heights Trail. The trail offers occasional views of the Burrard Inlet while by-passing through the urban areas of northern Burnaby. The trail passes through Eton and McGill Parks before meeting Willingdon Avenue near Penzance Drive at the Rainbow Creek Station Museum. Across the road, Confederation Park hosts playing fields, a skateboarding area and many other amenities.

Burnaby Heights   R. Mussio

At Penzance Drive, the Trans Canada Trail route proceeds along a new trail on the north side of the road. The route offers a nice walk or cycle as it passes through Confederation Park to the Capital Hill Conservation Area and the Scenic View Trailhead.

This urban park offers a number of exciting activities to the visitor. The park is separated into two sections divided by a north and south portion. In the southern section of the park there are a number of recreational opportunities available including lawn bowling, bocce, and other sports such as baseball. Other amenities in the southern portion of the park include a fitness centre, community centre, library, spray pool and the popular model steam railway, which operates on weekends during the summer. The northern portion of the park has been left in a near natural state offering a semi-wilderness experience complete with the fantastic Penzance Trail system.

> For an alternative route for hikers, there is a lovely 1.65 km forested loop trail that can be found at the parking area of Confederation Park. The trail meanders through some densely forested areas and offers some hidden trails that will take you down to the shoreline. The loop trail rejoins the Trans Canada Trail further east on Penzance Drive.

Southwestern BC Section 18-19

2.2 km

Scenic View Trail

To the east of Confederation Park lies Scenic Park and the continuation of the trail. The trail follows an established route called the Scenic Trail through Scenic Park, which is the quintessential urban retreat trail. Along the trail, it is easy to forget about the urban 'bustle' that occurs beyond the trail environment. Several vantage points offer good views of Burrard Inlet and Indian Arm. There is little noise to detract from the experience. The trail eventually passes Fell Street and finally ends at the meeting with Hastings Street.

At the intersection of Fell Street, it is recommended that bikers follow a different route south along Fell Street to just past Hastings Street and the entrance of Kensington Park. The route travels through the park via an urban trail. The urban trail connects with Union Street and heads east to Duthie Avenue. From Duthie Avenue, the route heads north to the Burnaby Mountain Parkway. Shortly along the parkway, there is a pedestrian activated traffic light, where the trail crosses the parkway to Burnwood Avenue. The biker route then veers north along Burnwood Avenue to Hastings Street where it connects with the main Trans Canada Trail.

Southwestern BC Section 19-20

2 km

Hastings Trail

Near Hastings Street, the Trans Canada Trail route follows the north side of Hastings Street east to the corner of the Kensington Intersection. The trail then follows a path behind the gas station, which eventually passes a golf range leading back to Hastings Street.

The route continues east along Hastings Street under a pedestrian overpass to an intersection with the Barnet Highway. The route crosses the intersection and continues on the much less busy section of Hastings Street. Follow Hastings Street towards Burnaby Mountain Park and the trailhead of the Burnaby Mountain Park Trail.

This small Burnaby park offers visitors the chance to practice their golf on its pitch and putt green. There are also several sports fields for various activities such as soccer and softball. The park is also home to an oval track, outdoor pool, tennis courts and the Kensington Arena.

Southwestern BC Section 20-22

6.5 km

Burnaby Park Trail

The Burnaby Park Trail begins near the end of Hastings Street. Here the trail starts to climb along a path on the westside of the Burnaby Mountain Park. The forested trail crosses a road within the park named Centennial Way and passes a familiar looking Trans Canada Trail Pavilion. Occasional glimpses of Burrard Inlet and the city beyond can be enjoyed in this area. Continuing on a new trail that leads up towards Simon Fraser University one will find themselves on a much more tranquil forested section of the route. The trail levels off and skirts University Drive before joining a local trail called Joe's Trail. Joe's Trail continues east and starts to descend through a mixture of second growth coniferous and deciduous trees until it meets a BC Hydro right-of-way.

Burnaby Mountain Trails   *W. Mussio*

From the hydro right-of-way, the Trans Canada Trail route travels north about 200 metres and enters the forest on a fairly steep hill. Continue downhill all the way to the noisy Barnet Highway and the beginning of the new Inlet Trail. This downhill route loses about 220 m (720 ft). Cyclists will require a good set of brakes to safely negotiate this lovely forested trail.

The eastern side of Burnaby Mountain is riddled with trails. The SFU Mountain Bike Club originally built these, many of which still exist today. Whether on foot or on bike, there are many excellent trails to explore. These trails cut through the forested slopes of Burnaby Mountain and range from gentle to extreme.

The Burnaby Mountain Park was established to preserve an integral natural portion of the Burnaby area from the sprawl of urban development. Protected within the park is a mixed conifer/deciduous forest creating prime habitat for hundreds of animal species, including bald eagles. Recreation opportunities have been developed within the park with its ecological interests in mind and are comprised of a few main hiking/biking trails, including a viable horseback alternative for the Trans Canada Trail.

The city of Burnaby lies within the centre of the Lower Mainland region and was first settled by Europeans in the mid 1800's. Unlike the urban sprawl of today, the original settlers had to carve their homes out of lush rainforest vegetation towered by giant fir and cedar trees. Up until the extension of the Canadian Pacific Railway through the townsite in 1887, development of the area was quite slow. In 1892, the town of Burnaby was established, named after one of the original settlers and explorers of the area, Robert Burnaby. Built on an economic base of forestry and agriculture, Burnaby soon grew to include schools, a post office and church. Today, Burnaby boasts a population fast approaching 200,000 and is one of the leading centres for industrial and technological business growth in the Lower Mainland.

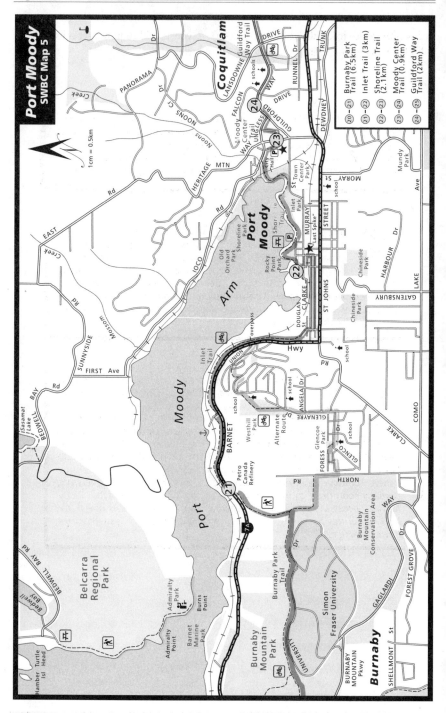

Port Moody
SWBC Map 5

1cm = 0.5km

20 – 21 Burnaby Park Trail (6.5km)
21 – 22 Inlet Trail (3km)
22 – 23 Shoreline Trail (2.1km)
23 – 24 Moody Center Trail (0.9km)
24 – 25 Guildford Way Trail (2km)

Southwestern BC Map 5: Port Moody

Southwestern BC Section 21-22

4.5 km
Inlet Trail

The Inlet Trail is a new, welcome addition to the trail network in Port Moody. The trail starts after the crossing of the busy Barnet Highway at the traffic lights in front of the Petro-Canada Industrial Site. The trail quickly dives towards the inlet as it undulates through a surprisingly peaceful forested setting. You are afforded many views of Burrard Inlet, which features a number of industrial sites lining the Port Moody Harbour. Interpretative signs featuring both natural features and the industries of the harbour area will be added along this trail. Outside of a tricky jaunt on the Reed Point Marina Road, this 3 km section of the Trans

Vines on Inlet Trail   R. Mussio

Canada Trail route is on an easy to follow trail.

Port Moody Arm is 560 ha in size and features many Industrial sites. The eastern portion of the waterbody is an extensive inter-tidal mudflat. Waterfowl and a wide variety of marine life can be seen in this area.

After passing the giant yellow sulphur piles of Pacific Coast Terminal as well as Melrose and Schoolhouse Creeks, you will soon exit onto a paved path leading onto Short Street. Follow Short Street to Douglas Street, which travels south to Clarke Street. Clarke Street is one of the main streets in the Old Port Moody area and the trail follows the street east through the heart of the town. There are many interesting shops or restaurants to visit, including a bike shop for those in need of supplies. At the end of Clarke Street, you will need to cross over the railway tracks on the overpass leading to Rocky Point Park. Bikers may find the sidewalk a better alternative since there is no shoulder on the road. After passing the Port Moody or Last Spike Museum on Murray Road, you will meet up with a paved multi-use pathway that marks the beginning of the Shoreline Trail.

> Beneath the ramp to Rocky Point Park, you will find the Old Port Moody Rail Station Museum. The Museum is full of fantastic artifacts and information about the rail line in Port Moody and the history of the 'Last Spike'.

Southwestern BC Section 22-23

2.1 km
Shoreline Trail

The Shoreline Trail is a popular paved path that is enjoyed by walkers, joggers, in-line skaters and cyclists. It is a gentle, scenic path that skirts the Port Moody shoreline and the pier area of Rocky Point Park. There are several separate walking paths in the area for people on foot to enjoy.

The path heads east along the water and through the forested Inlet Park, which offers a fantastic display of west coast fauna. Shortly after the route veers north along the inlet, the Trans Canada Trail meets up with a trail that travels east over the railway tracks towards the Port Moody Civic Centre. If you cross the bridge over Noons Creek, you have gone too far.

Southwestern BC Section 23-24

0.9 km
Moody Centre Trail

The Moody Centre Trail takes the Trans Canada Trail route through Port Moody's new town centre. This section is mainly on sidewalks.

The route begins from the railway tracks heading past the soccer field towards the Port Moody Arena. After the railway crossing the route follows the tracks north to

Noon's Creek. Stay parallel to Noon's Creek until you reach Ioco Road. Go south toward the sidewalk and cross over to the main entrance to Pioneer Park. Follow the trail southward until it comes out on another sidewalk along Ioco Road. Go south to the traffic lights, cross Ioco Road and proceed through Newport Village, which soon connects to Ungless Way. The Trans Canada Trail continues along Ungless Way east to Guildford Way, where you will begin to traverse along the Guildford Way Trail.

Southwestern BC Section 24-25

2 km
Guilford Way Trail

The Guildford Way Trail is the part of the Trans Canada Trail route that travels east out of the town of Port Moody and towards the Coquitlam Town Centre. The trail traverses the Eagle Ridge Neighbourhood along a nicely planted boulevard called Guildford Way. You will pass Falcon Drive, Lansdowne Drive and Johnson Street before meeting Hoy Creek and the trailhead to the Town Centre Trail.

Shoreline Trail   L. Lebrun

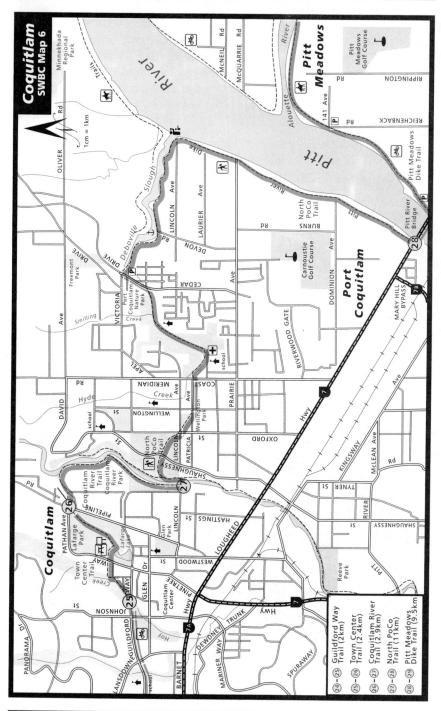

Coquitlam
SWBC Map 6

1cm = 1km

Minnekhada Regional Park

Tsil Tsil Trails

OLIVER Rd

Pitt Meadows

Pitt Meadows Golf Course

RIPPINGTON

McNeil Rd

McQuarrie Rd

141 Ave

REICHENBACK Rd

River

Alouette

Deboville Slough

Dike

Pitt River

Pitt

Pitt River Bridge

Pitt Meadows Dike Trail

28

LINCOLN Ave

LAURIER Ave

DEVON

CEDAR

Port Coquitlam Nature Park

BURNS Rd

North PoCo Trail

Carnoustie Golf Course

DOMINION Ave

RIVERWOOD GATE

Port Coquitlam

MARY HILL BYPASS

7B

Hwy 7

Freemont Park

DRIVE

VICTORIA

Smilling

Creek

Ave

school

MERIDIAN Rd

APEL

COAST Ave

PRAIRIE Ave

OXFORD

Hwy 7

KINGSWAY

McLEAN Rd

Hyde St

David

school

WELLINGTON

Creek

Wellington Park

North PoCo Trail

LINCOLN

PATRICIA St

SHAUGHNESSY

27

TYNER St

RIVER St

SHAUGHNESSY

Coquitlam

PATHAN Ave

Lafarge Park

26

PIPELINE Rd

Coquitlam River Trail

Coquitlam River Park

HASTINGS St

LOUGHEED

Reeve Park

PITT

Town Center Trail

Lafarge Lake

Glen Park

Glen Dr

LINCOLN St

WESTWOOD

Hwy

25

JOHNSON

Creek

PINETREE

Coquitlam Center

DEWDNEY TRUNK

7A

Hwy 7

PANORAMA Dr

LANSDOWNE

GUILDFORD

Hoy

BARNET

MARINER WAY

SPURAWAY

24–25 Guildford Way Trail (2km)
25–26 Town Center Trail (2.4km)
26–27 Coquitlam River Trail (2.9km)
27–28 North PoCo Trail (11km)
28–29 Pitt Meadows Dike Trail (9.5km)

24–25 Guildford Way Trail (2km)
25–26 Town Center Trail (2.4km)
26–27 Coquitlam River Trail (2.9km)
27–28 North PoCo Trail (11km)
28–29 Pitt Meadows Dike Trail (9.5km)

Southwestern BC Map 6: Coquitlam

Southwestern BC Section 25-26

2.5 km
Town Centre
Trail

In the town of Coquitlam, the Town Centre Trail marks the beginning of a more peaceful section of the trail as it joins two nice parks. Both areas provide good access points, while the Town Centre Park, surround-

Lafarge Lake   R. Mussio

ing picturesque Lafarge Lake, offers picnic tables and latrines.

The route begins at the crossing of Guildford Way along the Hoy Creek greenway. The trail heads northeast through a forested setting along the Hoy Creek, through the David Lam College and Pinetree Secondary School Campus and crosses Pinetree Way before traversing past scenic Lafarge Lake. In the park, which was once a large gravel pit, the route follows a bike path past Lafarge Lake. Anglers may want to test their luck for the small stocked rainbow trout in this man-made lake. Towards the northeast corner of the lake, the trail passes a Trans Canada Trail Pavilion and a sports stadium before meeting Pipeline Road. The Trans Canada Trail route continues across Pipeline Road to an old road that meets a waterline right-of-way. This gravel path marks the beginning of the Coquitlam River Trail.

Southwestern BC Section 26-27

2.9 km
Coquitlam River Trail

The Coquitlam River Trail begins at the junction of Pathan Avenue and Pipeline Road. There is a small gravel parking area available as well as the familiar route markings to guide the way. The route starts on a former road before meeting a short path that spills out onto a short residential road before accessing the rest of the Coquitlam River Trail.

The Trail travels south and passes through a secluded forest environment and past a number of fish channels before meeting the Patricia Pedestrian Bridge over the river. A large portion of the trail travels through the Coquitlam River Park, which helps protect a portion of the river shoreline from urban expansion. On the east side of the river lies the town of Port Coquitlam and the beginning of the North PoCo Trail.

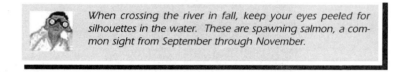

When crossing the river in fall, keep your eyes peeled for silhouettes in the water. These are spawning salmon, a common sight from September through November.

Southwestern BC Section 27-28

11 km
North PoCo Trail

The newly surfaced North PoCo trail begins after the pedestrian bridge over the Coquitlam River. You will actually have to turn right and loop under the bridge. In addition to the familiar Trans Canada Trail logo, you will find the route marked with the PoCo Trail signs. Pedestrians, cyclists and equestrian riders will enjoy this easy, urban route, which joins a series of small park trails to make one long trail.

The route heads north from the pedestrian bridge and away from the river through a mixed forest section. The trail crosses Shaughnessy Street into another wooded area of the Coquitlam River Park and eventually crosses Oxford Street at Lincoln Avenue. After the crossing, the trail continues southeast through Wellington Park. The Trans Canada Trail route follows a small pathway through the park and meets up with Patricia Avenue. The route then follows Patricia Avenue east crossing Wellington Street and Coast Meridian Road.

Cycling the PoCo Trail   R. Mussio

After the crossing of Coast Meridian Road, the Trans Canada Trail follows a local trail named the Hyde Creek Trail. The Hyde Creek Trail is a well-used trail that treks along the south side of the Hyde Creek, past a recreational centre and a school to the mixed forest environment of the Port Coquitlam Nature Park. The trail leaves the northeast corner of the park and then turns north parallel to Cedar Drive. The Trans Canada Trail route crosses the Hyde Creek over a pedestrian bridge and then begins to travel along an access road to the corner of Victoria Drive and Cedar Drive. The route then crosses Cedar Drive and travels on the south side of the Deboville Slough.

During the fall months (late October/early November), thousands of spawning salmon can be viewed in Hyde Creek. If you have never witnessed this natural marvel, you should definitely plan to if possible, it is quite an amazing event.

A cement marker at Hyde Creek Recreation Centre marks the starting location of the Home Town Terry Fox Run. This run, held each September, celebrates Terry Fox who died in 1981 during a cross Canada run to raise cancer awareness.

The Deboville Slough makes another fine access point. The Trans Canada Trail route follows this popular dike trail east along the south shoreline of the scenic slough that is surrounded by farmland and the distant peaks of Golden Ears Park. Bird enthusiasts will want to take some time when travelling along the slough as the wetland is a fantastic viewing area for waterfowl and other resident birds. River otters, deer and coyotes also frequent the area.

Continue past the marina to a fabulous viewpoint at the junction of the Deboville Slough and the Pitt River. This is a good place to have lunch and soak in the peace and tranquility before the long trek south to the busy Pitt River Bridge.

From the viewpoint, the Trans Canada Trail route follows the west side of the Pitt River. Along the dike, there are great views of the river and the resident waterfowl, especially blue herons. On clear days, Mount Baker can be seen to the southeast and the equally majestic Golden Ears can be seen to the east. To the west, views of the surrounding farmland areas dominate the landscape.

The Pitt River is the southern extension of Pitt Lake to the north. Both the river and the lake are tidal water bodies and offer a unique inland water environment. Pitt Lake is actually the largest tidal lake in the world. Historically, the H.M.S. Plumper carried out Admirality surveys along the river. Today, tugboats, paddlewheelers and pleasure craft can be seen cruising the water way.

The PoCo Trail is a 35 km nature trail that completely surrounds the city of Port Coquitlam. It was offically recognized in 1975 after a determined group of volunteers brought the trail to life. Today, cyclists, hikers, joggers and horseback riders enjoy the natural environment of the trail.

Southwestern BC Section 28-29

9.5 km

Pitt Meadows Dike Trail

The Pitt Meadows Dike Trail takes the Trans Canada Trail through the farmlands of Pitt Meadows and towards Maple Ridge. The trail begins on the sidewalk of the busy Pitt River Bridge. The route crosses the bridge and then heads north along the Pitt River Dike. From this point on, horseback riders will be able to follow most of the Trans Canada Trail route through the Fraser Valley.

Similar to the dike trail along the west side of the river, the Pitt Meadows Dike Trail offers splendid views of great blue herons and other waterfowl, along with scenic sights of the surrounding rolling agricultural land. The trail eventually meets a tributary to the Pitt River named

Pitt Meadows Dike Trail   R. Mussio

the South Alouette River. The route passes through a marina down by the river before following the dike trail east along the Alouette River.

The dike system along the Alouette River is more established. It offers numerous interpretive signs and park benches. Mount Baker continues to offer an impressive background.

The route crosses Harris Road, which is a popular access point and a site of a Trans Canada Trail Pavilion. Along with scenic views of the Alouette River, the Pitt Meadows Dike Trail also provides picturesque sights of the surrounding farmlands, the Pitt Polders, the UBC Research Forest and Golden Ears Provincial Park. At the junction of Neaves Road, the Pitt Meadows Dike Trail ends and meets the Maple Ridge Dike Trail.

Interpretive signs and benches are strategically placed along the Alouette River section of this dike system. The signs will help you learn more about the history and diverse ecosystem surrounding the dikes.

Along the Pitt Meadows Dike Trail, horses must take a detour north along Harris Road to access the North Alouette River Dike Trail. The trail follows the dike along the North Alouette River before heading back to a trail south of the Alouette River named the Trans Ridge Trail. From the south side of the Alouette River, most of the route is along established trail, although there are a few areas where horses will have to travel on the side of the road or cross roadways. The last leg of the trail, which heads south towards the Albion Ferry, is mainly along quiet roads.

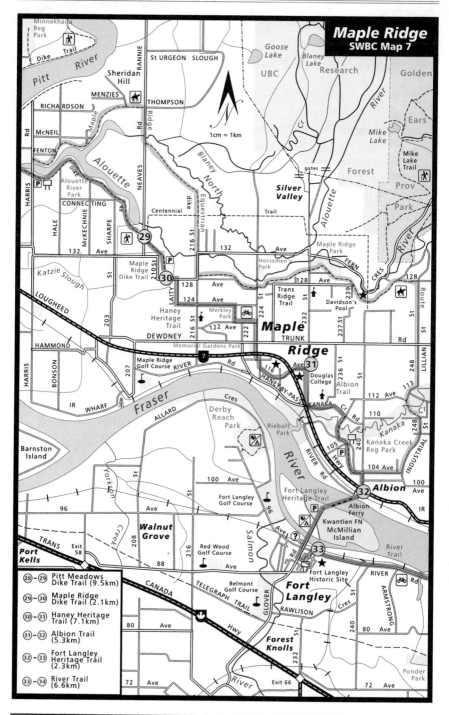

Maple Ridge
SWBC Map 7

1cm = 1km

28–29 Pitt Meadows
Dike Trail (9.5km)

29–30 Maple Ridge
Dike Trail (2.1km)

30–31 Haney Heritage
Trail (7.1km)

31–32 Albion Trail
(5.3km)

32–33 Fort Langley
Heritage Trail
(2.3km)

33–34 River Trail
(6.6km)

Southwestern BC Map 7: Maple Ridge

Southwestern BC Section 29-30

2.1 km
Maple Ridge Dike Trail

At Neaves Road near the Alouette River, in the northwest end of Maple Ridge, you will find the beginning of the Maple Ridge Dike Trail. The Maple Ridge Dike Trail is a short route at 1.5 km in length, which travels from the Neaves Road parking area south along the South Alouette Dike to 128th Avenue. On the south side of 128th Avenue, you will find the beginning of the Haney Heritage Trail.

Laity Farm   S. Shabacon

 Former Hudson Bay Company workers and other Crown servants initially settled the site of Maple Ridge. Most of the first settlers homesteaded along the Fraser River for the ease of transportation and access to fishing supplies. The town grew slowly, as word spread of the fantastic farming capabilities in the valley. In 1874, the municipality of Maple Ridge was incorporated and only a few years later the town had its first post office. Similar to the multiculturalism of Maple Ridge today, the region began with a varied influx of settlers ranging from Quebec to the Maritimes and even the United States.

Southwestern BC Section 30-31

7.1 km

Haney Heritage Trail

Through the heart of Maple Ridge, the Trans Canada Trail follows a local route we are calling the Haney Heritage Trail. From the south side of 128th Avenue, the

Haney Heritage Trail heads east along 128th Avenue approximately 30 metres to Laity Street. The trail follows Laity Street south to 124th Avenue, where the route then heads east through a magnificent stand of urban fir trees. Along 124th Street, the trail crosses 216th Street before the route heads south through Merkley Park.

Taking in the View   R. Mussio

Along 124th Avenue, be sure to watch for the Merkley Park entrance on the south side of the street. The Trans Canada Trail travels through the small urban park and past a local secondary school to 122nd Avenue. The trail then follows 122nd Avenue east to 224th Street. The route travels along 224th Street south into the Maple Ridge City Centre, known as Haney.

Within the Maple Ridge City Centre, the Trans Canada Trail route follows 224th Street over the Dewdney Trunk Road and into the Old Haney Shopping Area. Continue to follow 224th Street south over the Lougheed Highway (Highway 7) to the Haney Heritage House, where the route then begins to follow the Heritage Walk Trail. The trail travels along 116th Ave east uphill through a section of new home development and over Burnett Street before reaching the Lougheed Highway. The rest of the Haney Heritage Trail is under construction. In the interim, it is easier to follow 116th Street to 232nd Street.

In the near future, the route will be much more interesting. Although it is not signed, walkers can still piece it together.

Continue on 116th Street across the Lougheed Highway to the Thomas Haney School Campus. The route then enters the campus and follows the sport fields. From there, the route travels north to the edge of a ravine. From the north end of the ravine, the trail traverses southeast along what is currently a rustic trail, to a set of tennis courts. The Trans Canada Trail route follows a pathway along the tennis courts to 232nd Street and the beginning of the Albion Trail.

Southwestern BC Section 31-32

5.3 km
Albion Trail

This route takes the Trans Canada Trail down to the Fraser River shoreline and to the Albion Ferry. The route begins on 232nd Street and follows the street south to Kanaka Creek Road and into picturesque Kanaka Creek Regional Park. The route then follows a paved pathway along Kanaka Creek Road east and later traverses the scenic Kanaka Creek on a magnificent new bridge.

In the near future, there are plans in place to build a trail along Salamander Creek to Kanaka Creek Road. In addition to viewing salmon in the fall, this new trail will add a peaceful green section to the Trans Canada Trail route.

After the park, the route cuts through a residential area and the Albion Fairgrounds before meeting 240th Street along 104th Avenue. The route continues south towards the Fraser River along 240th Street and crosses the Lougheed Highway once again before meeting River Road. Follow River Road to the Albion Ferry terminal where the Albion Trail ends. A Trans Canada Trail Pavilion can be found in a little park before reaching the arena.

Bruce's Market would make a nice break before the ferry terminal. Inside the market, you can find everything from fresh seafood chowder to fishing artifacts.

Southwestern BC Section 32-33

2.3 km
Fort Langley Heritage Trail

From the Albion Ferry terminal, the Trans Canada Trail takes a water journey across the historic Fraser River via the ferry. The ferry charges a nominal fee and crosses every 15 minutes. The Ferry lands on McMillan Island and travels along Glover Road through the Kwantlen First Nations Reserve and onto the bridge over the Bedford Channel. There is a privately run campground on the island.

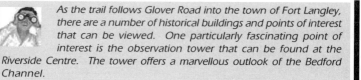

As the trail follows Glover Road into the town of Fort Langley, there are a number of historical buildings and points of interest that can be viewed. One particularly fascinating point of interest is the observation tower that can be found at the Riverside Centre. The tower offers a marvellous outlook of the Bedford Channel.

Continuing on Glover Road, you will enter the quaint heritage town of Fort Langley. There are plenty of historical sites to see as well as many shops to explore. The Trans Canada Trail route heads east on Francis Avenue to Church Street.

Fort Langley   R. Mussio

The route then follows Church Street north to Mary Avenue and travels east along Mary Avenue to King Street.

The Trans Canada Trail follows King Street north to Mavis Street where you will find the historic Fort Langley, a national historic site. Other local sites of interest include The Langley Centennial Museum & National Exhibition Centre as well as the Farm Machinery museum.

The current site of Fort Langley was established in 1839 as an important link in the framework of the fur trading ambitions of the Hudson's Bay Company. The fort later adopted large scale farming practices as well as the establishment of early salmon packing. The fort was integral in helping develop the Fraser Valley for settlement. The sanctity of the fort created a sense of security for settlers. In 1858, the fort was also the site of the official proclamation of the Colony of British Columbia by James Douglas. This historical event makes it one of the most significant landmarks in B.C's history.

Today, the fort site has been reconstructed complete with seven buildings and an original structure from the fort. Staff, all clothed in the appropriate era attire, create a real sense of the 1800's when visiting. While at the fort, you can also visit the Langley Centennial Museum. The museum has a fine display of First Nations artifacts of the native Sto:lo nation along with artefacts from the era of the first settlers. For more information on admission fees or special events, call 1-604-513-4777.

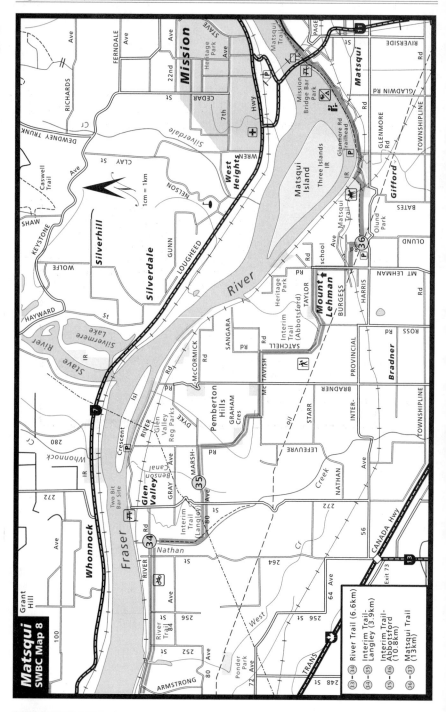

Matsqui
SWBC Map 8

1cm = 1km

Legend
33–34 = River Trail (6.6km)
34–35 = Interim Trail-Langley (3.9km)
35–36 = Interim Trail-Abbotsford (10.8km)
36–37 = Matsqui Trail (13km)

Southwestern BC Map 8: Matsqui

Southwestern BC Section 33-34

6.6 km
River Trail

Beginning at the junction of Mavis Street and River Road lies a Trans Canada Pavilion and the beginning of another portion of the Trans Canada Trail. We are calling this section the River Trail since it follows River Road (88th Avenue) and the Fraser River east to Glen Valley. Since the road is relatively busy and has virtually no shoulder to walk or cycle on, an off-road route is being planned.

Southwestern BC Section 34-35

3.9 km
Interim Trail (Langley)

At the junction of the Nathan Creek Dike and River Road, there is a small parking area. This dike trail is a popular dog walk for locals that continues further south to 272nd Street. Since this section of the Trans Canada Trail route is unsigned, be alert for a wooden shed and the double gates about 1.6 km along the dike. This is where you will need to get off the dike and onto 80th Avenue. Follow 80th Avenue east past 272nd Avenue and to Lefeuvre Road. Where the rough 80th Avenue turns in to the newly paved Marsh-McCormick Road, you are starting the Interim Trail (Abbotsford). Tiny Trans Canada Trail signs mark the way along these lovely country roads.

Interim Dike Trail   R. Mussio

Southwestern BC Section 35-36

10.8 km

Interim Trail (Abbotsford)

From Marsh-McCormick Road, turn south on Lefeuvre Road. This scenic road climbs from the river delta up Pemberton Hills. The rollercoaster route continues on McTavish, Satchell and Taylor Roads back down to Mount Lehman (past the Mount Lehman Elementary School). Turn south on Mount Lehman and east on Burgess Road just before the railway tracks. Follow Burgess Road east over a set of railway tracks to Ohlund Road (which looks very much like a private drive) and then progress along Ohlund Road south until the road ends at a trailhead, which is the beginning of the Matsqui Trail. There are a few tricky turns in this section, so please keep on the lookout for the tiny Trans Canada Trail signs that point the way.

> Please note that these interim trails are proposed to be changed. Be sure to check with Trails BC, www.backroadmapbooks.com or locally for any current route changes

Southwestern BC Section 36-37

13 km

Matsqui Trail

The Matsqui Trail is one of the feature sections of the Trans Canada Trail route through Southwestern B.C. Initially, the trail skirts a farm, before cutting through the deciduous forest, which is part of the Matsqui Indian Reserve. This section of the trail is popular with equestrian riders and is lined with soft, spongy bark mulch that makes cycling more difficult. You will cross over the Southern Railway Tracks and then under the CP Railway Tracks before meeting McLennan Creek. Glenmore Road lies just to the east of the creek mouth where you will find a parking area for the

Horses on the Matsqui Trail   R. Mussio

Glenmore Road Trailhead of the Matsqui Trail.

For day trippers from Vancouver or other points west, it is good to know that across the Mission Bridge on the north side of the Fraser River travellers can find the West Coast Commuter Train Terminal. This train terminal is the last stop east along the line. The train travels west to Vancouver stopping along the way at all major centres.

The Matsqui Trail continues along a dike trail along the south bank of the mighty Fraser River. A pair of binoculars is highly recommended to view the many different sites along the river. This is a very popular recreational area where all sorts of activities including bar fishing, camping and hiking are enjoyed year round. There are picnic facilities and washrooms at the Mission Bridge Bar Park as well as another familiar Trans Canada Trail Pavilion Trail Marker. The trail continues under Highway 11 where you start to drift away from the river towards the Page Road Trailhead at the foot of Sumas Mountain. The more adventurous may wish to travel the rougher trails that follow the original dike along the edge of the river.

Intrepretive signs are found along the Matsqui Trail. These signs provide interesting tidbits on the diverse ecosystem surrounding the area.

The area is rich in history. The legendary Billy Miner once held up a train here, while a devastating flood occurred in 1948. You can learn more about these events and other interesting facts in a guided cycling tour offered by the park.

The Matsqui First Nations Reserve was allotted in 1879. The name "Matsqui" comes from the Salish lingual word meaning "easy travel". It is thought that the name was derived due to the easy portage route from Sumas Lake to the Fraser River.

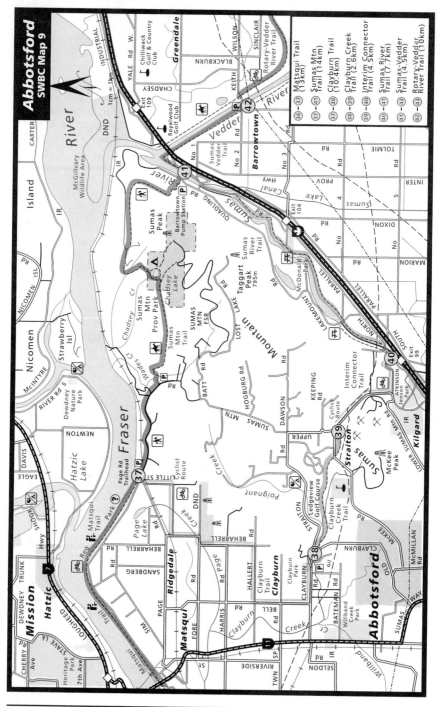

Abbotsford
SWBC Map 9

36 – 37	Matsqui Trail (13km)
37 – 41	Sumas Mtn Trail (14km)
37 – 38	Clayburn Trail (10.4km)
38 – 39	Clayburn Creek Trail (2.6km)
39 – 40	Interim Connector Trail (4.5km)
40 – 41	Sumas River Trail (7.7km)
41 – 42	Sumas-Vedder Trail (4.5km)
42 – 43	Rotary-Vedder River Trail (10km)

Southwestern BC Map 9: Abbotsford

Southwestern BC Section 37-41

14 km

Sumas Mountain Trail

At the Page Road Trailhead, there are two options for the Trans Canada Trail route. The more adventurous route is the Sumas Mountain Trail, which is recommended for hikers only at this time. Cyclists must follow the Clayburn Trail, a series of country roads heading south from Page Road. We will describe that route later.

Chadsey Lake   L. Lebrun

You begin the Sumas Mountain Trail by following the gravel road called the Upper Sumas Mountain Road. The gravel road winds its way up the shoulder of the long mountain and provides great views of the Fraser River and the valley below. About 2.2 km along the road you will find the original trailhead for the Old Centennial Trail up Sumas Mountain. The Trans Canada trailhead is found at the end of Carlyle Road.

No matter which route you choose, it is more challenging. Expect to climb through thick underbrush and a mixed forest. After about 5.5 km, the trail crosses Chadsey Creek before reaching Chadsey Lake near the top of the range. The change in elevation from the beginning of the Sumas Mountain Trail to the top is approximately 650 m (2,150 ft).

> Reaching picturesque Chadsey Lake and the Sumas Mountain Park is rewarding indeed. It makes a fine wilderness camping location and the lake offers small rainbow trout for the ardent fisher. An adventurous side trip is to trek up to the mountain peak from the east end of the lake. The peak offers spectacular panoramic views of the surrounding area including the Fraser River Valley and the United States to the south.

From Chadsey Lake, the trail continues east down the mountain along a mainly overgrown trail. After a few knee-popping kilometres, the trail culminates at the Barrowtown Pump Station, a popular fishing area for valley residents looking for Steelhead or salmon. Near the shore of the Sumas River you join up with the Sumas-Vedder Trail.

> Please note that the section from the end of the Matsqui Trail to a new Centennial Trailhead is under development and subject to route changes. Be sure to check with Trails BC, www.backroadmapbooks.com or locally for any current route changes.

Southwestern BC Section 37-38

10.4 km
Clayburn Trail

At the Page Road Trailhead of the Matsqui Trail, cyclists are encouraged to follow this route around the Sumas Mountain. The route follows a series of quiet country roads south past several farms and the Department of National Defence. Sumas Mountain looms in the background and you are more than likely going to hear the firing range in the area.

The Clayburn Trail begins by following Page Road south over the CNR Tracks on Little Street to a junction with Gallagher Road. The trail then heads west along Gallagher Road to Beharrell Road. Follow Beharrell Road south and along a short side section west (Fore Road) and continuing on Beharrell Road to Hallert Road. The Trans Canada Trail route travels west along Hallert Road to the junction with

Bell Road, where the trail then heads south to Clayburn Road.

Sumas Backroads   *R. Mussio*

When you get to the busier Clayburn Road, you will begin the more challenging hill section of this alternative route. Clayburn Road takes you through the village of Clayburn and turns into the Old Clayburn Road. Before entering a creek draw, keep your eyes peeled for Straiton Road and the trailhead of the Clayburn Creek Trail.

Southwestern BC Section 38-39

2.6 km
Clayburn Creek Trail

The Clayburn Creek Trail follows an old railbed that used to travel to the clay factory in Clayburn. From the Straiton Road trailhead, the trail follows the old railbed trail east along the north shore of the creek. The trail travels through a mainly forested area, home of second growth timber and many birds and small mammals. The trail ends up at the Auguston Subdivision, where the Trans Canada Trail route continues along McKee Road.

The *MSA* Museum and Archives offers an interesting display of the colourful history of Abbotsford and the surrounding settlements. There is also a gift shop at historic Clayburn Village.

Southwestern BC Section 39-40

4.5 km

Interim Connector Trail

The Interim Connector Trail starts at the McKee Road and Upper Sumas Mountain Road junctions. The Sumas Mountain Road is a pretty road that winds its way downhill through a deciduous forest. You will need to be alert for large trucks on the road as well as the Atkinson Road junction. Follow this short road to a gated service road and the short downhill to the bridge over the Sumas River (at the junction of Eldridge and North Parallel Road).

 There are future plans to re-route the cycling route from McKee Road all the way to the Sumas River. Be sure to check with Trails BC, www.backroadmapbooks.com or locally for any current route changes.

Southwestern BC Section 40-41

7.7 km

Sumas River Trail

The Sumas River Trail is the last leg of the alternate route around Sumas Mountain and begins by crossing the bridge and following the south Sumas River Dike Trail going east. This flat 7.7 km section is a true delight. You pass by farms and several small parks with washrooms and picnic facilities.

The scenic river is home to a variety of small animals and waterfowl. The humming in the back

Sumas River Dyke   R. Mussio

ground is the Trans Canada Highway.

The dike trail passes by a small park named McDonald Park, which makes for a great resting place or lunch stop. North of McDonald Park, the route veers onto the old westbound highway lane and continues north to the Barrowtown Pump Station and the connection with the end of the Sumas Mountain Trail (38-42).

If there is a distinctive pungent smell in the air, you are being acquainted with the odor associated with mushroom farms identified by large, long buildings with rows of vents coming out of their walls.

Southwestern BC Section 41-42

4.5 km
Sumas Vedder Trail

After the crossing of the Sumas River, the Trans Canada Trail follows the Sumas River Dike east to the Vedder Canal Dike. You will find plenty of activity in these areas as people drive the dikes to access the river and to camp.

The Trans Canada Trail route proceeds along the Vedder Canal Dike southeast to a traversing under the Trans Canada Highway. The route continues to follow the dike along the Vedder River all the way to the Keith Wilson Bridge. In the fall and winter, this stretch of river is lined with fishermen hoping to land a salmon or steelhead trout. The beginning of the Rotary Vedder River Trail is found on the east side of the bridge.

In the spring runoff period, a portion of the trail under the Trans Canada Highway can flood. If the section is flooded it is recommended to back pedal to the Barrowtown Pump Station and cross on North Parallel Road onto the Old Interprovincial Highway. This Road quickly becomes a trail that leads under the highway on the east bank of a canal that flows into the Sumas River. Continue on the Old Interprovincial Highway westward for about 150 metres to Number 2 Road. Follow Number 2 Road south to a parking lot (staging area) just before the Keith Wilson Bridge. This parking lot accesses the Vedder River Dike, where you can rejoin the Trans Canada.

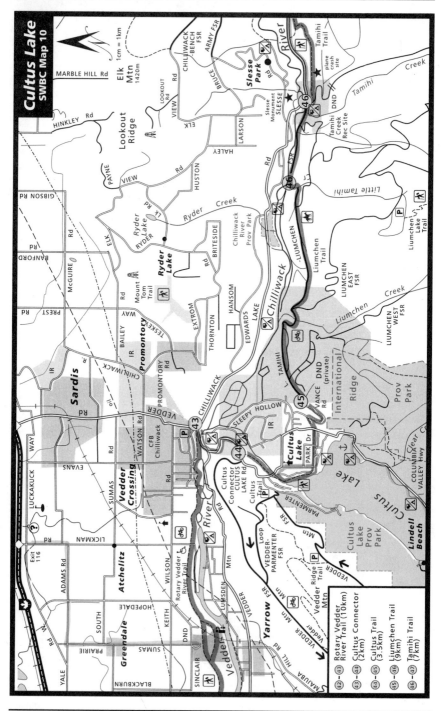

Cultus Lake
SWBC Map 10

1cm = 1km

MARBLE HILL Rd

Elk Mtn 1420m

HINKLEY Rd

Lookout Ridge

PAYNE

VIEW Rd

Ryder Lake Rd

Ryder Creek

Ryder Lake

GIBSON Rd

BANFORD Rd

McGUIRE Rd

Mount Tom Trail

PREST Rd

Promontory

TESKEY Rd

BAILEY Rd

ELK

BRITESIDE

BRACEWELL Rd

BRUCE

LARSON

Slesse Monument SLESSE

Slesse Park

plane crash site

Tamihi Trail

CHILLIWACK BENCH FSR

ARMY FSR

HALEY

HUSTON

EXTROM Rd

THORNTON

HANSOM

EDWARDS

Chilliwack

Chilliwack River Prov Park

LIUMCHEN

Little Tamihi

Tamihi Creek

Tamihi Creek Rec Site

Tamihi DND

Liumchen Trail

Liumchen Lake Trail

Liumchen Creek

LIUMCHEN EAST FSR

LIUMCHEN WEST FSR

Ridge

Prov Park

International

Sardis

VEDDER Rd

CHILLIWACK

WATSON Rd

CFB Chilliwack

PROMONTORY

CHILLIWACK

VEDDER

Sleepy Hollow

IR

VANCE DND (private)

Cultus Lake

PARK Dr

Cultus Lake Prov Park

Lindell Beach

Cultus Lake

COLUMBIA VALLEY HWY

Clear Creek

WAY

LUCKAKUCK WAY

EVANS

SUMAS Rd

Vedder Crossing

Exit 116

LICKMAN Rd

ADAMS Rd

SOUTH Rd

HOPEDALE

KEITH

WILSON

LUMSDEN

VEDDER

Rotary Vedder River Trail

Cultus Connector

CULTUS LAKE Rd

Cultus Trail

VEDDER-PARMENTER FSR

Mtn FSR

Vedder Ridge Mtn Trail

VEDDER Mtn Rd

MAJUBA Hill Rd

Yarrow

Vedder

Atchelitz

Greendale

PRAIRIE

YALE Rd

BLACKBURN Rd

SUMAS

SINCLAIR Rd

DND

42 — 43 Rotary Vedder River Trail (10km)
43 — 44 Cultus Connector (2km)
44 — 45 Cultus Trail (3.5km)
45 — 46 Liumchen Trail (9km)
46 — 47 Tamihi Trail (7km)

Southwestern BC Map 10: Cultus Lake

Southwestern BC Section 42-43

10 km
Rotary Vedder River Trail

The Trans Canada Trail continues its eastward journey along the Rotary Vedder Trail, which begins at the east side of the Keith Wilson Bridge over the Vedder River. This long stretch of trail offers a variety of different views and terrain. Portions of the trail traverse along various dikes along the river, while sections travel through semi-wooded and agricultural areas. Much of the trail is made up of hard packed gravel suitable for all, including wheelchairs. Near the end of the trail, the route passes by the old Canadian Forces Base Chilliwack. It ends at the junction of Vedder Mountain Road.

Vedder River Bridge   W. Mussio

The western end of this trail is not nearly as busy as the eastern end. Vehicles are allowed to access portions of the route and there is a rustic camping area across the scenic river.

 The Rotary Vedder Trail also passes by the Great Blue Heron Reserve, which is home to a colony of Great Blue Herons as well as the Rotary Interpretive Centre. There are also a number of interpretive signs along the trail explaining various interesting natural facts of the area.

Southwestern BC Section 43-44

2 km
Cultus Connector Trail

From the Vedder River, the Trans Canada Trail route heads south up the busy Cultus Lake Road. The road snakes its way uphill all the way to the Cultus Lake Provincial Park and the beginning of the Cultus Trail at the park entrance sign.

Southwestern BC Section 44-45

3.5 km
Cultus Trail

Beginning at the Cultus Lake Provincial Park sign, the route follows what we call the Cultus Trail. The route travels through a portion of the park to the Sweltzer River Hatchery. At the hatchery, a short section of the trail is under construction. Follow the pink flagging tape until they are replaced with more permanent signage.

Vedder Canal   R. Mussio

Hikers can cross the road at the hatchery and continue across a parking lot to a small footbridge leading to the shore of Cultus Lake. The hiking route follows the shoreline of Cultus Lake south to a boat launch, where the trail then veers east to Park Drive.

The biking/equestrian route follows the Columbia Valley Highway (Cultus Lake Road) south to Sunnyside Boulevard. The bike/equestrian portion of the route then follows the boulevard to Park Drive where it meets the hiking portion of the trail.

The Trans Canada Trail route continues east along Park Drive and past the semi-urban setting of the north end of Cultus Lake. Heading east, Park Drive soon comes to an end. The trail then begins to follow a few tricky directions. From the end of the road, the route continues along a short section of established trail towards the Columbia Valley Highway. Just before you reach the highway, pick up the trail that follows the highway south. The route then crosses the highway at the pub and continues on the other side along a trail uphill to Elizabeth Road. The route follows Elizabeth Road east to Vance Road, where we begin the Liumchen portion of the Trans Canada Trail.

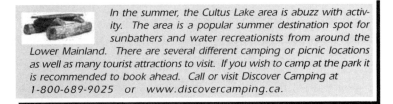

From Vedder Crossing through to Cultus Lake, there are plans to make changes to the routing. At the end of the Rotary Vedder River Trail, plans are to find an off-road alternative. At Cultus Lake, it is hoped to continue the route south to enter the Cultus Lake Provincial Park and its many amenities. A trail then will lead back to Vance Road. Be sure to check with Trails BC, www.backroadmapbooks.com or locally for any current route changes.

In the summer, the Cultus Lake area is abuzz with activity. The area is a popular summer destination spot for sunbathers and water recreationists from around the Lower Mainland. There are several different camping or picnic locations as well as many tourist attractions to visit. If you wish to camp at the park it is recommended to book ahead. Call or visit Discover Camping at 1-800-689-9025 or www.discovercamping.ca.

Southwestern BC Section 45-46

9 km
Liumchen Trail

The Liumchen Trail offers travellers from the Lower Mainland area the first real sense of space and wilderness. The route enters the beautiful Chilliwack River Valley along Vance Road. The road winds its way up a steep section and eventually meets the Lower Tamihi Liumchen Forest Service Road. The trail follows the road east through Department of National Defense property and over the Liumchen Creek. Continue along the Lower Tamihi Liumchen Forest Service Road to a crossing of the Little Tamihi Creek.

Along the way, the route travels along a quiet logging road. The road starts out along an open area with a couple nice vantage points before descending into the valley bottom surrounded by a dense second growth forest ecosystem. The road can be quite wet in this section and there are many side roads branching off the main route that can lead you astray.

One of the highlights of this section of the Trans Canada Trail route is the Liumchen Creek Canyon. The canyon is quite majestic and is a great foreshadowing of the scenery that lies ahead.

Southwestern BC Section 46-47

7 km
Tamihi Trail

The Tamihi Trail starts after the crossing of the Little Tamihi Creek along the Lower Tamihi Liumchen Forest Service Road. After the creek crossing look for the Centennial Trail on your left. Follow the Centennial Trail along the south side of the Chilliwack River all the way to the Tamihi Creek

Tamihi View   L. Lebrun

Forest Recreation Site. The large, open campsite is found next to a bend in the river, where whitewater kayakers can be seen negotiating the rapids. The Trans Canada Trail route then follows Chilliwack Lake Road east to the Anderson Creek and the beginning of the Thurston Trail. A trail higher up on the hillside is currently under construction between the Tamihi Creek Rec Site and Anderson Creek.

The Tamihi Creek Forest Recreation Site marks the beginning of a series of rustic camping areas in the valley. Established by the BC Forest Service, there are two levels of campsites. Larger, more popular sites such as Tamihi Creek and Thurston Meadows have a host on-site from May through October and charge a $10 fee ($5 is you have an annual pass). The smaller, more rustic sites have a nightly fee of $8 or an annual fee of $27 and are user maintained with very basic facilities. Regardless of which type of site you visit, one should expect a wilderness type camping area. Picnic tables, fire rings and outhouse or two may or may not be available.

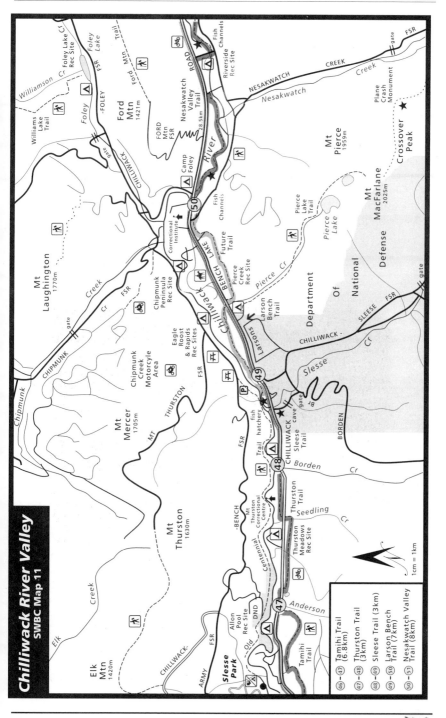

Chilliwack River Valley
SWBC Map 11

Foley Lake Cr
Foley Lake Rec Site
Williamson Cr
Williams Lake Trail
Foley
Foley Lake
Foley FSR
FORD -FOLEY
Ford Mtn 1421m
Ford Mtn Trail
Nesakwatch Valley Trail
28.5km Trail
ROAD
Fish Channels
Riverside Rec Site
NESAKWATCH
CREEK
Creek
gate FSR
Nesakwatch
FORD Mtn FSR
Nesakwatch
Camp Foley
River
Plane Crash Monument
Mt Pierce 1959m
Crossover Peak
CHILLIWACK
gate
50
Correctional Institute
Fish Channels
Future Trail
Mt MacFarlane 2025m
Chipmunk Peninsula Rec Site
BENCH LAKE
Pierce Lake Trail
Pierce Lake
Department
Mt Laughington 1770m
Creek
Cr FSR
CHIPMUNK
gate
Eagle Roost & Rapids Rec Sites
Chipmunk Creek Motorcyle Area
CHILLIWACK
Pierce Creek Rec Site
Pierce Cr
Larson Bench Trail
Of National Defense
SLEESE FSR
gate
Chipmunk
MT THURSTON
FSR
Larsons
49
CHILLIWACK ·
SLEESE Cr
Slesse
Mt Mercer 1705m
P
fish hatchery
Br
Slesse cave
BORDEN
gate
Mt Thurston 1630m
Trail Head
CHILLIWACK
48
Slesse Trail
Borden
Borden Cr
Elk Creek
-BENCH
FSR
Mt Thurston Correctional Centre
Thurston Trail
Seedling
Cr
Thurston Meadows Rec Site
Centennial
Elk Mtn 1420m
CHILLIWACK-
ARMY
Old
DND
47
Anderson
1cm = 1km
Slesse Park
Allon Pool Rec Site
FSR
Tamihi Trail

- 46 — 47 Tamihi Trail (6.8km)
- 47 — 48 Thurston Trail (3km)
- 48 — 49 Slesse Trail (3km)
- 49 — 50 Larson Bench Trail (7km)
- 50 — 51 Nesakwatch Valley Trail (8km)

131

Southwestern BC Map 11: Chilliwack River Valley

Southwestern BC Section 47-48

3 km
Thurston Trail

The Thurston Trail begins by travelling along Chilliwack Lake Road. The paved road is not very busy. Shortly along the road past Anderson Creek, the route veers south into a gravel pit. The pit should be easily noticed off the south side of the road. The trail leading east from the pit travels through a mixed forest and along the fish channels eventually crossing Chilliwack Lake Road to the Thurston Meadows Recreation Site. A 1.3 km trail continues east from the campsite along a series of fish channels of the Chilliwack River to the Borden Creek.

Thurston Meadows Campsite   W. Mussio

 The Chilliwack River is another Southwestern BC stream that hosts spawning salmon in the fall. The fish channels at Borden Creek are an excellent place to see this natural phenomenon. When walking next to the river keep your eyes peeled as pretty well any large pool of water may be holding resting salmon.

Southwestern BC Sections 48-49/49-50

3 km/7 km

Slesse Trail/Larson Bench Trail

In the not too distant future there are plans in place to develop the trail from Borden Creek to near the Chilliwack Lake Road crossing of the Chilliwack River at Camp Foley. This future trail is still a work in progress.

Currently both the Slesse Trail and the Larson Bench Trail travel strictly along the Chilliwack River Road. However, this portion of the trail is still a fantastic section of the route since the wide cut of the road creates fantastic views of the surrounding mountains, including picturesque sights of Mount MacFarlane and Mount Laughington.

Chilliwack River Fisherman   J. Marleau

Rustic camping is offered at both the Pierce Creek and Camp Foley Recreation Sites. The Pierce Creek Site is a little quieter as it is off the road.

The trailhead to the Pierce Lake Trail is found at the Pierce Creek Recreation Site. This is a difficult trail leading to a picturesque mountain lake. If you have a couple extra days you can even climb Mount MacFarlane.

Southwestern BC Section 50-51

8 km
Nesakwatch Valley Trail

There are two options along this section of the Trans Canada Trail route. Beginning at the bridge over the Chilliwack River (or Camp Foley), bikers and equestrian riders must continue on Chilliwack Lake Road to a yellow gate on the south side of the road. Go through the gate and follow this forestry road east towards Centre Creek.

Hikers will find a trail that leads from Camp Foley along the fish channels. This trail is undeveloped but will lead back to the Chilliwack Lake Road. Continue onto the Riverside Recreation Site where all travellers will turn south past the yellow gate. Another trail branches from this forestry road and leads along the Centennial Fish Channels before rejoining the road. This is the start of the Centre Creek Trail.

Chilliwack Valley Trail　　　*R. Mussio*

 Similar to most settlements of the Fraser Valley, the Chilliwack area was first inhabited by the Sto:lo first nations some 5,000 to 10,000 years ago. European settlers arrived in the mid 1800's and began clearing the land for the establishment of agriculture. The town of Chilliwhack was established in 1873 and the current name Chilliwack (minus the 'h') was chosen in 1908 when the city of Chilliwack was formed.

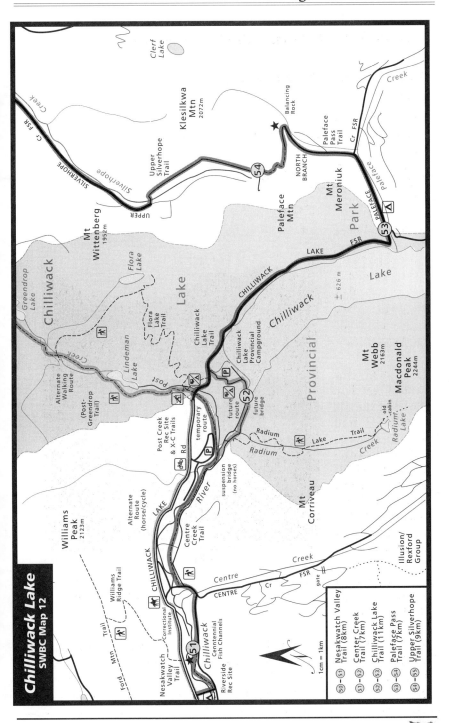

Chilliwack Lake
SWBC Map 12

Clerf Lake

Klesilkwa Mtn
2072m

Balancing Rock

Upper Silverhope Trail

Cr FSR

Paleface Pass Trail

NORTH BRANCH

Mt Meroniuk

Paleface Mtn

54

UPPER SILVERHOPE Creek

Cr FSR

Mt Wittenberg
1952m

Flora Lake

LAKE

FSR

PALEFACE

53

Paleface

Greendrop Lake

Chilliwack

Lake

Flora Lake Trail

Chilliwack Lake Trail

CHILLIWACK

± 626 m

Lake

Chilliwack

Lindeman Lake

Chilliwack Lake Provincial Campground

Provincial

Mt Webb
2163m

Macdonald Peak
2244m

Alternate Walking Route
(Post-Greendrop Trail)

Creek

Post Creek

Post Creek Rec Site & X-C Trails

P

52

future route

future bridge

Radium

old cabin

Radium Lake

Lake Trail

Radium Creek

Rd

temporary route

P

suspension bridge
(no horses)

Radium

Mt Corriveau

Provincial

Alternate Route
(horse/cycle)

CHILLIWACK LAKE

RIVER

Centre Creek Trail

Williams Peak
2123m

Creek

Illusion/Rexford Group

Williams Ridge Trail

ford   Mtn   Trail

Centre

Cr FSR

gate

CENTRE

Nesakwatch Valley Trail

Correctional Institution

CHILLIWACK LAKE

51

Chilliwack

Cenntennial Fish Channels

Riverside Rec Site

1cm = 1km

50—51 Nesakwatch Valley Trail (8km)
51—52 Center Creek Trail (7km)
52—53 Chilliwack Lake Trail (11km)
53—54 Paleface Pass Trail (7km)
54—55 Upper Silverhope Trail (9km)

135

Southwestern BC Map 12: Chilliwack Lake

Southwestern BC Section 51-52

5 km

Centre Creek Trail

At the east end of the Centennial Fish Channels all travellers will follow the forestry road east towards Centre Creek. You will join the Centre Creek Forest Service Road and follow this road southeast over Centre Creek. Pick up the trail off the east side of the road before the bridge over the Chilliwack River.

This portion of the Centre Creek Trail is part of the old Centennial Trail and travels through a tranquil coastal rainforest environment for 3 km to a bluff. The bluff, which provides impressive views of the river and the forest environ-

Chilliwack Lake   J. Marleau

ment, will present a challenge to cyclists but it is passable. Once past the bluff the Trans Canada Trail continues on the south side of the Chilliwack River to Chilliwack Lake.

Sometimes during the fall of 2001 a bridge will be constructed across the head of the Chilliwack River. In the meantime it will be necessary to cross the Chilliwack River over a suspension bridge at Post Creek. This suspension bridge is not passable for horses and is very difficult for cyclists. Until the bridge is built equestrian riders can ford the river at the mouth of the lake. The easier option for horses and cyclists is to simply follow the Chilliwack River Road from Riverside Forestry Recreation Site to Chilliwack Lake.

The Centennial Trail was completed in 1969, in recognition of Canada's centennial birthday. This great hicking/biking trail connects Horseshoe Bay in the west all the way to Joe Lake near Keremos to the east.

Southwestern BC Section 52-53

11 km
Chilliwack Lake Trail

Large portions of the desired trail route along this section of the Trans Canada Trail route are to be completed during the summer of 2001. In the interim, follow the Centennial Trail past the bluff to the suspension bridge over the Chilliwack River. Traverse over the bridge and follow the trail to another bridge over Post Creek. Continue along the trail on the north side of the creek until you reach the Chilliwack Lake Road.

The Trans Canada Trail route passes the entrance to the Chilliwack Lake Provincial Campground where the road turns into the Chilliwack Lake Forest Service Road. The gravel road skirts the eastern shore of the scenic Chilliwack Lake. The Chilliwack Lake Trail ends at the junction of

Post Creek Suspension   L. Lebrun

the Chilliwack Lake Road and the Paleface Creek Forest Service Road.

Chilliwack Lake is a spectacular lake where mountain views create a post card British Columbia backdrop. The Chilliwack Lake Provincial Park has recently been expanded to protect this scenic unlogged viewscape. Although the lake sees its fair share of boaters throughout the summer period, a canoe or kayak would make the perfect craft for an intimate exploration of the lake's waters and shoreline.

The Chilliwack Lake Provincial Park Campground is a popular retreat for Lower Mainland residents. It offers over 100 vehicle access campsites as well as a separate boat launch and picnic area with a fine beach. The fee-based campsite offers basic facilities including pump water and pit toilets and is usually full during weekends throughout the summer.

An alternate hiking route along this section of trail is to continue across Chilliwack Lake Road to the Post-Greendrop Trail. The trail is somewhat rustic and even experienced travellers should be prepared for the trek. The trail travels north along the north side of the Post Creek past Lindeman and Greendrop Lakes, eventually meeting the Hicks Creek Forest Service Road. The route then follows Hicks Creek Forest Service Road between Mount Nowell and Mount Holden before descending to the Silver Skagit Road in the Silverhope Valley. The route through this section of the park offers fabulous views of the surrounding mountains and traverses past two very picturesque park lakes. Be sure to bring your fishing rod if you choose this route.

Southwestern BC Section 53-54

7 km

Paleface Pass Trail

The new Paleface Pass Trail is part of the Trans Canada Trail route that helps the route traverse over the mountain range between the Chilliwack Lake Valley and the Silverhope Creek Valley. From Chilliwack Lake to the Paleface Pass you can expect to ascend some 575 m (1,917 ft) to a sub-alpine environment at 1,280 m (4,200 ft).

The route begins on the Paleface Creek Forest Service Road near the old Paleface Forest Service Site and heads east along the forest service road. The road comes to a defined fork and the Trans Canada Trail route proceeds along the north fork (North Branch) and ascends towards higher elevations of the Paleface Pass. The route traverses along a steep switchback before continuing north to the top of the pass and the beginning of the Upper Silverhope Trail.

Paleface Pass in Winter   B. Smith

 Caution: Along portions of this section of roads, decommission trenches have been built across some of the roads. This section of the route is very remote and has little or no vehicle traffic at times. Please be aware that logging trucks can be active in the area.

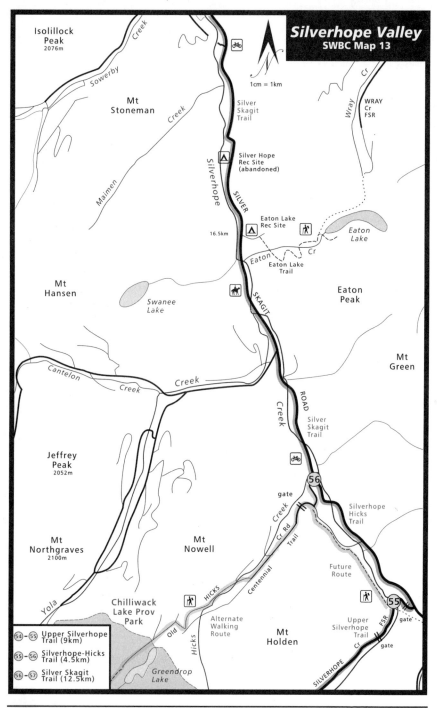

Silverhope Valley
SWBC Map 13

Isolillock Peak 2076m

Sowerby Creek

Mt Stoneman

Maimen Creek

Silverhope

Silver Skagit Trail

1cm = 1km

Silver Hope Rec Site (abandoned)

16.5km

Eaton Lake Rec Site

SILVER

Eaton Cr

Eaton Lake Trail

Eaton Lake

Wray Cr

WRAY Cr FSR

Mt Hansen

Swanee Lake

SKAGIT

Eaton Peak

Mt Green

Cantelon Creek

Creek

ROAD

Creek

Silver Skagit Trail

Jeffrey Peak 2052m

Mt Northgraves 2100m

Mt Nowell

Creek

Cr Rd

Centennial Trail

56

Silverhope Hicks Trail

Future Route

Upper Silverhope Trail

55

Yola

Chilliwack Lake Prov Park

Old

HICKS

Hicks

Alternate Walking Route

Mt Holden

FSR

gate

Greendrop Lake

SILVERHOPE

Cr

gate

54–55	Upper Silverhope Trail (9km)
55–56	Silverhope-Hicks Trail (4.5km)
56–57	Silver Skagit Trail (12.5km)

Southwestern BC Map 13: Silverhope Valley

Southwestern BC Section 54-55

9 km
Upper Silverhope Trail

At the Paleface Pass, the Upper Silverhope Trail starts to descend into the Silverhope Creek Valley. The trail follows the Upper Silverhope Creek Forest Service Road downhill about 9 km to a junction with the Silver Skagit Road. Along the way down, the trail (road) crosses the Silverhope Creek and it may be necessary to travel around a few gated areas (to keep vehicles out). The trail travels through a rugged mountain environment combined with dense forest and some newer forest sections. This portion of the Trans Canada Trail route can be quite secluded and offers a good taste of the backcountry of beautiful British Columbia.

Upper Silverhope Trail   L. Lebrun

Southwestern BC Section 55-56

4.5 km
Silverhope Hicks Trail

There are grand plans for this part of the Trans Canada Trail, with changes planned to be completed by the year 2002. The 4 km trail under construction leads along the west side of the Silverhope Creek to the junction with the Hicks Creek Road. Presently, the route continues along the Silverhope Creek Forest Service Road to the Silver Skagit Road, where the route then heads north along the main road to Hicks Creek.

Southwestern BC Section 56-57

12.5 km
Silver Skagit Trail

The Silver Skagit Trail offers Trans Canada Trail travellers several scenic mountain views as it follows the Silver Skagit Road north towards Silver Lake Provincial Park. Along the road, there are several opportunities to snap an exquisite photo of the surrounding mountain countryside, as well as the Silverhope Creek. The trail ends near the site of a future bridge and trail over the Silverhope Creek south of Silver Lake.

Silver Skagit Trail   *L. Lebrun*

Along the way to Silver Lake, the road passes the old Silver Hope Recreation Campsite as well as the Easton Lake Recreation Campsite. Both sites offer great camping areas, although the Silver Hope site is currently not maintained. The Eaton Lake Recreation Campsite lies near the trailhead to the popular fishing destination of Eaton Lake.

Caution: The Silver Skagit Road is an active log-hauling road and large logging trucks are frequently encountered along the road. Be sure to stay alert and always give the trucks the right-of-way.

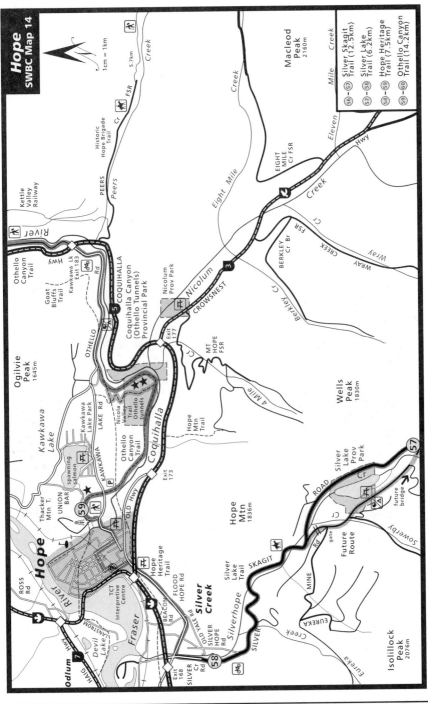

Hope
SWBC Map 14

1cm = 1km

56 — 57	Silver Skagit Trail (12.5km)	
57 — 58	Silver Lake Trail (6.2km)	
58 — 59	Hope Heritage Trail (7.5km)	
59 — 60	Othello Canyon Trail (14.2km)	

Macleod Peak
2160m

Eleven Mile Creek

Eight Mile Creek

EIGHT MILE Cr FSR

WRAY CREEK

Wray Hwy

BERKLEY Cr Br

Berkley Cr FSR

Creek

5.7km

FSR

Kettle Valley Railway

Historic Hope Brigade Trail

PEERS

Peers Cr

Othello Canyon Trail

Goat Bluffs Trail

Kawkawa Lk Exit 183

OTHELLO Rd

COQUIHALLA

Coquihalla Canyon (Othello Tunnels) Provincial Park

Nicolum Prov Park

Nicolum River

CROWSNEST

3

Exit 177

MT HOPE FSR

4 Mile Cr

Wells Peak
1830m

Ogilvie Peak
1645m

Kawkawa Lake

Kawkawa Lake Park

LAKE Rd

Nicola Valley Trail Othello tunnels

Othello Canyon Trail

Coquihalla

Hope Mtn Trail

Exit 173

spawning salmon

Thacker Mtn T.

UNION BAR

59

P

KAWKAWA

OLD Hwy

Exit 173

Hope Mtn
1836m

Silver Lake Prov Park

SKAGIT

Cr

ROAD

57

future bridge

Sowerby

Hope

ROSS Rd

Fraser River

LANSTROM

HAIG Hwy

Devil Lake

7

odium

TCT Interpretive Centre

Hope Heritage Trail

BEACON Rd

FLOOD HOPE Rd

OLD YALE Rd

OLD SILVER HOPE Rd

SILVER Cr Rd

Exit 168

58

Silver Creek

Silver Lake Trail

Silverhope Creek

SILVER

Future Route

gate

MINE Rd

EUREKA

Eureka Creek

Isolillock Peak
2076m

Southwestern BC Map 14: Hope

Southwestern BC Section 57-58
6.2 km
Silver Lake Trail

In the future, the Trans Canada Trail is planned to traverse over the Silverhope Creek across a bridge and then down into Silver Lake Provincial Park along an old road. Currently, the Trans Canada Trail route continues to follow the Silver Skagit Road north past Silver Lake Provincial Park. Access to the lake is quite easy from the roadside and it is even possible to cast the odd fly or lure from shore. From the lake, the trail follows the road as it winds its way out of the valley and eventually back to civilization at the paved Silver Creek Road.

Creek Crossing   N. Mussio

 Silver Lake Provincial Park is a lovely park that offers 50 vehicle access campsites available for a fee on a first-come, first-serve basis. There is a separate picnic area and boat launch for day-trippers.

Southwestern BC Section 58-59

7.5 km

Hope Centre Trail

The Trans Canada Trail begins its trek into the town of Hope from Silver Creek Road. Hope makes a fine break from the wilderness trek both east and west of the city. Be sure to stock up on any supplies necessary to continue along the route. It could be a few days before you are back in contact with civilization.

Othello Tunnels   Joanne

The Hope Centre Trail follows Silver Creek Road north, past a few rural homes to the junction with the Flood Hope Road. The trail follows the Flood Hope Road east under the cut off to Highway 5 (the infamous Coquihalla Highway) and proceeds to the Hope Information Centre. From the information centre, the Trans Canada Trail route travels east along Hudson's Bay Street to Fraser Avenue. Follow Fraser Avenue north to Wallace Street and then proceed east to 6th Avenue. The trail then travels along 6th Avenue to the town recreation centre and park, where the route continues along a trail found behind the recreation centre buildings. Trans Canada Trail signs can be easily followed through the park all the way to Kawkawa Lake Road. Follow Kawkawa Lake Road east over the Coquihalla River and then head south along the Kettle Valley Road to its end and the beginning of the Othello Canyon Trail.

Routing is well underway from the bridge over the Coquihalla River to follow the old Kettle Valley Railway. The more adventurous might like to try it by turning north at the bridge and look for a trail that starts across from the fish channels at Sucker Creek. This is much more scenic route that loops back to the beginning of the Othello Canyon Trail.

The first major influx of Europeans in the Hope area began around 1858 with the discovery of gold in the Fraser River north of Hope. By 1859, Fort Hope was established by James Douglas, governor of the newly constituted colony of B.C. Fort Hope was one of the first in a series of posts built throughout the region to help maintain control and sovereignty of the region. The Dewdney Trail was initiated in 1860 from Fort Hope as the first all Canadian route to link the Pacific with the Rockies. By 1889, the groundwork for the future economy of Hope was established with the construction of the first sawmill and some forty years later the village of Hope was incorporated.

Perhaps Hope's greatest claim to modern Canadian historical fame is the Hope Slide. In 1965, the largest earth and rockslide in British Columbia occurred as the side of Johnson Peak came crashing down over Highway 3. The mass of the slide actually displaced an entire lake, spread giant rock debris onto the other mountainside of the valley and crushed two unfortunate vehicles in its wake. Today, a rest stop and a small plaque off the side of the highway mark the slide. Eerily, as you drive past the ends of the slide, you can actually see where the old highway once travelled. The asphalt still in good shape.

Southwestern BC Section 59-60

~14.2 km

Othello Canyon Trail

East of the town of Hope, the Trans Canada Trail reaches a fantastic portion of the route called the Othello Canyon Trail. The trail traverses along the historic Kettle Valley Railway east to the Coquihalla Canyon Provincial Park. The route travels through the spectacular Othello Canyon carved out over thousands of years by the Coquihalla River.

This portion of the route treks along the generally easy to travel railbed and encounters the first of many rail tunnels that lie ahead between Hope and the Myra Canyon near the city of Kelowna. The first tunnel encountered is just over 100 metres in length. You must dismount from your bike and walk through all tunnels, as they can be hazardous and not lighted. Horseback riders need to take a trail around the tunnels starting at the park gate.

Often tunnels will have fallen ceiling rock debris along the tunnel floor and lighting in tunnels is very limited.

The trail traverses three more tunnels before passing by the old Othello Station site and meeting Tunnel Road. The longest tunnel of the three is 200 metres, while the shortest of the three is a mere 30 metres. As you travel through the canyon and tunnels, just imagine the engineering challenge that was overcome to build this fascinating portion of the old railway.

 The Othello Canyon Tunnels were created by an amazing engineering feat. They were originally known as the Quintet Tunnels, due to the fact that the second tunnel is partially open, creating the image that there are two tunnels.

At the end of the trail, the route continues along Tunnel Road to Othello Road, where the trail then follows Othello Road east, crossing under Highway 5. On the east side of the Coquihalla Highway the trail continues to follow what was the Othello Road and the former Kettle Valley Railway, although is now a CNR Microwave tower cable car access road. Currently, the trail ends at the future site of a bridge over the Coquihalla River.

In the meantime, cyclists can use the shoulder of the highway from near the cable car access. Continue up the highway to where it begins to descend back over the river. Do not cross the river. Instead watch for a way to get off the highway and push your bike along the riverbank under the highway to the the Trans Mountain Pipeline service road. If you do not mind the highway travel, simply continue up the highway to the Carolin Mines Exit 195.

 The Coquihalla Highway (Highway 5) was completed in 1986 in time for the World Exposition in Vancouver. It is a toll highway that has made travel to and from the interior of B.C. much quicker and easier. Trans Canada Trail travellers will quickly learn that it is a very scenic route that eventually leads up and over a spectacular alpine pass. Unfortunately, they will also learn the terrain is quite steep and the busy highway is not a joy to cycle and is out of bounds for walkers and equestrian riders, hence the need of an expensive bridge over the Coquihalla River near Jessica.

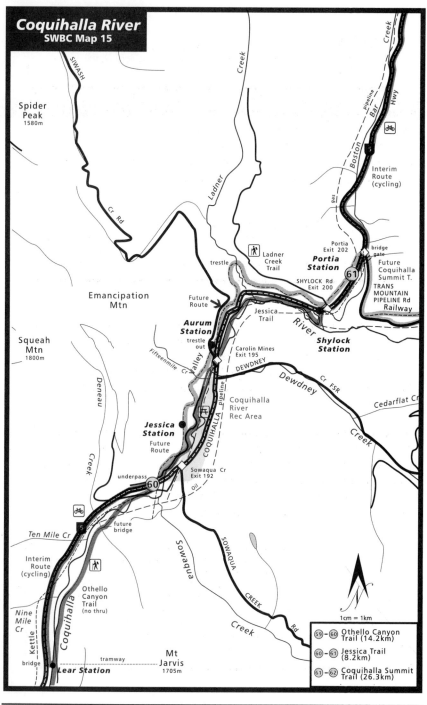

Coquihalla River
SWBC Map 15

Spider
Peak
1580m

SIWASH

Cr Rd

Ladner

Creek

trestle

Ladner
Creek
Trail

Portia
Exit 202

Portia
Station

bridge
gate

Boston

Bar

pipeline

Hwy

5

Interim
Route
(cycling)

gas

61

Future
Coquihalla
Summit T.

TRANS
MOUNTAIN
PIPELINE Rd

SHYLOCK Rd
Exit 200

Railway

Emancipation
Mtn

Future
Route

Jessica
Trail

River

Aurum
Station

trestle
out

Carolin Mines
Exit 195

DEWDNEY

Dewdney

Cr FSR

Shylock
Station

Cedarflat Cr

Squeah
Mtn
1800m

Fifteenmile Cr Valley

Pipeline

COQUIHALLA

Coquihalla
River
Rec Area

Deneau

Creek

Jessica
Station

Future
Route

Sowaqua Cr
Exit 192

Creek

underpass

60

oil

5

Ten Mile Cr

future
bridge

Interim
Route
(cycling)

Sowaqua

SOWAQUA

CREEK

N

Nine
Mile
Cr

Othello
Canyon
Trail
(no thru)

Creek

Creek

Rd

1cm = 1km

Kettle

Coquihalla

bridge

tramway

Lear Station

Mt
Jarvis
1705m

59–60 Othello Canyon
Trail (14.2km)

60–61 Jessica Trail
(8.2km)

61–62 Coquihalla Summit
Trail (26.3km)

Southwestern BC Map 15: Coquihalla River

Southwestern BC Section 60-61

~8 km

Jessica Trail

After crossing under the highway to the service road on the other side, it is a rather scenic route next to the river. The road also parallels the old Kettle Valley Railway and the future Trans Canada Trail route. Continue north and up to the Carolin Mines Exit.

From the Carolin Mines Exit (Exit 195), the Trans Canada Trail currently follows the cut-off road be-low the highway and then north towards Ladner Creek. As the road begins to veer east, it crosses Ladner Creek and continues along the north side of the scenic Coquihalla River. The trail hops back onto Highway 5 at the Shylock Road cut off (Exit 200). The route follows the high-way shoulder again un-til it meets the Portia Station cut off (Exit 202).

Substantial work needs to be done in this area to follow the historic Kettle Valley Railway. When the route is com-plete, it will cross some truly amazing areas. The Slide Creek Bridge and the Ladner Creek Trestle are two of the sites careful travellers can visit.

Slide Creek Bridge   B. Wearing

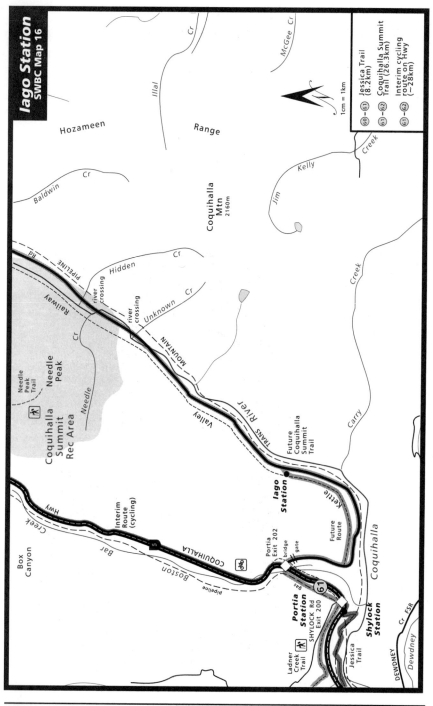

Iago Station
SWBC Map 16

Hozameen

Range

Coquihalla Mtn
2160m

1cm = 1km

60 — 61 Jessica Trail
(8.2km)

61 — 62 Coquihalla Summit
Trail (26.3km)

61 — 62 Interim cycling
route on Hwy
(~28km)

McGee Cr

Kelly Creek

Jim Creek

Baldwin Cr

Hidden Cr

PIPELINE Rd

Railway

river crossing

river crossing

Unknown Cr

Needle Cr

MOUNTAIN

Needle Peak Trail

Coquihalla Summit Rec Area

Needle Peak

VALLEY

TRANS River

Carry Creek

Future Coquihalla Summit Trail

Iago Station

Kettle

Box Canyon

Creek Hwy

Boston Bar Hwy

Interim Route (cycling)

COQUIHALLA

pipeline

Future Route

Coquihalla

Portia Exit 202

bridge

gate

see 61

Portia Station

SHYLOCK Rd
Exit 200

Ladner Creek Trail

Jessica Trail

Shylock Station

DEWDNEY Cr FSR

Dewdney

Southwestern BC Maps 16/17: Iago Station & Coquihalla Summit

Southwestern BC Section 61-62

~28 km
Coquihalla Summit Trail

The Coquihalla Summit Trail is a route that takes the Trans Canada Trail up and over the Coquihalla Summit. At the summit, there is some sign of civilization, otherwise one should expect to travel isolated wilderness sections. Unfortunately, until the Trans Mountain Pipeline Road is open to the public, hikers and horse-back riders do not have an option to explore.

The interim route simply follows the Coquihalla Highway. Cyclists will find this a

Zopikos Ridge   R. Mussio

relentless grunt up an extremely steep grade but the scenery is spectacular. From Hope to the Coquihalla Lakes, the highway climbs nearly 1,200 m (4,000 ft) in elevation.

 The route up and over the Coquihalla Summit takes you through some remote, mountainous terrains. Be prepared for sudden weather changes. Fog and snow are common throughout the year!

> *The Coquihalla Summit Recreation Area is a mountaineer's paradise. There are several mountain peaks, which can be accessed from a number of different trails. Anglers will also find fish in any one of a number of sub-alpine lakes in the area.*

Continue up past the Boston Bar Summit Rest Area, over the amazing Dry Gulch and through the toll booth. You can rejoin the Trans Canada Trail by taking the first road to the right after the toll booth.

The future route will hopefully follow the Trans Mountain Pipeline Road along the Coquihalla River. The 26.3 km road offers a hard packed gravel surface and a much easier grade up towards the summit. The pretty Coquihalla Lakes mark the end of the Coquihalla Summit Trail.

> *Facilities are few and far between in this area. One should be prepared for a wilderness experience. Camping is certainly possible and you may find a few rumi-nants of previous campsite. Please respect the environment by practicing no-trace camping.*

Coquihalla Lakes   L. Lebrun

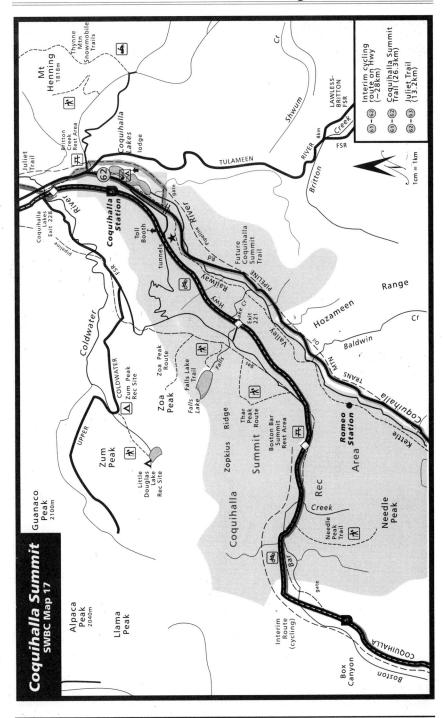

Coquihalla Summit
SWBC Map 17

Interim cycling route on Hwy (~28km)   61 – 62

Coquihalla Summit Trail (26.3km)   61 – 62

Juliet Trail (13.2km)   62 – 63

1cm = 1km

Guanaco Peak 2100m

Alpaca Peak 2040m

Llama Peak

Zum Peak

Zoa Peak

Coquihalla Summit

Zopkius Ridge

Thar Peak

Needle Peak

Coquihalla

Rec

Creek

Bar

Box Canyon

Interim Route (cycling)

Boston

Needle Peak Trail

Romeo Area Station

Baldwin

Hozameen Range

TRANS MTN

Oil

Kettle (Coquihalla)

gate

Boston Bar Summit Rest Area

Falls Lake Trail

Falls

Falls Lake

Zoa Peak Route

Thar Peak Route

Little Douglas Lake Rec Site

Zum Peak Rec Site

COLDWATER

UPPER

Coldwater

River

FSR

pipeline

Coquihalla Lakes Exit 228

Coquihalla Station

Toll Booth

tunnels

HWY

Railway

Rd

PIPELINE

Exit 221

Jake Cr

Valley

Future Coquihalla Summit Trail

62

Coquihalla Lakes lodge

TULAMEEN

RIVER

8km

LAWLESS-BRITTON FSR

Britton

Creek

Shwum

Cr

Britton Creek Rest Area

Juliet Trail

Mt Henning 1818m

Thynne Mtn Snowmobile Trails

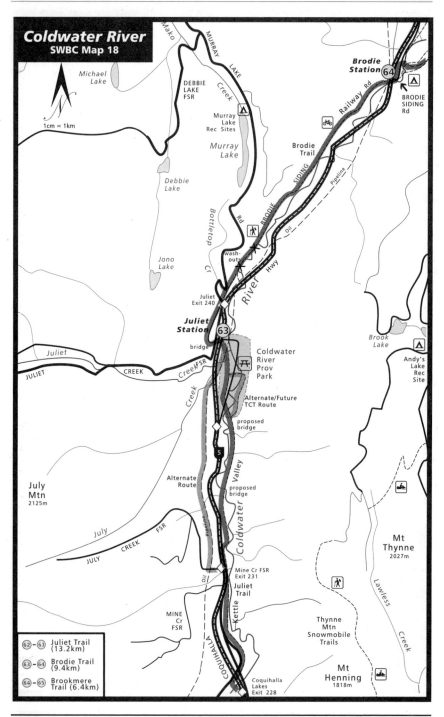

Coldwater River
SWBC Map 18

1cm = 1km

Michael
Lake

Mako Creek

MURRAY LAKE

DEBBIE
LAKE
FSR

Murray
Lake
Rec Sites

Murray Lake

Debbie
Lake

Jono
Lake

Bottletop Cr

Rd

BRODIE SIDING

Oil

River Hwy

wash-outs

Juliet
Exit 240

Juliet
Station

63

bridge

Juliet CREEK FSR

JULIET

Creek FSR

Coldwater
River
Prov
Park

Alternate/Future
TCT Route

proposed
bridge

5

July
Mtn
2125m

July CREEK FSR

JULY

Alternate
Route

Pipeline

Coldwater Valley

proposed
bridge

Mine Cr FSR
Exit 231

Juliet
Trail

MINE
Cr
FSR

Oil

Kettle

COQUIHALLA

Coquihalla
Lakes
Exit 228

Brodie Station 64

Railway Rd

BRODIE
SIDING
Rd

Brodie
Trail

Brook
Lake

Andy's
Lake
Rec
Site

Mt
Thynne
2027m

Lawless Creek

Thynne
Mtn
Snowmobile
Trails

Mt
Henning
1818m

62 – 63 Juliet Trail
(13.2km)

63 – 64 Brodie Trail
(9.4km)

64 – 65 Brookmere
Trail (6.4km)

Southwestern BC Map 18: Coldwater River

Southwestern BC Section 62-63

13.2 km
Juliet Trail

The Juliet Trail portion of the Trans Canada Trail begins at the north end of the Coquihalla Lakes, which form the headwaters of the Coquihalla River. The section of trail is not well developed at this time but it does begin a much-appreciated downhill grade.

The trail begins by continuing along the former Kettle Valley Railway (KVR) north to the Coquihalla Lakes Exit off Highway 5. The trail then travels west over the highway and the former railway bridge over the Coldwater River. The route leads back underneath the highway and follows the railbed north along the east side of the highway all the way to the Mine Creek Forest Service Road Exit.

Falls above KVR   *L. Lebrun*

An interim route travels underneath the highway again and picks up along the Westcoast Energy Gas Pipeline right-of-way. The trail proceeds north along the right-of-way all the way to Juliet Station Exit road.

If you do not mind getting your feet wet, it is possible to continue north on an undeveloped trail. This route requires crossing the upper Coldwater River, which shouldn't be too deep or swift to cause any problems. On the east side of the river a service road continues north to another river crossing and the section through the lovely Coldwater River Park.

A more viable option for bikers is to follow the shoulder of Highway 5 from the Coquihalla Lakes Exit (Exit 228) to the Juliet Station Exit (Exit 240). The main route above is passable on a bike, although traverses over some challenging terrain.

Day-trippers can access the trail from the Britton Creek Rest Area. Washrooms and picnic tables are provided at the rest area. The undeveloped Coldwater River Provincial Park also makes a nice picnic area.

Southwestern BC Section 63-64

9.4 km

Brodie Trail

At Juliet Station, the Trans Canada Trail picks up along the historic Kettle Valley Railway bed along the west side of the highway. You must first cross the highway and then follow the road that parallels the highway. The road follows the formerrailbed although remnants of the railway and old Juliet Station are not visible. Along the way, you will encounter a fence, which is periodically locked (Trails BC is looking into this problem). If the gate is locked, there is a way through the fence to the south, where you will find a one-way animal access to the opposite side of the fencing.

Once on the north side of the gate, the Trans Canada Trail route continues along the old railbed north to Brodie Station. This road is known as Brodie Siding Road and makes for a nice riverside route. Unfortunately, there are two significant wash outs that have been created by the Coldwater River. The areas are passable on foot, although the footing can be quite tricky, hence not recommended for bikers or equestrian riders.

Just before the route crosses the highway, you will notice the actual KVR can be seen to the north of Brodie Road. However, follow the road underneath the highway where it picks up the KVR again for the journey east.

Cyclists may wish to travel along the shoulder of Highway 5 from Juliet to Brodie Station. When following this option, travellers can continue north to the Larson Exit (Exit 250) and then return to the Bordie StationBridge via the Bordie Station service road. More sure-footed travellers can scramble down the embankment at the south foot of Larson Hill, just north of the Coldwater River Bridge and use the one-way wildlife gate to access the KVR right-of-way, thus saving several kilometers.

Coldwater River Bridge   M. Shewchuk

 Facilities are few and far between in this area. One should be prepared for a wilderness experience. Camping is certainly possible and you may find a few ruminants of previous campsite. Please respect the environment by practicing no-trace camping.

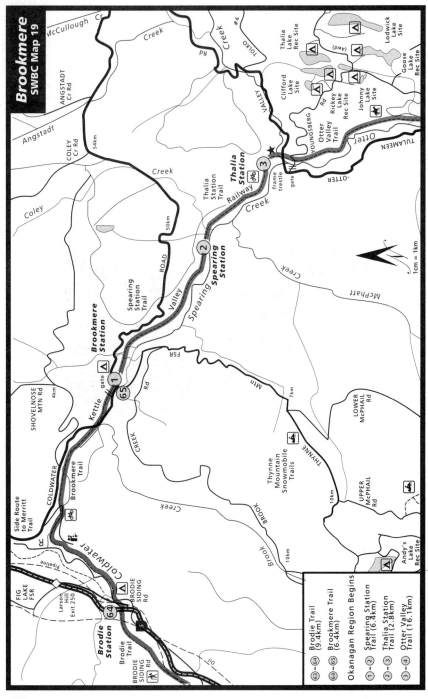

Brookmere
SWBC Map 19

McCullough Cr

Creek

Creek #4

TOLKO

Thalia Lake Rec Site

Lodwick Lake Site

ANGSTADT Cr Rd

VALLEY

Clifford Lake Site

(4wd)

Goose Lake Rec Site

Rd

Angstadt

Rickey Lake Rec Site

Johnny Lake Site

COLEY Cr Rd

54km

Creek

YOUNGSBERG

Otter Valley Trail

Coley

Rd

Thalia Station

Thalia Station Trail

Railway

3

frame trestle

gate

OTTER

TULAMEEN

Coley

50km

Creek

Creek

2

Spearing Station

Spearing Station Trail

ROAD

Valley

Spearing

Creek

McPhatt

1cm = 1km

Brookmere Station

FSR

Mtn

7km

LOWER McPHAIL Rd

1

65

gate

Kettle

CREEK Rd

THYNNE

Thynne Mountain Snowmobile Trails

UPPER McPHAIL Rd

SHOVELNOSE MTN Rd

4km

COLDWATER

Brookmere Trail

Creek

BROOK

10km

Andy's Lake Rec Site

Side Route to Merritt Trail

Coldwater

Brook

10km

FIG LAKE FSR

Larson Hill Exit 250

Pipeline

BRODIE SIDING Rd

64

5

Brodie Station

Brodie Trail

BRODIE SIDING Rd

63	Brodie Trail (9.4km)
64–65	Brookmere Trail (6.4km)

Okanagan Region Begins

1–2	Spearing Station Trail (6.4km)
2–3	Thalia Station Trail (2.8km)
3–4	Otter Valley Trail (16.1km)

Southwestern BC Map 19: Brookmere

Southwestern BC Section 64-65

6.4 km
Brookmere Trail

After crossing underneath Highway 5, Brodie Siding Road veers north and away from the railway. Trans Canada Trail travellers should follow the railbed east to the Coldwater River, where the bridge over the river has been removed. Follow the Merritt Subdivision (railway terms for a divide in the rail line) north along the west side of the river to the railway bridge over the river. Once across the river, the Merritt Subdivision section of the KVR links back up to the main line.

The remaining portion of the route to Brookmere Station is a marginal uphill

Brookmere Station   J. Klein

climb along the old railbed that is still in good condition. This area offers fantastic backcountry scenery, including a fabulous viewpoint overlooking the Coldwater River.

Brookmere is the dividing point between the Southwestern BC and Okanagan Regions of the Trans Canada Trail. This historical location made a good regional divide as it has more recently been used as the beginning or end of the world-renowned Kettle Valley Railway cycling route.

 Brookmere used to be the dividing point of the KVR and the Vancouver, Victoria & Eastern Railway (VV&E). In its heyday, the station served both railways and became the focal point of the small settlement of Brookmere. The Brookmere water tower is the last standing water tower on the KVR and is a historic landmark of the era. Today, Brookmere marks the begining of the famous Kettle Valley Railway recreational route.

The Dogwood BC's Official Flower   L. Timbs

SWBC SERVICE PROVIDERS

Accommodations

HI-Vancouver Jericho Beach
Scenic natural beachside location.
Numerous programs and activities.

1515 Discovery Street
Vancouver, BC, V6R 4K5
1-888-203-4303
1-604-224-3208
www.hihostels.bc.ca

HI-Vancouver Downtown
Located Downtown Vancouver with
easy access to Stanley Park.

1114 Burnaby Street
Vancouver, BC, V6E 1P1
1-888-203-4302
1-604-684-4565
www.hihostels.bc.ca

C&N Backpackers Hostel
Accomodations for
backpackers&budget travellers.

927 Main Street
Vancouver, BC, V6A 2V8
1-604-682-2441
www.cnnbackpackers.com

www.**backroadmapbooks**.com

Tours and Guides

travel@britishcolumbiatours.com
1-800-797-6335

Attractions

MSA Museum Society
Discover Abbotsford BC's Heritage
house, garden/lake tours, & gift shop.

2313 Ware Street
Abbotsford, BC, V2S 3C6
1-604-853-0313
www.abbotsford.net/MSAMuseum

Okanagan

The majority of the Trans Canada Trail through the Oakanagan follows the historic Kettle Valley Railway bed. The old rail bed makes for a superb trail base as it is well laid out and tackles steeper climbs much easier than other parts of the Trans Canada Trail due to its original design. The Kettle Valley Railway is a historic railway that was the main route of transportation and supply into and from the B.C. interior well before the establishment of an efficient road network.

Generally, all outdoor travellers including horseback riders can travel the Trans Canada Trail through the Oakanagan region. The trail is perhaps the best multi-use trail section of the Trans Canada Trail in British Columbia and traverses through some spectacular geography along the route. The most impressive section of the Oakanagan section is the portion through the Myra Canyon north of Kelowna. Coupled with the many phenomenal trestles and tunnels, this portion of the route is unbelievable. A definite problem for horse riders is the section through the town of Penticton and Summerland. Since the route travels through the urban centres of both areas, it may be required to skip these areas and start back up just north of Penticton.

Much of the Trans Canada route through the Oakangan has been well established. Since the route follows the old Kettle Valley Railway bed, there are very few problems compared to other sections of the trail. Although the route is well established, this section is not without its problems. Lately, a few areas have come under dispute and will hopefully be solved in the future. One particular area is the portion of the Kettle Valley rail bed that travels through the local native reserve just outside of Summerland. There are also a few places along the rail bed just north of Rock Creek that have been reclaimed by local residents and farmers. Trails BC is attempting to negotiate with locals, however, in the interim, we have established route alternatives. For up to date route changes and information be sure to check in with Trails BC or on the web at **www.backroadmapbooks.com**

Throughout the Oakangan, help is usually not far away. Although the Trans Canada Trail travels through some remote areas, the route is very easy to follow and is never too far away from rural residents or urban areas. Perhaps the most remote section of the trail is from Penticton to Rock Creek. In reality, along much of this portion of the trail it is quite easy to travel to a busy road or urban area from the main route. Although civilisation is well at hand, the Trans Canada Trail through the Okanagan is an amazing journey and truly one of the main highlights of the entire Trans Canada Trail in British Columbia.

Okanagan Region

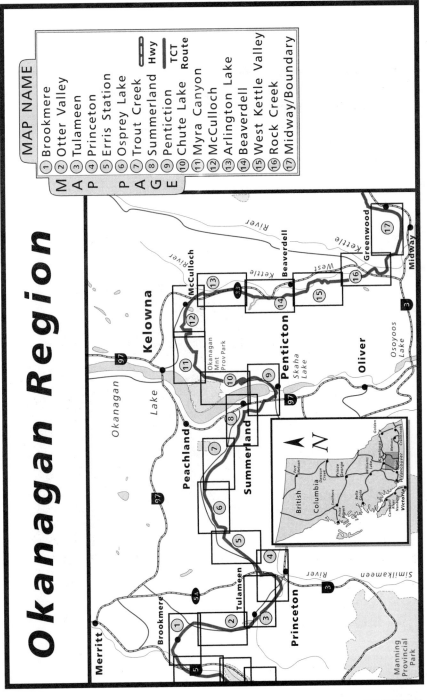

MAP NAME

M
- (1) Brookmere
- (2) Otter Valley

A
- (3) Tulameen

P
- (4) Princeton
- (5) Erris Station

P
- (6) Osprey Lake
- (7) Trout Creek

A
- (8) Summerland

G
- (9) Penticton
- (10) Chute Lake

E
- (11) Myra Canyon
- (12) McCulloch
- (13) Arlington Lake
- (14) Beaverdell
- (15) West Kettle Valley
- (16) Rock Creek
- (17) Midway/Boundary

Hwy
TCT Route

Okanagan Map 1: Brookmere

Okanagan Section 1-2

6.4 km
Spearing Trail

The Okanagan portion of the Trans Canada Trail begins at the old Brookmere Station of the historic Kettle Valley Railway. The railway was officially abandoned in 1990 and the tracks have been removed (in most sections anyways) to help form a world-class cycling destination. The remote setting, the gentle grade and the historical significance makes this route a logical choice for the Trans Canada Trail to follow.

Brookmere Watertower   M. Shewchuk

The Spearing Trail portion on the route leads you into a much more remote area as it takes the traveller further away from the busy Highway 5. The old railbed leads past a few of the old Brookmere Station buildings and around a gate. The route continues along the railbed crossing Brookmere Road and eventually across a small bridge over Spearing Creek. The trail the hugs bank above the creek and the small canyon, all the way to the former site of Spearing Station.

The Kettle Valley Railway is an amazing engineering feat that was orchestrated by Scottish engineer Andrew McCulloch. Started in 1910 it took five years to complete the 525 kilometre project between Hope and Midway. The development of the Crowsnest Highway (Hwy 3) and the high maintenance costs of the railway finally led to its' demise by 1990. Today the rails have been removed and it is now a popular recreational trail cutting through the mountains, deserts, orchards and forests of British Columbia's southern interior.

Okanagan Section 2-3

2.8 km
Thalia Station Trail

From Spearing Station, the Trans Canada Trail follows the KVR through a tight canyon as it proceeds eastward towards Thalia Station. There is very little room in the canyon other than for the creek and the railbed, making for quite an exhilarating trek. Approximately 1 km down the trail, there is a major washout of the railbed that locals have constructed a short detour around. As the route approaches the old Thalia Station site, the canyon begins to open up.

Thalia Station was originally named Canyon Station for its location in the canyon area of the Spearing Creek.

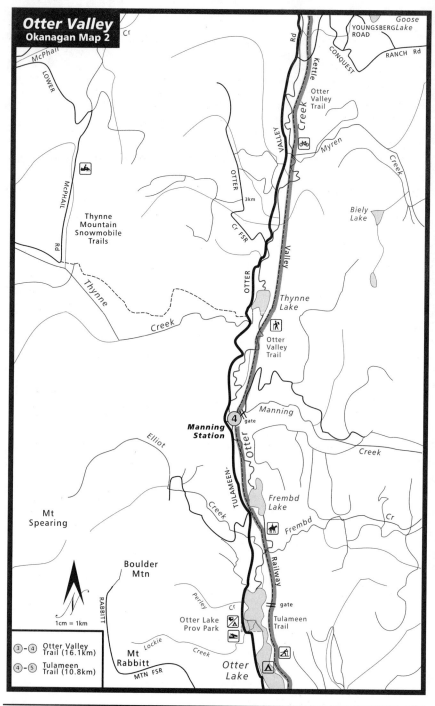

Otter Valley
Okanagan Map 2

Goose Lake
YOUNGSBERG
ROAD
RANCH Rd
CONQUEST
Kettle Rd

Cr
McPhall
LOWER
VALLEY
Creek

Otter
Valley
Trail

Myren Creek

McPHAIL Rd

OTTER
3km
Cr FSR

Biely
Lake

Thynne
Mountain
Snowmobile
Trails

OTTER

Thynne
Creek

Thynne
Lake

Otter
Valley
Trail

Mt
Spearing

Elliot

Creek

TULAMEEN-

Manning
Station

4 gate

Manning

Creek

Otter

Frembd
Lake

Frembd Cr

Boulder
Mtn

RABBITT

Railway

1cm = 1km

N

3 – 4 Otter Valley
Trail (16.1km)

4 – 5 Tulameen
Trail (10.8km)

Perley

Cr

gate

Tulameen
Trail

Otter Lake
Prov Park

Mt
Rabbitt

Lockie Creek

MTN FSR

Otter
Lake

Okanagan Map 2: Otter Valley

Okanagan Section 3-4

16.1 km
Otter Valley Trail

Shortly after the former Thalia Station site, the Trans Canada Trail veers off the railbed to skirt the former pile trestle that once crossed Otter Creek. There is a new trail leading from the trestle area, across the creek and up to the Tulameen-Otter Valley Road. The road will bring you back to the old railbed. The trestle was badly damaged by fire sometime in 1996 and has not been repaired.

Otter Lake   *P. White*

 Several BC Forest Recreational Campsites can be found further east along Youngsberg Road. There is a series of small interior lakes that offer a scenic camping and good fishing alternatives.

south along the railbed along the east side of the Otter Creek. Between Youngsberg Road and Manning Station the trail traverses over eight short trestles that help the route navigate its way south. The longest trestle is a mere 41 metres (135 ft), although they are all quite exciting to cross, as Otter Creek can be seen rushing below.

As the rail trail reaches Thynne Lake, it passes along the east side of the Otter Valley wall and provides splendid views of the remote lake. Continuing south of Thynne Lake a washout has damaged the upcoming trestle; however, a group of determined bikers have repaired much of it. Along the next one km of trail, the route passes over three trestles before reaching a fourth trestle that is slightly damaged. This is the beginning of a number of small washouts from here to the Manning Station, which are all easily passable.

At Manning Station, one will find a few remains of the old station. The cleared area offers patches of old concrete that remind us of the bustling railway of yesterday. One barrier to be aware of is the fencing that has been erected across the trail for ranching purposes. When opening any ranching gate, be sure to replace the gate to its original state.

Okanagan Section 4-5

10.8 km
Tulameen Trail

From the former site of Manning Station, the Trans Canada Trail continues its trek south along the KVR. However, when leaving Manning Station, the railbed has been ploughed over by a local farmer, making the bed unnoticeable. The ploughed section is only about 500 m (1,640 ft) in length and the railbed is easily found on the other side of this field. Shortly after the trail begins to follow the railbed again, the route passes over a bridge across Otter Creek and then across another trestle over an old channel of the creek.

The route then skirts along the west side of the marshy shores of Frembd Lake before the trail crosses the creek and begins its trek on the east side of the valley. The trail meets Otter Lake and travels along the canyon wall on the east side of the lake. There is a gate, which can be easily travelled around, across the trail soon after the route meets Otter Lake. As the trail approaches the town of Tulameen, the trail crosses Otter Creek again and passes by Otter Lake Provincial Park. The park has a separate camping and picnic area and makes for a rewarding rest area.

The former site of the Tulameen Station is recognized by the concrete base that once held a water tower. This signifies the end of the Tulameen Trail portion of rest area.

Otter Lake Provincial Park offers a rustic camping experience as well as a separate day-use closer to Tulameen. The lakeshore campsite makes a fine place to rest while enjoying the sights and sounds of this quiet area. A fantastic beach and good fishing also attract visitors to the area.

As the trail travels through the town of Tulameen, the former Tulameen KVR station house can be found within the town. It is now a private residence. Tulameen is a full service centre, providing basic amenities such as food and supplies, accommodation and even bicycle repairs.

The former site of the Tulameen Station is recognized by the concrete base that once held a water tower. This signifies the end of the Tulameen Trail portion of the Trans Canada Trail.

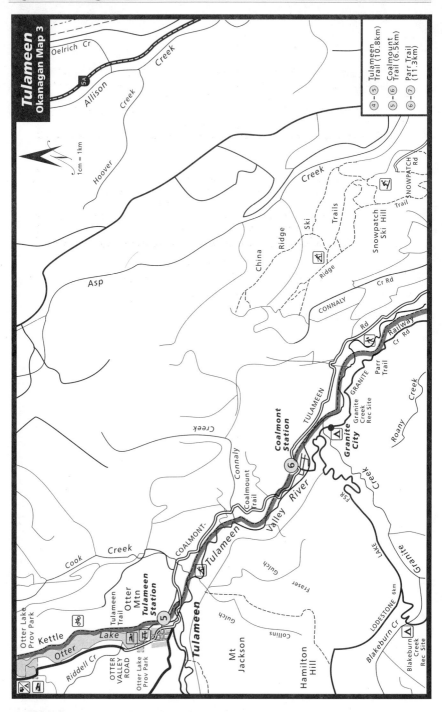

Okanagan Map 3: Tulameen

Okanagan Section 5-6

6.5 km
Coalmont Trail

The Coalmont Trail leads the Trans Canada Trail out of the town of Tulameen along the KVR. The trail crosses Otter Creek before proceeding south east towards the Tulameen River. Just out of town, the trail crosses the Coalmont-Tulameen Road before meeting a fenced cow pasture. The route continues on the east side of the river and crosses the Coalmont-Tulameen Road again before reaching the town site of Coalmont.

Parr Tunnel   *P. White*

Coalmont received its name from the massive supply of coal the town industry revolved around. In the early 1900's the town was booming but as the industry floundered, the town all but disappeared. Today, the town resembles more of a ghost town.

>
> When in Coalmont, be sure to take the time to visit both the general store and the historic Coalmont Hotel. The hotel is still operational but the general store is closed. The two sites are original structures of the town that have been restored. The hotel in particular is unique, since its interior and exterior have been refurbished complete with 19th Century furnishings. Just wandering past these buildings will give you a small sense of the 'old west'.

Okanagan Section 6-7

11.3 km
Parr Trail

From Coalmont, the Trans Canada Trail follows the KVR east out of town. The route parallels the road and the river while the former site of Granite City can be seen across the river. The old city is found just upstream from a Forestry Recreation Site found at the junction of Granite Creek and the Tulameen River.

About 2 km from the Granite City site, the trail crosses a 100 m (328 ft) trestle over

> Granite City was the largest settlement in BC's interior in 1886 with approximately 2,000 residents. The town boomed due to the discovery of gold in Granite Creek before becoming deserted by 1890 once gold prospects dwindled. Today, all that remains are mine tailings and remnants of log structures.

the Tulameen River. Substantial work has been done in the area by the Vermilion Trails Society to improve the tunnels, trestles and washouts that once posed as barriers to the route. Remember that over time washouts and irregularities are bound to happen along the route. Please be careful and be alert for potential dangers.

> One particularly noticeable natural feature along much of this portion of the trail is the brilliantly rust coloured slopes that are found throughout the canyon. The Tulameen River is named after this red colouration, since 'Tulameen' is a native Salish word meaning 'red earth'.

The trail crosses the Tulameen River again and proceeds to the Parr Tunnel. The

The trail crosses the Tulameen River again and proceeds to the Parr Tunnel. The curved tunnel is quite interesting as it is almost 150 m long. When you are in the middle of the tunnel, the ends are not visible. This can be unnerving to some visitors. Shortly after leaving the Parr Tunnel, the trail reaches the former site of the Parr Station. A small gazebo has been erected here.

Be sure to check on conditions of this section before heading out. If washouts do occur, an alternative to this section is to follow the Coalmont-Tulameen Road from Coalmont to Princeton.

Emerald Pool   P. Kivinen

Parr Station was the site of a short spur along the KVR. The station is named after the engineer who was in charge of the Parr Tunnel construction. Today, very little remains of the old station site.

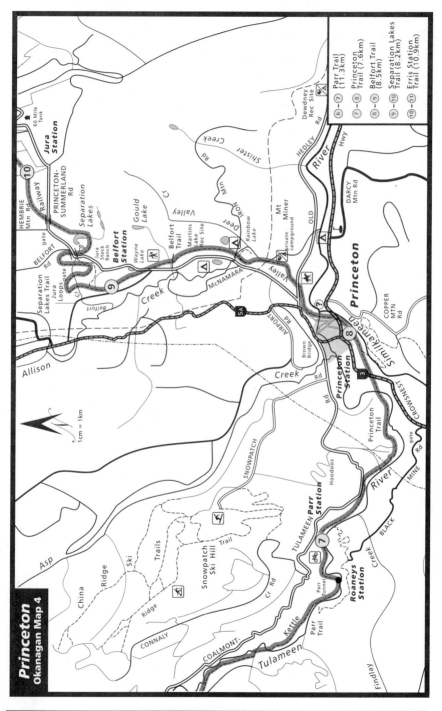

Princeton
Okanagan Map 4

Legend:
- ⑥–⑦ Parr Trail (11.3km)
- ⑦–⑧ Princeton Trail (7.6km)
- ⑧–⑨ Belfort Trail (8.5km)
- ⑨–⑩ Separation Lakes Trail (8.2km)
- ⑩–⑪ Erris Station Trail (10.9km)

1cm = 1km

Okanagan Map 4: Princeton

Okanagan Section 7-8

7.6 km
Princeton Trail

The Princeton Trail portion of the Trans Canada Trail picks up from the end of the Parr Trail and progresses east towards the town of Princeton. The railbed hugs the Tulameen River as it travels east and provides excellent views of the river and its bright red banks. About 3 km down this portion of the trail, Hoodoos are visible along the south shore of the river. These fascinating anomalies were created by wind eroding the soft soil along the cliffs.

Hoodoos   *P. Kivinen*

 Around 1885, the Tulameen River was the site of a major gold and platinum rush. Today, prospectors can still find the odd piece of gold along the river. If you are interested in trying your luck gold panning, the local travel information centres should have a list of tour operators in the area. Please do not attempt to dig on an existing place claims.

Just before the trail enters the town of Princeton, the route traverses a trestle crossing the Tulameen River and then passes through the lite Princeton Tunnel underneath Highway 3. The trail heads into the city Princeton and across Auburn Crescent before reaching the site of the Princeton Station found on the south side of Highway 3. The old station house is still standing; however, it is now home to a Subway restaurant and a real estate office. As can be expected, the city offers anything a traveller could want. Food and supplies, accommodation and a host of service operators are easily found in this small city.

The Vancouver, Victoria & Eastern Railway (VV&E) constructed the 324 m (1,063 ft) Princeton Tunnel in 1910. The VV&E owned the track heading west all the way to Coalmont but the Kettle Valley Railway operated along the rail line under an agreement with the VV&E.

The town of Princeton was once named Vermilion Forks, although the name was changed in 1860 in honour of the Prince of Wales. The name 'Vermilion' was derived from the red colour of the Tulameen River banks soil. Vermilion is the name of the natural compound, which creates the bright red colouration in the soil. Be sure to visit the local museum to learn more about the mining history of the area and the historical rail line through Princeton.

Okanagan Section 8-9

8.5 km

Belfort Trail

Beginning at the Princeton Station site, the Trans Canada Trail follows the old Kettle Valley Railway as well as a new 2 km trail next to Burton Avenue. Continuing northward through Princeton towards the Tulameen River the obstacles include the highway that interrupts the old railbed. The railbed trail is easily found again on the other side of the highway and leads to the crossing of the Tulameen River, where the KVR trestle is out of commission. Instead, the route crosses the river along the road bridge, running parallel to the trail.

The route picks up again on the railbed and starts up a decent grade. En route to the former site of the Belfort Station, the Trans Canada Trail/Kettle Valley Railway will cross Allison Creek and the Princeton-Summerland Road.

Princeton Bridge　　　　M. Skewchuck

Day-trippers from Princeton often like to explore the 120 km section between Brookmere and Osprey Lake in two separate journeys. Due to the steeper grade leading up to Osprey Lake, a shuttle is recommended. From Osprey Lake it is a nice 50 km cruise back down to town.

The Princeton Travel Information Centre is located across the Similameen River. There are washrooms and picnic tables as well as area information boards. A good map has also been produced by a memeber of the Summerland Trans Canada Society for the Princeton-Summerland Road and the Trans Canada Highway in this area. Trail users may find it valuable as it references numbered tags placed along the trail for construction and maintenace purposes.

Okanagan Section 9-10

8.2 km
Separation Lakes Trail

Belfort Station is hardly noticeable, other than the widening of the railbed marking the former site of the station. From Belfort Station, the trail continues to climb along the grassy hills characteristic of the Okanagan and begins a series of large switchbacks in order to climb towards Jura Station. The trail travels through cattle ranch areas as it meanders eastward and meets a gated fence once at the Princeton-Summerland Road. The trail picks up again on the other side of the road, re-accessing the railbed via another gate. As the trail traverses towards Separation Lakes, it passes through the Jura Stock Ranch.

The Separation Lakes are small water bodies that can dry significantly during the hot summer months and are set amid the rolling fields. In late spring and early summer, the fields in this section of the route bloom with wildflowers. The lakes also host a slew of migratory birds and are fine birding areas.

The trail eventually meets up with the Princeton-Summerland Road again as well as gated fences on either side of the road. The trail continues on the north side of the road and eventually comes to the former site of the Jura Station. The wider railbed and the water tower base mark the site of the former KVR stop.

The Belfort Station was named after the French military garrison that was famed for its mountain resistance to invading German armies in 1870. The garrison repelled much larger German forces while taking refuge in the Jura Mountains of Europe. The Jura Station next along the line was named after the mountain range famed for the same event.

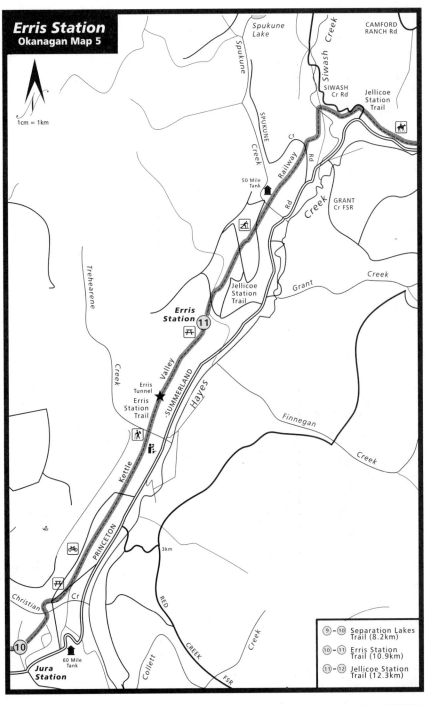

Erris Station
Okanagan Map 5

1cm = 1km

Spukune Lake

Siwash Creek

CAMFORD RANCH Rd

Spukune

SIWASH Cr Rd

Jellicoe Station Trail

SPUKUNE Creek

Cr

Railway Rd

50 Mile Tank

Rd

Creek

GRANT Cr FSR

Jellicoe Station Trail

Grant

Creek

Trehearene

Erris Station (11)

Creek

Valley

Erris Tunnel
Erris Station Trail

SUMMERLAND

Hayes

Finnegan

Creek

Kettle

PRINCETON

3km

RED

Christian

Cr

CREEK

Creek

(10)

60 Mile Tank

Jura Station

Collett

FSR

⑨–⑩	Separation Lakes Trail (8.2km)
⑩–⑪	Erris Station Trail (10.9km)
⑪–⑫	Jellicoe Station Trail (12.3km)

Okanagan Map 5: Erris Station

Okanagan Section 10-11

10.9 km
Erris Station Trail

As the Trans Canada Trail heads further east, the trail incline begins to slow somewhat compared to the portion of trail from Princeton to the Jura Station. The route traverses along the west side of the Princeton-Summerland Road crossing the Christian Creek before providing excellent views of the Hayes Valley found below the trail. About 2 km before Erris Station, the trail passes through the Erris Tunnel. The tunnel is approximately 90 m (295 ft) in length and is unique because wooden timbers support the tunnel roof and walls. At Erris Station, the station site is noticeable due to the widening of the railbed and the remains of a shed found down the side of the hill.

Wildflowers by the Route   *P. White*

Okanagan Section 11-12

12.3 km
Jellicoe Station Trail

The Trans Canada Trail continues east along the KVR through the semi-wooded hillside atop the Princeton-Summerland Road. The trail crosses the Spukunne Creek along a short trestle and the remains of an old water tower named the Fifty

Mile Tank.

The number of water tanks in the area should be a good indication of just how hot and dry it can get in the Okanagan. Be sure to carry plenty of water and try to avoid travelling in the heat of the day.

The route then crosses the Pinewood Creek Road before traversing over Siwash Creek. The trail crosses the Siwash Creek Road before heading along the final stretch of this portion of the Jellicoe Station Trail, which ends at the former site of the Jellicoe Station.

Leaving the Tunnel   N. Balcolm

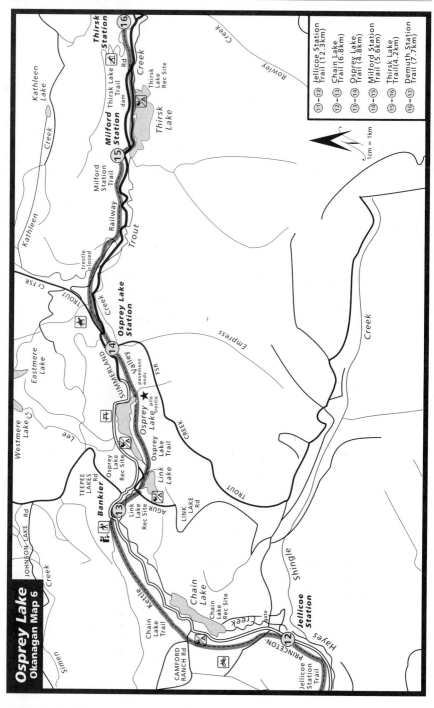

Osprey Lake
Okanagan Map 6

1cm = 1km

11 – 12 Jellicoe Station Trail (12.3km)
12 – 13 Chain Lake Trail (6.8km)
13 – 14 Osprey Lake Trail (4.8km)
14 – 15 Milford Station Trail (5.6km)
15 – 16 Thirsk Lake Trail (4.2km)
16 – 17 Demuth Station Trail (7.7km)

Okanagan Map 6: Osprey Lake

Okanagan Section 12-13

6.8 km
Chain Lake Trail

From Jellicoe Station the Trans Canada Trail heads north along the KVR towards Chain Lake. The trail skirts north of the lake well above the valley, offering splendid views of the surrounding countryside. Views of the area include the scenic Chain Lake, which is host to a number of cottages and homes as well as a recreation site for camping. The trail crosses the Penticton-Summerland Road just before the trail passes by the settlement and former KVR stop of Bankier.

Osprey Lake Boardwalk   *L. Grant*

Bankier is a very small settlement made up of mainly vacation residences. The community does have a general store that can be found just to the north of the trail.

183

Okanagan Section 13-14

4.8 km

Osprey Lake Trail

Travelling east from Bankier, the Trans Canada Trail crosses Augur Road just before reaching Link Lake. The trail traverses along the lake's northern shore and crosses Link Lake Road about 400 m (1,310 ft) before Osprey Lake. The old KVR continues along Osprey Lake's southern shore and crosses over an impressive pile trestle near the lake's eastern shore. Just after the pile trestle, the route passes the highest point between Princeton and Summerland. After this, it is a slow descent towards Summerland and Penticton. The concrete base of the former station water tower and station house marks the Osprey Lake Station.

Osprey Lake is a quiet summer destination and is a great spot for an afternoon picnic. Similar to nearby Chain and Link Lakes, there is a nice forestry recreation site that offers a good place to base camp. Perhaps the most popular pastime is fishing for the abundant rainbow trout found in this lake chain. The FISHING BC Okanagan book highlights this and other lakes in the region.

Okanagan Section 14-15

5.6 km

Milford Station Trail

The Trans Canada Trail begins to travel into more remote territory as it follows the KVR east from Osprey Lake Station. About 500 m (1,640 ft) from the Osprey Lake Station, the trail crosses the Penticton-Summerland Road and then over a small creek. Shortly after the creek crossing, it is necessary to take the first road encountered south down to the Penticton-Summerland Road. Continue down the road to the bridge crossing Trout Creek and take the next trail on the left back up to the KVR. The ironwork of the railway crossing over Trout Creek has been removed and only the cement abutments remain.

The Milford Station site is found about 3 km east from the Kathleen Creek although is not recognizable. As the trail nears the former site, the railbed becomes the Penticton-Summerland Road and the trail uses the former road section that runs adjacent to Thirsk Lake. The trail provides access to Thirsk Lake, where camping (for a fee) and fishing are possible.

The dam at Thirsk Lake is being raised and some sections of the former road and the campsite will become flooded in the future. Until this happens, the trail will use the lower road.

Okanagan Section 15-16

4.2 km

Thirsk Lake Trail

This portion of the Trans Canada Trail heads into characteristic Okanagan terrain marked by grassy semi-forested slopes and desert climate plants such as tumbleweeds and even cactus. The terrain provides a real sense of solitude and unlike the lush rainforests of the coast, the dry Okanagan forests host some eerie looking snags. Coupled with some circling ravens above and you could have the authentic setting of the 19th Century Wild West.

Leaving Thirsk Lake from the lower road the trail makes a sharp left turn onto the Penticton-Summerland Road to access the KVR once again. Travel along the railbed continues slowly downhill and is generally uneventful, other than the great wilderness scenery. The Thirsk Station is barely noticeable by the widening in the railbed.

Drawdown on Thirsk Lake   J. Marleau

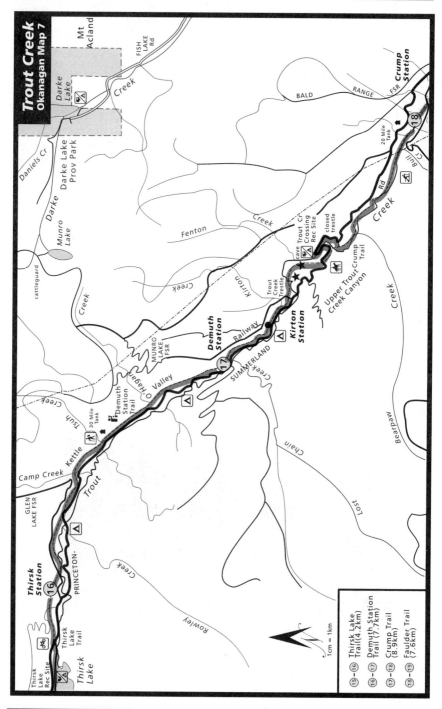

Trout Creek
Okanagan Map 7

1cm = 1km

- ⑮–⑯ Thirsk Lake Trail (4.2km)
- ⑯–⑰ Demuth Station Trail (7.7km)
- ⑰–⑱ Crump Trail (8.9km)
- ⑱–⑲ Faulder Trail (7.6km)

Okanagan Map 7: Trout Creek

Okanagan Section 16-17

7.7 km

Demuth Station Trail

East from Thirsk Station, the Trans Canada Trail crosses the Glen Lake Forest Service Road then over Tsuh Creek and past a cattle ranch as it continues its downward trek along the north side of the Princeton-Summerland Road. Shortly after Tsuh Creek, the trail passes by several fantastic natural viewpoints, which provide exceptional views of the Trout Creek Valley and the distant mountain slopes. The trail crosses O'Hagan Creek and a private access road before reaching the site of the Demuth Station. The station site is not noticeable.

Trout Creek Trestle   J. Marleau

Okanagan Section 17-18

8.9 km
Crump Trail

The Trans Canada Trail continues east along the KVR from Demuth Station, traversing through the arid, secluded Trout Creek Valley. The route passes the former Kirton Station site, although all that remains are concrete bases of the buildings of the past era. However, if you take a look over the nearby cliff, you will find the remains of the former Kirton Station House.

Beyond Kirton Station the trail crosses the Munroe Lake Forest Service Road before another short trestle crossing of Trout Creek. The trestle is scheduled for decking and guard rails in 2001. Continue past the trestle, and into the narrow canyon area. Recent work has been done in the area to prevent further erosion of the sandy slope into the creek. You will also pass a cave that has been shored with timbers. It is not known why the cave was used by the railway.

The steep rock walls surrounding Trout Creek are extremely unstable. Please avoid the temptation to scale them.

1.5 km past this trestle the trail meets the Penticton-Summerland Road again. A second trestle just beyond the road has been removed so it is necessary to use the road bridge to cross the creek. Just before the bridge, a Forestry Recreation Site offers an outhouse and picnic tables. Once across the bridge look for a bypass trail to the right. This new trail is rather rough but provides a pleasant bush hike back to the railbed. Cyclists are recommended to dismount along this rough trail.

Returning to the railbed the trail follows close to Trout Creek as it runs towards Summerland. The canyon is surrounded semi-open grasslands dotted with Douglas-fir and the odd rocky bluff. Shortly before Crump Station you will pass well below the powerlines. Little remains of Crump Station except the octagonal concrete base of the former water tank.

A short walk upstream from the Crump Station will lead to a beaver falling area. Several large Aspen, which are the beavers favourite food, have been felled.

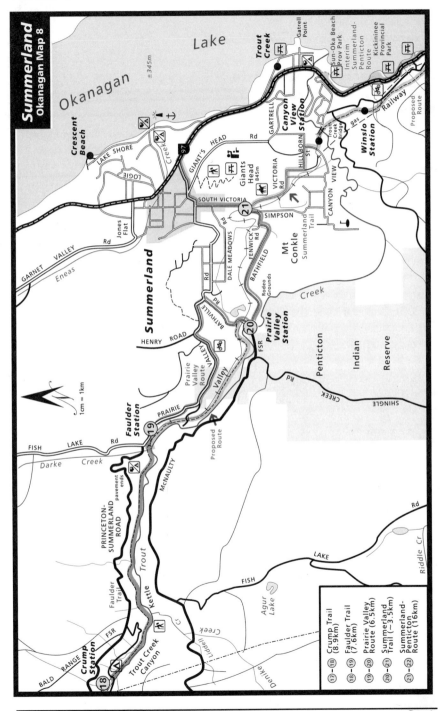

Summerland
Okanagan Map 8

Crescent Beach

Okanagan Lake

Trout Creek

Gatrell Point

Sun-Oka Beach Prov Park

Interim Summerland-Penticton Route

Kickininee Provincial Park

±345m

LAKE SHORE

LOGIE

Creek

GIANT'S HEAD

GARTRELL Rd

Canyon View Station

Railway

Proposed Route

Winslow Station

Trout Creek Bridge

gas

Giants Head 845m

VICTORIA Rd

HILLBORN St

CANYON VIEW

SOUTH VICTORIA

21

SIMPSON

DALE MEADOWS Rd

FENWICK Rd

BATHFIELD

Mt Conkle

Summerland Trail

GARNET VALLEY Rd

Jones Flat

Eneas

Summerland

HENRY ROAD

BATHVILLE Rd

VALLEY

Prairie Valley Route

Rodeo Grounds

20

Prairie Valley Station

FSR

Creek

Penticton

Indian

Reserve

SHINGLE CREEK Rd

1cm = 1km

Faulder Station

19

PRAIRIE

Proposed Route

FISH LAKE Rd

Darke Creek

pavement ends

McNAULTY

PRINCETON-SUMMERLAND ROAD

Trout

Kettle

Creek

Faulder Trail

FSR

BALD RANGE

Crump Station

18

Trout Creek Canyon

Liddell Cr

Deruyke Cr

FISH

LAKE

Agur Lake

Riddle Cr

Rd

17—18 Crump Trail (8.9km)
18—19 Faulder Trail (7.6km)
19—20 Prairie Valley Route (6.5km)
20—21 Summerland Trail (~3.5km)
21—22 Summerland-Penticton Route (16km)

Okanagan Map 8: Summerland

Okanagan Section 18-19

7.6 km
Faulder Trail

Below Crump Station the trail passes a usually dry creek washout and then a 4wd road. This area makes a good camping location. Further along, the trail crosses a cattleguard and rounds a corner where the semi-open grasslands give way to rocky canyon walls. Craggy rock bluffs tinged with red coloured lichens stand above the rocky slopes mixed with Douglas-fir. The historic KVR was masterfully constructed through this impressive natural barrier. Today, travellers should be aware of falling rocks and debris and of couse do not attempt to climb the rock falls. The rocky canyon area continues for about 3 km. As the trail finds its way out of the tight canyon, the route approaches the rural settlement of Faulder and the site of the former Faulder Station.

Okanagan Section 19-20

~6.5 km
Prairie Valley Route

Travellers will have to get off the KVR at Faulder Station since the next 16 km of track is still an active railway. The Kettle Valley Steam Railway Company operates a vintage steam train and is a popular attraction for the town of Summerland. The steam train plans to run to Faulder Station in the future and will be offering one-way travel with room for bicycles.

The Trans Canada Trail will eventually be constructed adjacent to the tracks between Faulder and Prairie Valley Station. Until then it is necessary to use the Princeton-Summerland Road to access the Prairie Valley Station. The active railway is private property, please do not trespass.

To access the Princeton-Summerland Road turn north off the railbed at Kettle Place Road. If you see tracks you have gone too far. The short road meets the paved but narrow Princeton-Summerland Road. Traffic is light but there is a windy downhill section to be wary of. At the bottom of this hill turn right at the junction with Bathville Road. At this point you may notice the vineyards and fruit orchards that characterize Summerland. Follow Bathville for 1.4 km past the landfill and down to the KVR crossing at Prairie Valley Station.

The Kettle Valley Steam Railway is a fantastic side adventure during your trip to Summerland. An authentic steam engine, similar to those that travelled along the original Kettle Valley Railway, has been refurbished to offer tourists a scenic tour. The old Kettle Valley Railway has been re-established from Prairie Valley Station to Canyon View Siding. The route is about ten kilometres and takes roughly 90 minutes return to ride. For more information call toll free at 1-877-494-8424 or (250) 494-8422. You can find out more about the history of the Kettle Valley Railway or take advantage of the gift shop and concession stand at the Prairie Valley Station.

Okanagan Section 20-21

~3.5 km
Summerland Trail

From the train station, the Trans Canada Trail resumes at the entrance to the Rodeo Grounds. The signed trail runs beside the fenced flume that supplies irrigation water to the Summerland area. Continue past the gate and follow an old flume grade through a mixed forest with great views of Okanagan Lake and it's surrounding orchards. Fortunate visitors may even catch a glimpse of the passing steam train. About 2.5 km from the Rodeo Grounds, stairs lead down to a fabulous gazebo, a recommended rest area.

Steam Train   T. Ernst

500 metres from the gazebo, follow the signs north along an old service road that leads to Fenwick Road. From Fenwick turn right on Fyffe and follow this road down to Simpson Road. Cross the railway tracks to Victoria Road South.

 In the late 1800's, a man named John Moore was one of the first to settle in the Summerland area. Moore saw the picturesque Okanagan Valley as a prime area for the establishment of fruit orchards. As the news of the promising climate spread, other settlers soon followed. Incorporated in 1907, Summerland has a rich history in agriculture. The Agriculture Canada Summerland Research Centre (now named Pacific Agri-Food Research Centre) was established as far back as 1914 and has long been a part of Canadian agriculture research.

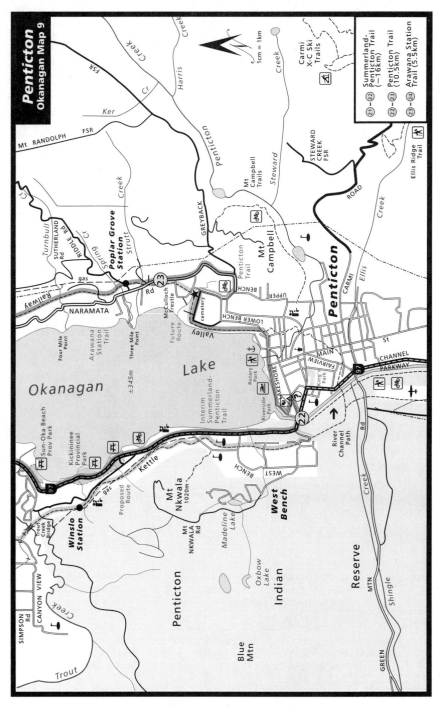

Map 9- Penticton p.192

Okanagan Map 9: Penticton

Okanagan Section 21-22

~ *16 km*

Summerland-Penticton Trail

There are two routes used by hikers and cyclists to access Penticton. Due to land disputes we recommend travellers follow the interim highway route.

Route above Okanagan Lake   *T. Ernst*

From the Simpson, Victoria Road junction, turn north on Victoria and continue to a 4 way stop. Turn east on what is now Prairie Valley Road, unless you prefer to visit downtown Summerland by simply continuing north. Proceed east down the hill to the next 4 way stop at the stone church building. Turn right keeping on Prairie Valley Road to the stop light on Highway 97. Another right leads towards Penticton while a left leads to the Summerland Travel Information Centre.

> *The route along Highway 97 to Penticton passes by Sunoka and Kichinee Provincial Parks. Both parks offer day-use facilities such as picnic areas and access to Okanagan Lake. The parks are also quite popular during the summer for their beach areas.*

Once down the hill and onto the highway, the route is relatively flat all the way to

Penticton. The four laned highway has a good bicycle path but traffic is constant with a 100 km/h speed limit. The wind can also be strong at times but the views of Okanagan Lake and Penticton are rewarding.

From Highway 97, the trail follows Eckhardt Avenue over the Okanagan River channel and then veers north along Riverside Drive. This portion of the trail ends at Riverside Park off Riverside Drive in Penticton.

The proposed route has long been used by cyclists and hikers. Unfortunately, the route follows the former KVR corridor where land ownership is being disputed. Travellers are encouraged to respect this claim until the courts decide. Another drawback is the Trout Creek Bridge has not seen the upgrading other trestles along the route have. The 10 cm (4 inch) wide gaps between the timbers allow for a daunting view of the creek valley more than 60 m (200 ft) below.

> *The Kettle Valley Railway provides a sensational off-highway alternative. Unfortuantely, land dispute claims have caused the re-routing of the Trans Canada Trail. If you do choose to follow the old railbed, you do so at your own risk. Be sure to check locally or visit www.backroadmapbooks.com for any updates on this section of the trail.*

To reach the bridge from the junction of Simpson and Victoria Road South, turn south and follow Victoria to it's end. Take a right on Lewes Avenue and a left on Hillborn Street. Continue east to the bottom of the hill where a right leads to Canyon View Road and the old KVR trestle.

From the bridge it is about 9 km to Penticton. Continue down the old railbed to the third overpass. A footpath leads up to the overpass. Cross the bridge and proceed downhill to Highway 97 and the bridge over the popular river channel. If time permits, a float down the channel is a very relaxing treat.

Okanagan Section 22-23

10.5 km
Penticton Trail

From Riverside Park, the route follows Riverside Drive to Lakeshore Drive along the southern shore of beautiful Okanagan Lake. For bikers, it is best to follow Lakeshore Drive, although hikers can choose to walk along the Okanagan Beach Promenade, which parallels the road. The trail leads into Rotary Park, the site of

Promenade, which parallels the road. The trail leads into Rotary Park, the site of the Penticton Trans Canada Trail Pavilion.

The best current route through this portion of Penticton is to continue along Lakeshore Drive east over the Penticton Creek to Vancouver Avenue. Vancouver Avenue eventually changes to the Lower Bench Road and is a good climb up to Corbishley Avenue. Lower Bench Road, similar to the highway portion, offers decent views of Okanagan Lake and the city of Penticton. Once at Corbishley Road, the route follows the road east to Upper Bench Road, which leads to McMillan Avenue. Follow McMillan Avenue for a short jaunt east to Naramata Road.

Once on Naramata Road, the Trans Canada Trail climbs along the steep grade of Okanagan Lake to Riddle Road and back to the Kettle Valley Railway grade. The return of the KVR is quite difficult to miss as the trailhead for the route is well signed off Naramata Road.

Penticton lies in the heart of the Okanagan wine country and is home to a number of fantastic British Columbian wineries. The wineries are unique and offer tasting tours throughout the year. For more information on local wineries and tours, it is best to drop into the local information centre that is found off Eckhardt Avenue in the west side of the city.

The name Penticton originates from the Okanagan Nations word "snpintktn", meaning a "place to stay for eternity". The Okanagan Natives were the first human settlers in the area and inhabited the area solely until the arrival of European settlers in the late 1800's. The first recorded settler of the Penticton area was the Irish immigrant Tom Ellis. Around 1890, Ellis sold large tracts of his land holdings to the Penticton Townsite Company and the town of Penticton was born soon after. Today, the community has established itself as one of the premier wine growing regions in North America. Other economic influences are the growing eco-tourism industry as well as other agricultural interests.

Okanagan Section 23-24

5.5 km

Arawana Station Trail

The section of trail from Penticton up to the Myra Canyon south of Kelowna travels over a fairly steep grade. For this reason, many travellers of the KVR choose to do this section from north to south in order to ride the grade down instead of upward.

From Riddle Road, the trail heads upward towards Arawana Station. This section of the trail is quite rewarding as the rail grade skirts along the east slope of Okanagan Lake through the orchards and vineyards surrounding the lake. The trail crosses over two forest access roads before reaching Arawana Station. The old station site is evident by the remains of the base of the former water tower.

Lookout north of Penticton   *D. Greenfield*

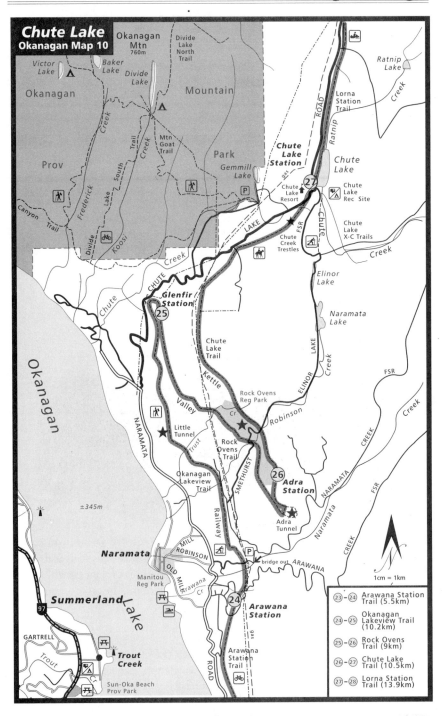

Chute Lake
Okanagan Map 10

Okanagan
Mtn 760m

Divide
Lake North
Trail

Victor
Lake

Baker
Lake

Divide
Lake

Okanagan

Mountain

Prov

Mtn
Goat
Trail

Park

Gemmill
Lake

Chute Lake
Station

Chute
Lake

Ratnip
Lake

Lorna
Station
Trail

Chute
Lake
Rec Site

Chute Lake
Resort

Canyon
Trail

Frederick

Lake

Koosi

Divide

South

Trail

Creek

Creek

CHUTE

LAKE

Chute Creek
Trestles

Chute
Lake
X-C Trails

Creek

Elinor
Lake

Glenfir
Station

25

Chute

Creek

Chute
Lake
Trail

Naramata
Lake

Kettle

Valley

Rock Ovens
Reg Park

Robinson

ELINOR

LAKE

Creek

FSR

Creek

Okanagan

Little
Tunnel

Trust

Rock
Ovens
Trail

Okanagan
Lakeview
Trail

SMETHURST

Adra
Station

26

CREEK

NARAMATA

FSR

±345m

NARAMATA

Railway

Adra
Tunnel

Creek

Naramata

MILL
ROBINSON

OLD MILL

Naramata

Manitou
Reg Park

Arawana
Cr

bridge out ARAWANA

P

Summerland

Lake

97

GARTRELL

Trout

Trout
Creek

Sun-Oka Beach
Prov Park

ROAD

24

Arawana
Station

Arawana
Station
Trail

1cm = 1km

N

23 - 24 Arawana Station
         Trail (5.5km)

24 - 25 Okanagan
         Lakeview Trail
         (10.2km)

25 - 26 Rock Ovens
         Trail (9km)

26 - 27 Chute Lake
         Trail (10.5km)

27 - 28 Lorna Station
         Trail (13.9km)

Okanagan Map 10: Chute Lake

Okanagan Section 24-25

10.2 km
Okanagan Lakeview Trail

This section of the Trans Canada Trail is named accordingly because of the endless views along the route of Okanagan Lake. A camera is a necessity along this stretch in order to capture the majestic grandeur of Okanagan Lake.

From the Arawana station site, the trail begins by crossing Arawana Creek and then soon after Naramata Creek. Both trestles over these creeks are gone and a crossing is required to continue along the trail. The creeks lie in gullies, which can be slippery and muddy during wet periods, but the crossings are generally easy.

Little Tunnel   P. Kivinen

After Naramata Creek, the trail crosses over Smethurst Road. Smethurst Road can be used as a short cut to bypass Glenfir Station if desired. The road meets up with the KVR just before and after Adra Station. The route continues by crossing over Robinson Creek and Trust Creek before reaching one of the other highlights of this section, the Little Tunnel.

Little Tunnel is 48 m (158 ft) in length and marks a great viewpoint area along the route. From both sides of the tunnel the views of Okanagan Lake and the surrounding mountains are fabulous. On a good day, you can see as far as Skaha Lake to the south of Penticton. From the tunnel, it is about 4 km to the former site of Glenfir Station. The station site is not readily noticeable, although was located just after the trail switchbacks and begins to head south.

Okanagan Lake is rich with history and has made its mark in Canadian folklore. The lake is rumoured to be the home of the legendary Ogopogo monster. Similar to the Loch Ness monster, Ogopogo resembles a serpent like creature and roams the deep, dark depths of the lake. Natives first introduced the story of Ogopogo to settlers in the area by telling stories of how Ogopogo would rise from the lake and engulf a canoe.

Okanagan Section 25-26

9 km
Rock Ovens Trail

Just past the switchback, or Glenfir Station, the Trans Canada Trail continues its climb towards the Adra Tunnel and Rock Ovens Park.

After passing the trail to the Rock Ovens, the route continues south along an uphill grade across the Smethurst Road and Robinson Creek.

Rock Ovens   P. Kivinen

After the trail crosses Trust Creek, look for a rough trail off the east side of the railbed. The road leads to the Rock Ovens, which were built during the construction of the KVR by Scandinavian rail workers. The ovens essentially look like large piles of rocks but played an important role in building the railway. The workers were able to provide fresh food to each other despite the fact they were far from any of the normal amenities of home.

After the Robinson Creek crossing, the trail continues towards the decommissioned Adra Tunnel. About 600 m before the tunnel, there is a bypass trail that must be taken to travel around the tunnel. The trail is a short 150 m uphill trek back onto the KVR. Once on the other side of the railbed, the trail changes direction and begins heading north along the uphill grade to Adra Station. Foundations of the buildings from the old station remain and mark the end of this somewhat challenging section of trail.

> Just after the creek crossing, look for another trail off the east side of the route. This trail leads to two more rock ovens.

Okanagan Section 26-27

10.5 km

Chute Lake Trail

The uphill climb continues from Adra Station to Chute Lake. The trail begins by crossing over the Robinson Creek and Smethurst Road again and eventually slows its ascent as the trail approaches Chute Creek. Before reaching Chute Lake, the trail crosses

Adra Tunnel   P. Kivinen

over Chute Creek several times and eventually joins up with Chute Lake Road. From the Chute Lake Road, you can access Chute Lake and

> ⚠ Adra Tunnel is the longest tunnel along the KVR at 489 m (1,604 ft) and is constructed in a large spiral. The tunnel is a masterful engineering feat for its time and it is too bad that it is unsafe for exploration. The entrances of the tunnel were partially sealed in the early 1990's to restrict any exploration of the tunnel. The ceiling of the tunnel is quite unsafe and there is also flooding problems.

the Chute Lake Forest Recreation site. The road passes by the Chute Lake Resort, which is the former site of the Chute Lake KVR Station. The resort is still using some of the original buildings. Be sure to stop in and sample some of their delicious home made apple pie.

Chute Lake has long been a favourite outdoor getaway location for Penticton and area residents. The Chute Lake Recreation Site is a user-maintained camping area that is a nice place to spend a night. The site is complete with picnic tables and outhouses and is found next to the shore of this fine fishing lake.

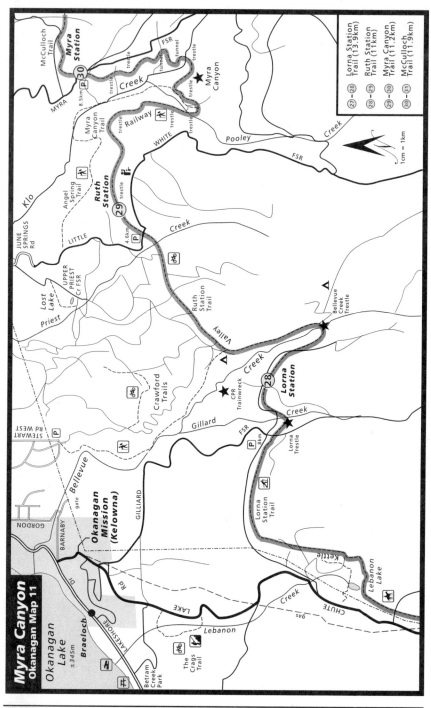

Myra Canyon
Okanagan Map 11

Lorna Station Trail (13.9km) ② - ②
Ruth Station Trail (11km) ② - ②
Myra Canyon Trail (11.2km) ② - ③
McCulloch Trail (11.9km) ③ - ③

1cm = 1km

Okanagan Map 11: Myra Canyon

Okanagan Section 27-28

13.9 km
Lorna Station Trail

The grade from Chute Lake to Lorna Station is generally easy, as a good portion of the climb from Penticton into the surrounding Okanagan Hills is complete. Along with the rustic and remote scenery, the trail passes by Lebanon Lake and a large cut block. The cut block was actually done to help control a pine beetle infestation in the early 1990's. The forest was replanted shortly after and is well on its way to becoming a new stand for the future.

Myra Canyon Trestle   J. Marleau

After Lebanon Lake, the trail crosses over evidence of logging roads including the Gilliard Forest Service Road. Shortly down the trail past the Gilliard Forest Service Road, the trail crosses over a fill area beside the former trestle across Gilliard Creek. Remnants of the original wooden trestle can be seen.

Lorna Station is about 1.5 km east of the creek, although it is very easy to miss.

Lorna Station is named after the youngest daughter of the former Kettle Valley Railway President J.J. Warren.

If so desired, the Gilliard Forest Service Road could be followed north down to the suburb of Okanagan Mission, south of the City of Kelowna. Supplies and accommodation can be found in the area.

Extensive work upgrading the railgrade has been done by Trails BC volunteers over the past few years. The railway primarily used wooden culverts to divert the water run-off from the hills above. Over time, these hollowed wooden pipes deteriorated and caused many washouts and pools. Through volunteer work, the railbed has been graded from Gillard Forest Service Road to June Springs and is know a much smoother surface to travel.

Okanagan Section 28-29

11 km
Ruth Station Trail

The section from Lorina Station to Ruth Station is a very scenic stretch offering several fantastic views of Kelowna and Okanagan Mission to the north. The ascent continues on a gradual grade and begins by veering south towards a crossing of the Bellevue Creek.

The Bellevue Creek Trestle is one of the longest in the area at 267 m (875 ft) and stands almost 122 m (400 ft) above the creek. The curved structure has recently been decked and guard rails have been added by Trails BC volunteers. Even with the safety work added, it can be an intimidating structure to cross.

The trail crosses the creek and switchbacks to head north. Just after the crossing with the Bellevue Creek, there is a trail/old logging road that heads south up to a small wilderness campsite. This trail also leads to Little White Mountain and is a favourite for avid mountain bikers.

As the route heads north it becomes part of another trail system named the

Crawford Trails. The Crawford Trails are popular with Kelowna residences as they travel up the mountainside to the old KVR. Travellers on the Trans Canada Trail/Kettle Valley Railway may notice the main Crawford Trail, which is a rustic staircase that travels down from the railbed towards Kelowna. At the bottom, there is a small rustic campsite available for overnight use. At this site, curious travellers can also see an old train wreck if they know where to look.

Myra Canyon Trestle   T. Ernst

The Ruth Station was originally named Kelowna Station, although was changed as the community of Kelowna grew in order to reduce confusion. The Little White Forest Service Road can be traveled north down to Kelowna to access everything a big interior city has to offer.

Kelowna's name is derived from the Native Salish word meaning Grizzly Bear. Grizzlies were once a natural part of this region but the ever increasing expansion of Kelowna and the surrounding communities has nearly eliminated the grizzly from this region. The original settlement of Kelowna began in 1860 by Father Pandosy at what is known today as the suburb of Mission. After Father Pandosy, other settlers followed as word of the prime growing conditions of the valley spread east. Throughout the late 1800's and the early 1900's settlers arrived in the Kelowna area setting up ranches and other agricultural operations. The City of Kelowna was incorporated in 1905 and it was during this time that the region began to establish itself as the economic centre of the Okanagan and the southern interior of British Columbia. After the arrival of the Canadian National Railway in 1925, Kelowna saw an even greater insurgence of settlers as the economic potential of the region dramatically increased with the renewed accessibility to eastern and coastal markets. Today, Kelowna is a fast growing city that has also been bolstered by forestry, eco-tourism and technological companies.

The trail eventually crosses Priest Creek and then the Little White Forest Service Road before reaching Ruth Station. The old station building was torched some five years ago and only the roof and foundation remain. The Little White Forest Service Road is used as a main access road to the Myra Canyon Portion of the Kettle Valley Railway. There is a small parking area available near the railbed.

Okanagan Section 29-30

11.2 km
Myra Canyon Trail

This portion of the Kettle Valley Railway is simply spectacular and is certainly the highlight of the Okanagan section of Trans Canada Trail. The Myra Canyon is a deep canyon that posed a formidable obstacle in the construction of the Kettle Valley Railway. The winding rail grade traverses high above the canyon along the tight canyon walls, amid the wilderness of the Okanagan Mountains. From Ruth Station to the site of the former Myra Station, the trail meanders in a "U" formation through the canyon across eighteen rail trestles and through two spectacular tunnels.

> *The rail grade has been upgraded considerably over the past years by the Myra Canyon Trestle Restoration Society. Today, all trestles and tunnels can be travelled safely as handrails and planking have been added to connect railway ties. The trestles are numbered 1-18 from west to east and are all a marvel of human engineering. To think that the system was built over eighty five years ago just increases the magnitude of this engineering accomplishment. The longest trestle in the canyon is an astonishing 220 m (722 ft) in length and was constructed in a curved shape to aid the route through the tight canyon. The first train to travel across this trestle occurred in October 1914 while the last train to add soot to the walls of this 55 m (180 ft) high marvel occurred in June 1973.*

From the Ruth Station to the Myra Station site the route is just over 11 km in length and takes about just over an hour to travel on bike, if you do not stop to take in the scenery. Parking areas are available at the Little White Forest Service Road west of Ruth Station and at the Myra Canyon Station site off the Myra Forest Service Road. Both parking areas also offer basic outhouse facilities while the roads leads down to the City of Kelowna.

There is one wash out area along the route; however, it is easily travelled around on bike or on foot. It is recommended to walk your bike through the tunnels, as the dim lighting can hide rocks and debris along the tunnel floors.

Myra Canyon Bikers　　　J. Marleau

 Today, on foot or by bike, the trestles amaze even the most avid outdoor travellers. During much of the route, you can glance across to the other side of the massive canyon and see the trestles passed or those still to come in the distance. The width of the canyon is so great that you can barely make out travellers on the other side, which can be up to 1.5 km wide in sections. If you have binoculars, it can be interesting to try to spot travellers on the distant trestles.

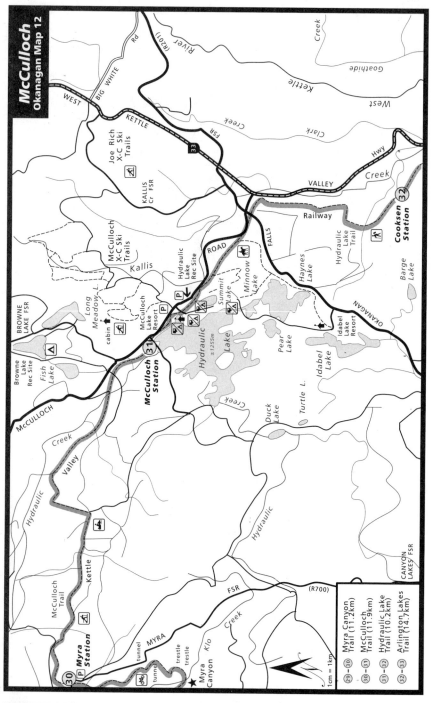

McCulloch
Okanagan Map 12

29–30 Myra Canyon Trail (11.2km)
30–31 McCulloch Trail (11.9km)
31–32 Hydraulic Lake Trail (10.2km)
32–33 Arlington Lakes Trail (14.7km)

1cm = 1km

Okanagan Map 12: McCulloch

Okanagan Section 30-31

11.9 km
McCulloch Trail

From the parking area near Myra Station, the Trans Canada Trail/Kettle Valley Railway continues east to McCulloch Station at Hydraulic Lake. The trail follows the railbed across a maze of logging roads and cut areas before reaching McCulloch Road and eventually McCulloch Station. Portions of this stretch of the railbed also double as an access road for logging operations so stay alert on these sections of the trail.

Raccoons   *J. Marleau*

 If you are interested in camping along the route, this portion of the Trans Canada has plenty to offer. A Forest Recreation site can be found on Browne Lake to the north or closer to the route on both McCulloch and Hydraulic Lakes. For a break from the rustic outdoor world, two full service resorts are also found in the area, one on Hydraulic Lake and the other to the south on Idabel Lake.

Okanagan Section 31-32

10.2 km
Hydraulic Lake Trail

From Hydraulic Lake, the KVR finally begins to travel along a downward grade. The trail begins by skirting the north side of Hydraulic Lake and then follows McCulloch Road for a short stretch until it reaches the resort, where it picks up the rail grade once again. The trail travels southeast past the small Summit Lake before reaching the Okanagan Falls Forest Service Road. The trail crosses the road and begins its descent south towards Rock Creek along the old railbed.

En route towards Cooksen Station some picturesque sights of the river and surrounding valley can be seen. A small red shack off the side of the trail marks Cooksen Station.

> The many lakes found on the plateau above Kelowna are known to hold some feisty rainbow and brook trout. Some of these fish can reach 2.5 kg (5 lbs) and can be caught by trolling, spincasting or fly-fishing with common trout lures or flies. Fishing in the spring or fall will improve your chances of landing one of these world famous sport fish.

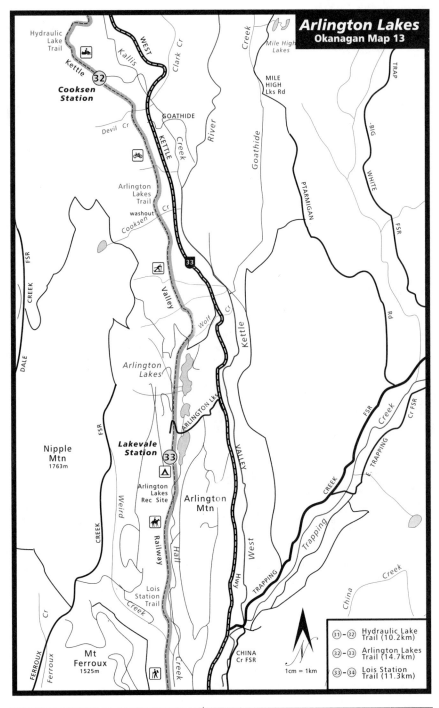

Arlington Lakes
Okanagan Map 13

Hydraulic Lake Trail

WEST

Kallis

Clark Cr

Creek

Mile High Lakes

KETTLE

Kettle

32

Cooksen Station

Devil Cr

GOATHIDE

Creek

River

Goathide

MILE HIGH Lks Rd

Mile High Lks Rd

TRAP

BIG

WHITE

FSR

PTARMIGAN

Arlington Lakes Trail

washout

Cooksen

Cr

33

Valley

Wolf Cr

Kettle Cr

Rd

DALE

CREEK FSR

Arlington Lakes

ARLINGTON Lks

FSR

Creek

FSR

Cr FSR

E. TRAPPING

Lakevale Station

33

Nipple Mtn
1763m

Arlington Lakes Rec Site

Arlington Mtn

ARLINGTON VALLEY

TRAPPING

CREEK

Railway

Weird

Hall

West Hwy

TRAPPING

Lois Station Trail

Creek

Creek

China

Cr

China Cr FSR

Ferroux

Mt Ferroux
1525m

Creek

N

1cm = 1km

31 – 32		Hydraulic Lake Trail (10.2km)
32 – 33		Arlington Lakes Trail (14.7km)
33 – 34		Lois Station Trail (11.3km)

Okanagan Map 13: Arlington Lakes

Okanagan Section 32-33

14.7 km
Arlington Lakes Trail

The trail continues its downward descent along the Arlington Lakes portion of the KVR. From Cooksen Station, the trail crosses Cooksen Creek along a washed out section of road that is passable on foot and bike. Further down the trail, the route crosses Wolf Creek and reaches a rock cut of the KVR that is overgrown. A short detour along a side road travels around the grown in section before rejoining the railbed.

Arlington Lake   *P. White*

Shortly after the detour, the trail reaches the Arlington Lakes. The Arlington Lakes are three interconnected lakes that make up the headwater for the Hall Creek. The old Lakevale Station site is located near the junction of the trail and the Arlington Lakes Road. Building foundations remain visible as evidence of the station.

> The Arlington Lakes Forest Recreation site is accessible just off the road and provides a basic rustic campsite for overnight use. Anglers will find a boat launch and a few areas to cast from shore. If needed, Arlington Lakes Road provides easy access to Highway 33.

Okanagan Section 33-34

11.3 km
Lois Station Trail

As the trail continues forging southward, the route passes between the small valley formed by Hall Creek. This is a remote stretch of trail with Arlington Mountain ascending to the east and the much larger Nipple Mountain and Mount Ferroux ascending to the west.

About 3 km south from the Arlington Lake Road, the route encounters a wash over of the old KVR. The section is easily navigable, although may involve some tricky footing. A further 3 km down the trail you will encounter another obstacle as the trail is covered by a rockslide. There is an established route around the slide, which is quite easy to traverse. Shortly after the rockslide, the trail crosses a rough road that can be used to access the highway and the picnic/rest area to the south. Lois Station is about 3 km further down the railbed and can be identified by the remaining shed and foundation. The station area is also just east of a branch of the Wilkinson Forest Service Road.

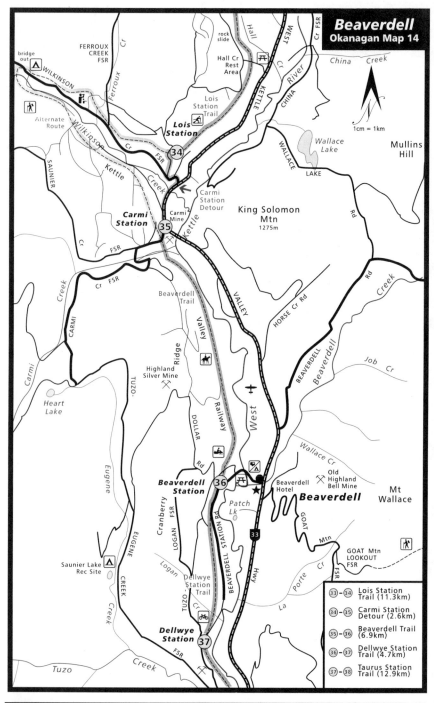

Beaverdell
Okanagan Map 14

FERROUX CREEK FSR

bridge out

WILKINSON

rock slide

Hall Cr Rest Area

China Creek

Lois Station Trail

Lois Station

Alternate Route

34

Wallace Lake

Mullins Hill

1cm = 1km

SAUNIER

Kettle

Wilkinson Cr FSR

Kettle Creek

Carmi Station Detour

King Solomon Mtn 1275m

Carmi Station

Carmi Mine

35

Cr FSR

Kettle

WALLACE LAKE

Rd

CARMI

Creek

Cr FSR

Beaverdell Trail

VALLEY

HORSE Cr Rd

Beaverdell

Beaverdell

Job Cr

Carmi

Creek

TUZO-

Ridge

Valley

Highland Silver Mine

Railway

West

Heart Lake

DOLLAR Rd

Wallace Cr

Old Highland Bell Mine

Mt Wallace

Eugene

Cranberry FSR

Beaverdell Station

36

Beaverdell Hotel

★

Beaverdell

LOGAN

Patch Lk

GOAT

Saunier Lake Rec Site

EUGENE

Logan Cr

Dellwye Station Trail

BEAVERDELL STATION Rd

33

Mtn

GOAT Mtn LOOKOUT FSR

TUZO-

Dellwye Station

37

La Porte Cr

Creek

Hwy

33–34	Lois Station Trail (11.3km)
34–35	Carmi Station Detour (2.6km)
35–36	Beaverdell Trail (6.9km)
36–37	Dellwye Station Trail (4.7km)
37–38	Taurus Station Trail (12.9km)

Tuzo Creek

Okanagan Map 14: Beaverdell

Okanagan Section 34-35

2.6 km
Carmi Station Detour

At Lois Station, the KVR veers northwest towards a switchback across the Wilkinson Creek, which lies approximately 6 km from Lois Station. Today, the bridge over the creek and gully gone and travellers not interested in getting their feet wet can detour around the switchback section entirely.

Beaverdell Hotel   P. White

In summer, Wilkinson Creek is easily forded. The water is quite shallow and the crossing is short. There are plans to replace the bridge when funds become available.

Near the former bridge site, there is a small wilderness campsite available off the railbed. The site is a great choice if needed, as the creek area and former bridge can be easily explored from the base camp area.

If you do want to detour around the creek crossing, a rough branch of the Wilkinson Creek Forest Service Road can be picked up about 800 metres west of Lois Station. It leads south to the main Forest Service Road, which links to the highway. Follow Highway 33 south for just over 1 km to the Carmi Creek Forest Service Road off the west side of the highway. The Carmi Creek Forest Service Road quickly leads back to the KVR at Carmi Station.

Highway 33 is not very busy and generally offers a decent sized shoulder for safe hiking/biking.

Carmi Station has a few residents, although in the early 1900's it was a thriving small mining town. The gold mine closed in 1939 and most of the residents of the town left in search of work. A few of the original buildings from the former town site remain intact, both as residences and as reminders of a past era.

Okanagan Section 35-36

6.9 km
Beaverdell Trail

The trail begins by crossing Carmi Creek. The old Carmi Mine can be found just to the north of the trail, while one of the town's original hotels still stands just off the south side of the trail. After the creek crossing, the Trans Canada Trail/Kettle Valley Railway descends to the valley bottom of the West Kettle River. The valley bottom is a very peaceful stretch of trail as it skirts close to the river channels.

Before the railbed reaches the former site of Beaverdell Station, the route veers off the KVR onto a trail that traverses around some tailing ponds from past mines. Look for the trail about 3.2 km from the Carmi Creek Forest Service Road. The

For supplies or lodging, it is recommended to venture into the town of Beaverdell found off Highway 33. The town is home to the oldest operating hotel in B.C., the Beaverdell Hotel. For overnight camping, there is a small campground situated along the south side of the West Kettle River just before entering the town. Basic supplies can be picked up in Beaverdell.

The town of Beaverdell is a small community found off Highway 33 that offers all the basic amenities, including accommodations, a few restaurants, a trading post and general store. The Beaverdell Hotel, found right off the side of the highway, is actually the oldest continuously operating hotel in British Columbia. The town was originally established around 1897 after the discovery of silver and gold in Mount Wallace. The town survived throughout the century on mainly the Highland Mine, although in the late 1980's the resources of the mine were finally exhausted. Today, Beaverdell survives primarily on the forest industry but there are high hopes eco-tourism will help surge the local economy in the future.

short detour takes you past the Kettle Valley Welding business and to Beaverdell Station Road. Follow the road west back to the railbed, which now doubles as part of the road. Not much is left of the Beaverdell Station, which is situated near the reconnection of the Trans Canada Trail with the former KVR.

Okanagan Section 36-37

4.7 km
Dellwye Station Trail

The Trans Canada Trail follows the Beaverdell Station Road south until the original railbed can be picked up again about 2 km down the road. The KVR travels parallel to the road almost all the way to Dellwye. The former station area was merely a wye (turnaround) site and has recently been cleared to accomodate campers.

Not far along the route from Beaverdell, you will pass an abandoned mill that was used to process ore from Highland Silver Mine. The mine lies atop Cranberry Ridge to the north.

For backcountry camping and fishing enthusiasts, there is a fantastic Forest Recreation Site found to the north of Dellwye on Saurnier Lake. To reach the site you must continue south about 2 km to the Tuzo Creek Forest Service Road. The site is found about 5 km down the road and is a user-maintained wilderness campsite.

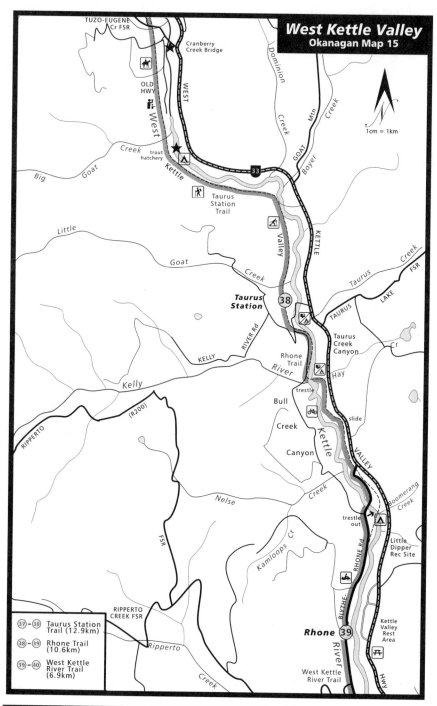

West Kettle Valley
Okanagan Map 15

1cm = 1km

TUZO-EUGENE
Cr FSR

Cranberry
Creek Bridge

OLD
HWY

West Kettle

Big Goat Creek

trout
hatchery

Taurus
Station
Trail

Little Goat Creek

Dominion Creek

GOAT Mtn Creek

Boyer

33

Valley

KETTLE

Taurus Creek

LAKE FSR

**Taurus
Station**

38

RIVER Rd

KELLY

Kelly

(R200)

RIPPERTO

Rhone
Trail

River

Taurus
Creek
Canyon

Cr

TAURUS

Hay

trestle

Bull
Creek
Canyon

Creek

Nelse

Kamloops Cr

FSR

slide

Kettle VALLEY

Boomerang Creek

trestle
out

Little
Dipper
Rec Site

RIPPERTO
CREEK FSR

Ripperto

Creek

RHONE Rd

BLYTHE

Kettle
Valley
Rest
Area

Rhone 39

West Kettle
River Trail

River

HWY

37–38 Taurus Station
Trail (12.9km)

38–39 Rhone Trail
(10.6km)

39–40 West Kettle
River Trail
(6.9km)

Okanagan Map 15: West Kettle Valley

Okanagan Section 37-38

12.9 km
Taurus Station Trail

The trek from Dellwye to the Taurus Station continues the descent through the remote West Kettle River Valley. The railbed crosses a few logging roads, including the Tuzo Creek Forest Service Road as well as a trestle that has been recently decked and guard rails.

The route descends towards the valley bottom before crossing Goat Creek. A little further on the trail meets the wild trout hatchery along the west bank of the West Kettle River. From the hatchery, the trail continues to skirt along the west bank of the river all the way to the Taurus Station site. The foundations of the former buildings mark the old station site and the end of this section of trail.

Cycling through the Canyon   T. Ernst

Near the wild trout hatchery, there is also a small rustic campsite area set along the scenic shore of the West Kettle River. Anglers interested in trying their luck for rainbow trout should not be disappointed. Try casting a small lure, a fly or even a baited hook into one of the many fine looking holes.

Okanagan Section 38-39

10.6 km
Rhone Trail

From Taurus Station, the Trans Canada Trail/Kettle Valley Railway continues its southerly trek along the valley to the scenic Bull Creek Canyon, which is locally referred to as Falls Canyon.

The impressive Falls Canyon has been formed by the West Kettle River cutting away at the gorge for thousands of years. Overtime, the river has taken the path of least resistance and can be seen winding it's way below the old railbed.

To traverse the canyon area, the KVR cuts across the river along a trestle, which has been recently re-decked by Trails BC volunteers. On the east side of the gorge, the trail is squeezed between the river and the highway all the way to an intersection with the Blythe-Rhone Road. At the intersection, the Trans Canada Trail begins following this paved road since the trestle further down the railbed has been removed.

At one point along the road, you can notice the intersection of the road and the old KVR. The Little Dipper Campground is found here. The route follows the Blythe-Rhone Road back over the West Kettle River and leads directly to the former station site of Rhone. The former Rhone Station site is recognizable by the old building foundations.

Rhone is named after the Rhone River found in southeast France. The Rhone River begins in the French Alps east of the city of Lyon and travels through Lyon then south all the way to the Mediterranean Sea.

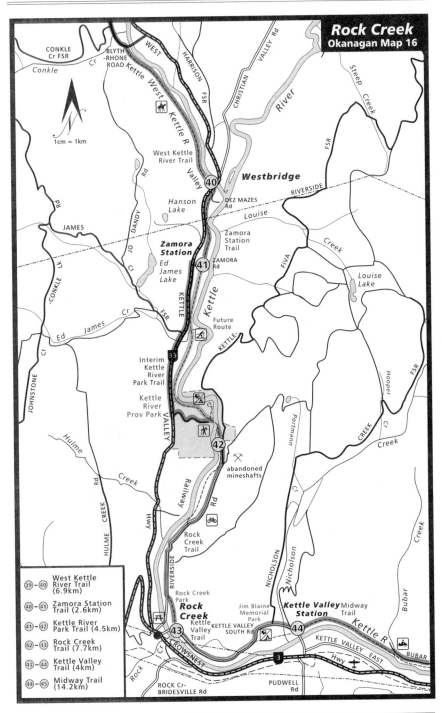

Rock Creek
Okanagan Map 16

1cm = 1km

CONKLE
Cr FSR
Conkle
BLYTH-RHONE
ROAD
WEST
Kettle
West
Kettle R
HARRISON
FSR
CHRISTIAN VALLEY Rd
River
Steep
Creek
FSR

West Kettle
River Trail
Valley
Rd
JO DANDY Cr

40
Westbridge
DEZ MAZES
Rd
RIVERSIDE

Hanson
Lake
Louise
Creek

JAMES
*Zamora
Station*
Zamora
Station
Trail
FIVA

Ed
James
Lake
41
ZAMORA
Rd
*Louise
Lake*

CONKLE Lk
Rd
Ed
James
Cr
FSR
KETTLE
Kettle
Future
Route
KETTLE
Hooper
Cr
FSR

JOHNSTONE Cr
Interim
Kettle
River
Park Trail
33
Kettle
River
Prov Park
42
abandoned
mineshafts
CREEK
Creek
Portmann

Hulme
Creek
Railway
Rd
Rd

HULME CREEK Rd
Rock
Creek
Trail
Nicholson
Cr
Nicholson
Creek
Bubar

RIVERSIDE
Rd
Rock Creek
Park
*Rock
Creek*
43
Kettle
Valley
Trail
Jim Blaine
Memorial
Park
*Kettle Valley
Station*
Midway
Trail
Kettle R
44
Bubar
KETTLE VALLEY EAST
BUBAR

Hwy
CROWSNEST
KETTLE VALLEY
SOUTH Rd
3
KETTLE VALLEY EAST Hwy
Rock
Cr
ROCK Cr-
BRIDESVILLE Rd
PUDWELL
Rd

39–**40** West Kettle
River Trail
(6.9km)

40–**41** Zamora Station
Trail (2.6km)

41–**42** Kettle River
Park Trail (4.5km)

42–**43** Rock Creek
Trail (7.7km)

43–**44** Kettle Valley
Trail (4km)

44–**45** Midway Trail
(14.2km)

Okanagan Section 39-40

6.9 km

West Kettle River Trail

The Trans Canada Trail continues south along the Blythe-Rhone Road over the Rippertoe Creek Forest Service Road and shortly after, Conkle Creek. Just past the creek crossing, the road branches from the KVR. The trail follows the railbed down the west side of the West Kettle Valley River all the way to the intersection of Highway 33 at Westbridge Station. Evidence of the station is no longer visible.

Mule Deer   W. Mussio

 For supplies, there is a small convenience store located across the river at the junction of Highway 33 and the Christian Valley Road.

For a semi-wilderness camping experience, you can follow the Rippertoe Creek Forest Service Road west to
Conkle Lake Provincial Park. The beautiful park encompasses Conkle Lake and offers plenty of camping sites along with outhouses. A fisherman's trail circles the lake and leads to a set of cascading
falls.

Okanagan Section 40-41

2.6 km
Zamora Station Trail

The Kettle Valley Railway bed continues south to the Zamora Station site. However, portions of the railbed travel through what are now farmer's fields. It is still
permissible to travel along the old railbed but please make sure you close the gates
after yourself. Also, sections along this stretch can be overgrown and hard to
track.

A good alternate option is to follow Highway 33 south from Westbridge to Zamora
Station. The highway is not very busy and there is a decent shoulder for travel.
Off the east side of the highway, you will come to Zamora Road, which travels east
back to the KVR and the site of the former Zamora Station. One of the original
station buildings continues to stand beside the railbed and has been converted to
a private residence.

During the early spring, as the grass begins to bud in the
valley bottom, an uncanny amount of mule deer can be spotted in the fields throughout this region. This is one of the
magnificent displays of nature that British Columbia has to
offer.

Okanagan Section 41-42

4.5 km
Kettle River Park Trail

From Zamora Station, it is actually best to continue along Highway 33 all the way
to the Kettle River Provincial Park. From Zamora Station to the park there are
currently land disputes in question and some pretty amusing obstacles in place
including a washout near Ed James Creek and an electric fence in one location.
Until Trails BC and the Provincial Government can settle these situations, it is best
just to use the side of the highway.

As the highway approaches Kettle River Provincial Park it is possible to re-access the KVR to travel through the park, although there is also an access road to the park off the highway.

> *The Kettle Valley River Provincial Park offers a favourite location for overnight camping. The sandy beach, refreshing river and well-kept campsites complete with picnic tables and fire rings make this a fine location to take a well-deserved rest. Large pine trees surrounded by open grasslands dominate the geography of the area.*

Okanagan Section 42-43

7.7 km
Rock Creek Trail

From within the Kettle River Provincial Park, the old railbed can be picked up off the park access road. The Trans Canada Trail/Kettle Valley Railway continues its journey over a trestle crossing the Kettle River. On the east side of the river, the trail continues along the old railbed until it reaches an intersection with Riverside Road.

Kettle River Park   *P. White*

From the intersection, the Trans Canada Trail route follows this rural road towards the town of Rock Creek. Be sure to have your camera ready as there are several picturesque sights of the Kettle River that can be seen along the way.

Rock Creek was established in the early part of the century when gold was discovered in Rock Creek near its intersection with the Kettle River. The town is home to two thriving convenience stores offering all the basic supplies. Overnight lodging is also available in the town. For day-use, the Rock Creek Park offers a nice picnic site on the north side of the river not far off the old KVR.

Okanagan Section 43-44

4 km
Kettle Valley Trail

The trek from Rock Creek to the former Kettle Valley Station site continues along the roadway (Kettle Valley South Road) as the KVR has been claimed by the road for much of the way to the former station. Not far from Riverside Road, the trail passes by an abandoned sawmill and shortly before Kettle Valley, Jim Blaine Memorial Park. Near the park, the old KVR can be seen, although it is best to stay on the road due to current land disputes over the railbed. In one section the old railbed has actually been reclaimed as farming field by the local farmer and has been ploughed under. The land is for sale (minus the railgrade) and it is hoped the new owner will support the Trans Canada Trail initiative.

The site of the former Kettle Valley Station is located near the bridge over the Kettle River.

Jim Blaine Memorial Park can be found just off the south side of the Kettle Valley Road and offers overnight camping along the scenic shores of the Kettle River.

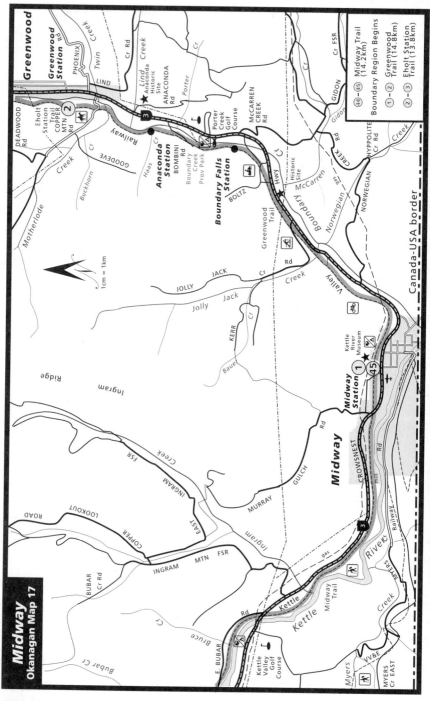

Midway
Okanagan Map 17

1cm = 1km

Midway Trail (14.2km)
Boundary Region Begins
Greenwood Trail (14.8km)
Eholt Station Trail (13.8km)

Okanagan Map 17: Midway

Okanagan Section 44-45

14.2 km
Midway Trail

The trail reconnects with the KVR just before the Kettle Valley South Road crosses over the Kettle River. The trail follows the old railbed through ranch country along the meandering shore of the Kettle River to East Bubar Road. The trail currently tracks onto the East Bubar Road and follows the road all the way to a junction with Highway 3. The temporary Trans Canada Trail route follows the highway into the town of Midway and to the Kettle Valley museum.

After construction of the new Trans BC Pipeline is complete, the route will follow the historical KVR into Midway. Unfortunately, as of May 2001, much of the old railbed will still be torn up or impassable due to construction. The planned route will follow the old railbed along the north side of the Kettle River bypassing the massive Pope and Talbot sawmill grounds, to a crossing of the highway. The route will eventually take you to the steps of the Kettle River museum.

Midway Museum   P. Kivinen

The Kettle Valley Museum is actually the old Midway Railway Station. The museum is well worth the visit as it exhibits artifacts and historical accounts that take you through the history of the railway and the town. The museum is also a popular starting point for travellers interested in following the Kettle Valley Railway west to Brookmere.

 Midway is a small sawmill town, which lies in the heart of British Columbia. The town lies in a flat valley area that is surrounded by ranchland and forested slopes. The town was actually named because of its location near the middle of British Columbia (from east to west). In the Kettle Valley Railway's heyday, the town and watering hole played an integral role in shipping from east to west as well as to the United States to the south. Today, it is a quiet interior B.C. town offering lodging, supplies and other amenities.

OKANAGAN SERVICE PROVIDERS

Accommodations

Tours and Guides

Boundary

The Boundary region of the Trans Canada Trail is the smallest portion of the route. The Boundary region is generally from around Rock Creek to Christina Lake, which includes Grand Forks. The trail through the Boundary region follows primarily the old Kettle Valley rail bed all the way from Rock Creek to Christina Lake. Through the city of Grand Forks, the trail follows a combination of side streets and local trail systems, eventually re-connecting with the Kettle Valley rail bed and heading east. Just south of Christina Lake, the Trans Canada Trail veers off the Kettle Valley rail bed for the last time and traverses north to Christina Lake via the Highway 3.

The Trans Canada Trail through the Boundary region is truly a multi-use trail system as bikers, hikers and horseback riders will all enjoy the route. Through the city of Grand Forks, there are a few alternatives that bikers and riders may want to consider. For bikers it may be best to follow Highway 3 through the city, linking back up with the Kettle Valley rail bed just to the east of Grand Forks. Horse back riders, on the other hand, should probably bypass the city, since the urban route is not suitable for horses and the highway can be very busy at times.

Although the Trans Canada Trail simply follows the old Kettle Valley rail bed most of the way through the Boundary region, there are a number of current problems along the way. The old rail bed travels through private land in a number of places in the Boundary region creating conflict with some property owners. Although, the rail bed is public property, some private residents have taken it upon themselves to reclaim the rail bed as their own, erecting fences and barriers and in one instance even ploughing over the rail bed completely. Trails BC is working on these cases and currently there are alternate routes around these trouble spots. I f you encounter a new or unfamiliar barrier along this section, be sure to notify Trails BC or e-mail info@backroadmapbooks.com and we will hopefully be able to pass the information on to other travellers.

As of spring, 2001, BC Gas had blocked off the Kettle Valley rail bed east of Grand Forks for gas line construction. The route along the rail bed is to be reconstructed and by fall, 2001 it was to be in full working order. Be sure to check locally, with Trails BC or www.backroadmapbooks.com for updates on this section of the trail.

One advantage of the Boundary section of trail for long distance travellers is that the route traverses through a number of urban areas. Long distance travellers will be able to find supplies in areas such as Rock Creek, Midway and Grand Forks before beginning the more remote Dewdney trail section of the West Kootenay Trans Canada Trail region. Outside of the urban areas, the trail traverses close to Highway 3, therefore in case of a problem, help is nearby.

Boundary

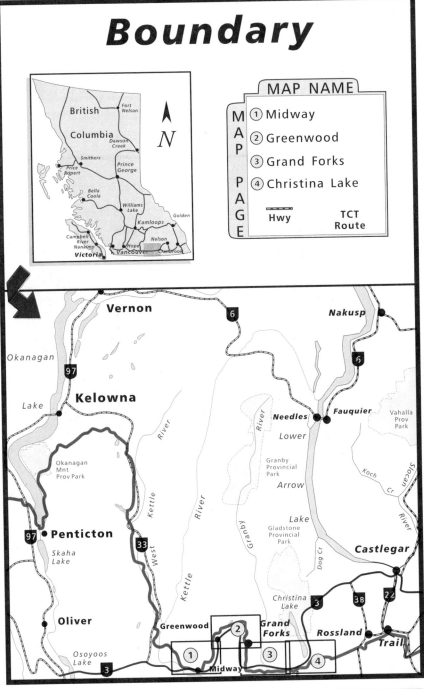

MAP NAME

① Midway
② Greenwood
③ Grand Forks
④ Christina Lake

----- Hwy   TCT Route

MAP PAGE

British Columbia

Fort Nelson
Dawson Creek
Smithers
Prince George
Price Rupert
Bella Coola
Williams Lake
Golden
Kamloops
Campbell River
Nanaimo
Hope
Nelson
Victoria Vancouver Cranbrook

N

Vernon
Nakusp
Okanagan
97
Kelowna
Lake
River
River
Needles
Fauquier
Vahalla Prov Park
Lower
Granby Provincial Park
Arrow
Okanagan Mnt Prov Park
Koch Cr
Slocan River
Lake
Gladstone Provincial Park
97
Penticton
Skaha Lake
33
Kettle
West
Granby
Kettle
River
Dog Cr
Castlegar
3
3B
22
Oliver
Greenwood
② ③
Grand Forks
Rossland
Christina Lake
Trail
Osoyoos Lake
3
① ④
Midway

Boundary Map 1: Midway

Boundary Section 1-2

14.8 km
Greenwood Trail

Beginning at the Kettle River Museum in Midway, the Trans Canada Trail continues its trek eastward by following the old Kettle Valley Railway. The old railbed has recently been the site of a massive BC Gas pipeline improvement project. Hopefully by July of 2001 most of the pipeline construction will be cleared and the route will regenerate into a fabulous cross-country trail.

Viewpoint   *J. Klein*

From the museum, the railbed trail leads out of the town and towards the city of Greenwood. The trail parallels Highway 3 much of the way and travels upward along a marginal grade through rock bluffs and open grasslands. The route passes by Boundary Creek Provincial Park and over Copper Mountain Road before reaching the former site of the Greenwood station.

Boundary Creek Provincial Park lies just off the side of Highway 3 and offers basic campsites and outhouses along the cascading Boundary Creek. To reach the park from the trail, you either have to forge the creek (which can usually be easily done) or access the highway from the Boltz Road to the south or the Bombini Road to the north.

The Greenwood area is rich in history and is known as B.C.'s smallest city. The city was established in the late 1800's as a coal and copper mining community. The town flourished throughout the early 1900's, although slowing demand for coal and later copper eventually forced the closure of the Greenwood mines. Today, the town relies mainly on the logging industry, although recently this quaint region of the province is slowly becoming a popular tourist site. The town has not changed much since the early 1900's and the refinished buildings can literally take you back in time. The historical character of the town has even attracted the eye of Hollywood producers looking to find that turn of the century backdrop for their productions.

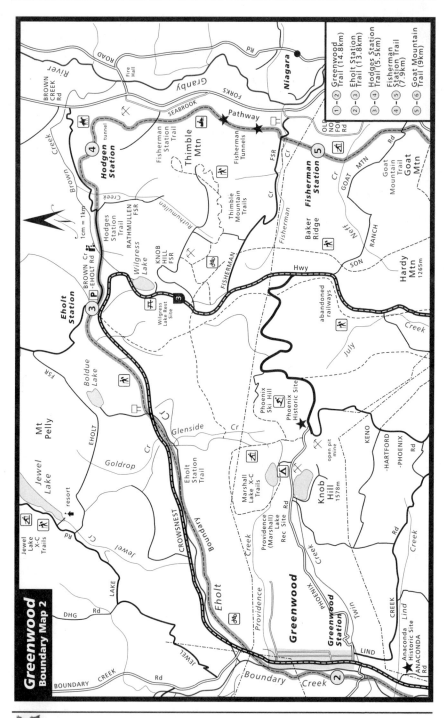

Greenwood
Boundary Map 2

①–②	Greenwood Trail (14.8km)
②–③	Eholt Station Trail (13.8km)
③–④	Hodges Station Trail (5.5km)
④–⑤	Fisherman Station Trail (7.9km)
⑤–⑥	Goat Mountain Trail (9km)

1cm = 1km

Boundary Map 2: Greenwood

In the hills surrounding Greenwood one can find many hidden gems. From historical sites to old mining artifacts, from fabulous backcountry roads to pretty mountain lakes the area makes for an interesting area to explore. To the east, one can find pretty Providence (Marshall) Lake as well as the former site of Phoenix (an old mining town). North of town, picturesque Jewel Lake is aptly named. This lake makes a fine destination and once produced a 25 kg (56 lb) rainbow trout.

Boundary Section 2-3

13.8 km
Eholt Station Trail

The subtle uphill climb continues from Greenwood to the former station and town site of Eholt. The route begins by following the former Columbia & Western (C&W) Railway. The old railbed is locally referred to as the Boundary Pathway and continues to parallel the highway through a mix of ranch land and thickly vegetated areas.

Eholt Trail   J. Klein

North of Greenwood, just before Boundary Creek Road, the route crosses over Highway 3. The trail then follows the old railbed parallel to Highway 3 and crosses the Eholt Creek before crossing over the highway again near the large Trans Canada Trail sign.

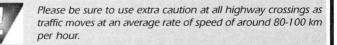

> *Please be sure to use extra caution at all highway crossings as traffic moves at an average rate of speed of around 80-100 km per hour.*

Just before the trail reaches the former station site of Eholt, the route crosses a few farming areas. There may be gated fences along the way. The site of Eholt is located simply amid a field area with very few reminders of the station or the town that once stood here.

> *Eholt was the site of the dividing point of the C&W Railway with one rail line running south towards the old mining town of Phoenix and the other east towards Grand Forks. By the turn of the century, Eholt was the home of five hotels and a growing, prosperous town. A number of different mine sites were developed in the area and the town quickly grew. However, with the great depression looming shortly after World War I, the mining-based economy of Eholt suffered immensely and the town soon turned into a ghost town. Today, other than the historical records, there is no remnant of the town. All the buildings that once stood have been torn down or moved. All that remains are a few old foundations amid the many quiet fields.*

Boundary Section 3-4

5.5 km
Hodges Station Trail

The route east from the field area known as Eholt Station to the former site of Hodges Station is relatively easy to follow and offers a nice wilderness setting. The trail begins by crossing the Eholt Road and follows the Brown Creek –Eholt Road, an interesting forestry road that also plays host to rumbling logging trucks on occasion. Shortly down the road, the railbed cuts its way through a wall of new growth and away from the road. The last couple kilometres slowly wind its way down to the old Hodges Station. The station site can be recognized by the remaining water tower foundation.

Boundary Section 4-5

7.9 km

Fishermen Station Trail

Shortly after the Trans Canada Trail/Boundary Pathway passes the Hodges Station area, the route begins to veer south towards Grand Forks along a more substantial downhill grade. After the first kilometre of this section of trail, the route passes a former railway tunnel. The tunnel is about 150 m (492 ft) in length and is one of the few tunnels that were constructed along the western portion of the C&W Railway. Another 4.6 km down the trail, the route encounters another tunnel of similar size. At the south end of the tunnel, you will find an old red shed that once offered maintenance storage along the rail line. The trail crosses over Fisherman Creek Forest Service Road and

Whitetailed Deer   R. Mussio

Goat Mountain Road before reaching the former site of the Fisherman Station. Not much remains of the station.

 For a further hiking/biking adventure, you can head west along the Fisherman Creek Forest Service Road to the Thimble Mountain Trails. The trail system is well maintained and is comprised of a mix of single and double track trails, which interconnect with the Knob Hill Forest Service Road. The trails can be followed to the top of Thimble Mountain where you can enjoy a fabulous view of the Granby River Valley.

 There is also a short hiking trail along the Fisherman Creek at the junction of the old railbed and the Fisherman Creek Forest Service Road. The rustic footpath treks through the forest cover on the north side of Fisherman Creek and leads to a scenic waterfall.

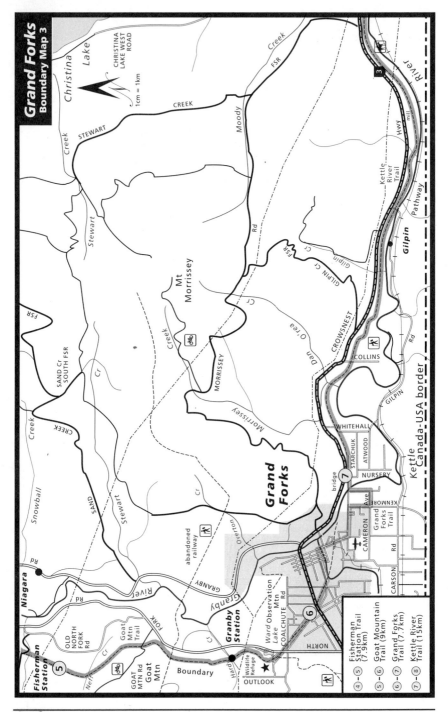

Grand Forks
Boundary Map 3

1cm = 1km

Christina Lake

CHRISTINA LAKE WEST ROAD

CREEK

STEWART Creek

Creek

Stewart

Stewart Creek

Mt Morrissey

Creek

Cr

SAND Cr SOUTH FSR

FSR

CREEK

Creek

Snowball

SAND

Stewart

Cr

MORRISSEY Creek

Morrissey

abandoned railway

GRANBY

River

Cr

Overton

Grand Forks

Moody

Rd

Dan O'rea FSR

GILPIN Cr FSR

Gilpin Cr

CROWSNEST

COLLINS

GILPIN

WHITEHALL

STARCHUK   ATWOOD

NURSERY

bridge   7

KENMORE

CAMERON Ave

Grand Forks Trail

CARSON   Rd

Rd

Kettle   Canada–USA border

Gilpin

Kettle River Trail

Hwy

Pathway

Moody Creek FSR

River

mill

3

Niagara Rd

OLD NORTH FORK Rd

Goat Mtn Trail

FORK

Nell Cr

GOAT MTN Rd   Goat Mtn

Boundary

Hardy   Cr

Wildlife Refuge

OUTLOOK

Ward Observation   Lake Mtn
COALCHUTE Rd

Granby Station

Granby

NORTH

6

Fisherman Station   5

	Fisherman Station Trail (7.9km)
4 – 5	
5 – 6	Goat Mountain Trail (9km)
6 – 7	Grand Forks Trail (7.7km)
7 – 8	Kettle River Trail (15km)

Boundary Map 3: Grand Forks

Boundary Section 5-6

9 km
Goat Mountain Trail

From the former Fisherman Station site, the Trans Canada Trail/Boundary Trail continues its downward trek along the old C&W Railbed. The route begins by crossing Neff Creek and then over Goat Mountain Road before reaching Hardy Creek and the former Granby Station site. You will probably not notice the site of the old station but cannot miss the view above Ward Lake. As the Trans Canada Trail/Boundary Pathway veers southeast towards Grand Forks, the route passes by the Columbia Station House Restaurant. The restaurant is certainly worth visiting since it is the original Grand Forks Station building.

Boundary Pathway   R. Mussio

 Along the section of trail from Hodges Station past Fisherman Station, there are several fantastic viewpoints of the Granby River Valley. Be sure to have your camera ready along this stretch as the railbed trail sits high above the scenic valley creating several ideal locations for a memorable snapshot.

Ward Lake is home to a waterfowl refuge, which is a fantastic site for viewing resident birds and waterfowl. The site was restored by Ducks Unlimited and plays an important role in migratory and resident bird life.

Boundary Section 6-7

7.7 km
Grand Forks Trail

Beginning at the Columbia Station House Restaurant, the route continues east into Grand Forks. The old railbed crosses over Highway 3 and travels towards the meandering Kettle River through the outskirts of town. Eventually you meet up with Kettle River Drive just before the river.

Currently, the official Trans Canada Trail route continues through Grand Forks east along Kettle River Drive to 8th Street. The route follows 8th Street north to 72nd Avenue and then heads east to 2nd Street. The route turns south along 2nd Street and crosses over the Kettle River where the road changes to International Road. Follow International Road south to Sagamore Avenue and then veer east along Sagamore Avenue to Kenmore Avenue. Follow Kenmore Avenue south to Cameron Avenue and then head east along Cameron to Darcy Avenue. Darcy Avenue will take you north to a trestle back over to the north side of the Kettle River and back onto the old C&W Railbed.

An alternate more scenic route is to cross the 2nd street bridge and then follow the footpath east along the south side of the river. Cross over or under the new bridge and continue on the side of the river until you come to a gate. Open and close the gate and continue until you come to the trestle that will take you

Near Grand Forks   C. Moslin

back over the Kettle River. This route is approved by the city and adjacent landowners and should become more developed over the next two years.

Shortly after the river crossing, the trail meets up with Nursery Road and the beginning of a temporary detour off the C&W railbed.

Grand Forks is one of the oldest European settlements in British Columbia and was founded in 1865. Initially the region thrived on the mining industry, although the industry collapsed after World War I during the Great Depression. The region eventually developed a forest industry, which continues to dominate much of the local economy to this day. The town is home to several historical turn of the century buildings and is famous for sunshine and borsch (a traditional Doukhobor dish). For more information on the historical sites in Grand Forks, it is best to visit the Boundary Museum or the local chamber of commerce.

Boundary Section 7-8

15 km
Kettle River Trail

In the fall of 2000, the C&W railbed heading east from Grand Forks towards Christina Lake was also completely torn up by new pipeline construction by BC Gas. The pipeline is scheduled to be restored with a crush gravel surface in 2001 and will make a fabulous path.

East of Midway   J. Klein

The route will begin near the Nursery Road intersection and head east along the old railbed passing through farmland with the odd home or barn dotting the landscape. On the way towards Christina Lake, the scenic route parallels Highway 3 and the Kettle River. The odd gate, a small mill and the necessary re-routing along the highway create a more challenging route than other old railway sections of the Trans Canada Trail route. Please stay on the trail, as this is all private land.

As you are heading east from Grand Forks, you may notice the highway signs warning of mountain sheep. At times, small collections of both mountain sheep and deer wander around the area, including along the old railbed.

Currently, the trestle crossing the Kettle River south of Highway 3/95 is in a state of disrepair. Adventurous travellers can continue over the trestle while those afraid of heights are recommended to take Highway 3 into Christina Lake. Travellers can access Highway 3 at the designated parking area just before the Gorge Trestle. Although there is no established trail, there are a number of easy access areas leading from the railbed to the highway. Follow Highway 3, which has a broad shoulder to travel on, to the junction with Highway 3/95.

Regardless of which route you choose, the old railway and trestle access a beautiful cascade gorge area that is worth the effort to visit. From the trestle, careful travellers can overlook the potholes and whirlpools created by the Kettle River as it falls towards the Columbia River to the south. If you follow the old railway east, you will cross Highway 3/95 and continue towards the beautiful Christina Lake Golf Course. After the golf course the trail comes to a long, high trestle crossing the Kettle River. Both trestles will be decked sometime in 2001.

The Kettle River Potholes are truly a magnificent site. The best time to see this area is during mid-day. At this time the bowl formed by the falls is filled with numerous rainbows. Aptly named Rainbow Rock offers the most spectacular viewing sight.

If travelling the route while it is still being restored by BC Gas, the best alternative is to follow Highway 3 all the way to the junction with Highway 395. Although there is a decent shoulder for travel along the highway, be sure to take extra caution along this stretch as the highway is normally busy with traffic.

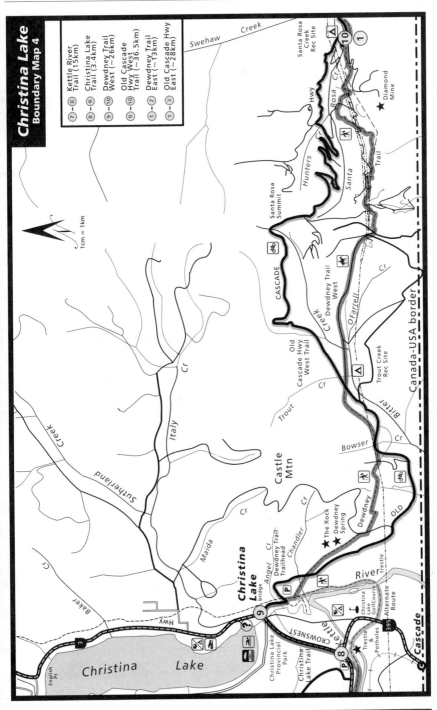

Christina Lake
Boundary Map 4

⑦—⑧	Kettle River Trail (15km)
⑧—⑨	Christina Lake Trail (3.4km)
⑨—⑩	Dewdney Trail West (~26km)
⑨—⑩	Old Cascade Hwy West Trail (~36.5km)
①—②	Dewdney Trail East (~13km)
①—③	Old Cascade Hwy East (~28km)

1cm = 1km

Boundary Map 4: Christina Lake

Boundary Section 8-9

3.4 km
Christina Lake Trail

The route from the junction of Highway 395 and Highway 3 requires you to climb up and over a small hill before dropping down to the town of Christina Lake. This section of trail will be busy with vehicle traffic so be sure to take advantage of the broad highway shoulder. At the bottom of the downhill section a few building mark the beginning of the town of Christina Lake. Look for Santa Rosa Road off the east side of the highway for the continuation of the Trans Canada Trail.

Trestle near Christina Lake   WildWays

Christina Lake is a popular resort town that comes alive in the summer. The lake itself boasts the warmest average annual water temperature in Canada. Every imaginable water sport, fishing and sunbathing make this a fine destination town. There is a friendly bike store that offers a good repair shop and you can even rent kayaks and canoes to enjoy the water with. They also carry an excellent map to help you explore the numerous local trails if you want to get off the beaten path. The area is also host to countless numbers of places to stay. From resorts to campgrounds and motels, every level of accommodation can be found.

Christina Lake Provincial Park lies along the southern shore of Christina Lake and is the site of a popular beach and picnic area. The day-use park makes an ideal place to spend a few hours lazing in the sun.

Boundary Section 9-10

~*26 km*
Dewdney Trail West

The historic Dewdney Trail trailhead is located off the south side of the Santa Rosa Road. The 38 km pack trail takes you over two different summits and through some challenging wilderness terrain. For this reason, this section of the Trans Canada Trail route is intended for hikers and horseback riders. Experienced mountain bikers are allowed on the trail providing they give all other travellers the right of way. For loaded cyclists looking for an easier route, see the Old Cascade Highway description below.

The Cascade Highway is not really a highway. Locals called it a highway some 70 years ago, because it was the only major route west from the Kootenays. In fact, the highway is and always has been a rough gravel road.

The Dewdney Trail was constructed in 1865 by the crew of Edgar Dewdney, who was a civil engineer contracted for the job by the governor of the colony of British Columbia. The trail was devised to be the first all Canadian route through the lower interior of British Columbia. Before the trail, much of the access to the interior was via the south through the United States. As the prospects of natural treasures such as gold and other minerals grew, the trail became a necessity for the government. When the trail was complete, it stretched from Hope to Wild Horse Creek, the eventual site of Fort Steele. By the late 1800's, train access and newer transportation routes rendered the Dewdney Trail obsolete and the route quickly fell into disrepair. By the 1880's, the West Kootenay section had become so rough that many areas were not even passable on foot.

The noted junction of the Santa Rosa Road and the Dewdney Trail is currently quite difficult to spot; however, there should be signs posted in the near future designating the trailhead off the road. The trailhead is located off the right side of the Santa Rosa Road at the first switchback, or you can skip the first steep part of the trail by following the Santa Rosa Road to 3.5 km and take the road off to the left marked with the Dewdney Trail sign.

The Dewdney Trail begins by travelling eastward over Chandler Creek. The trail then crosses over the old Cascade Highway and parallels the highway to the east. Shortly after the highway, crossing the trail passes by the Dewdney Spring, which is a natural water spring from the rocky ground. The trail continues eastward and crosses the Cascade Highway again and from here on, the old trail has become the base for a logging road for a number of kilometres. The road/trail crosses Bitter Creek and underneath the powerline before branching off the road system eastward toward the Santa Rosa Summit. Look for the arrows to the right of the road after the Trout Creek Campsite. This section of the Dewdney Trail is much as is was over a century ago, a beautiful single-track trail winding through mature forest cover and mossy rocks. You can almost hear the sound of the mules as they carried their loads of ore through these mountains.

South of Christina Lake   *J. Klein*

As the trail passes over the summit, there are several great views available from the mountain. The trail continues eastward past the vicinity of an old diamond mine and eventually crosses the Cascade Highway again near the Santa Rosa Creek Forest Recreation Site.

> *The summit is known as the dividing point between the Boundary and West Kootenay Regions. For purposes of this book we will use the Santa Rosa Creek Forest Recreation Site since all Trans Canada Trail users will pass by this point.*

> *Much of the Dewdney Trail goes through private lands. It is important for trail users to obey all signs and to stay on the trail when going through private land. Also, please note that recent construction of the BC Gas pipeline has temporarily torn up some of the trail. The route is scheduled to be reconstructed by late 2001. In the interim, the old Cascade Highway may be the best possible route.*

Boundary Section 9-10

~36.5 Km

Old Cascade Highway West

This is the alternate route to the Dewdney Trail intended as an easier route for cyclists. The road is shared with 4wd vehicles, ATV's, horseback riders and even hikers. Bikers should expect a good workout on this mountain route. When first constructed in the early 1900's, the old Cascade Highway was regarded as a highway despite only being a rough gravel road travelling over the Santa Rosa and Rossland Summits. The 60.6 km road remains a rough windy road and traverses along a few very steep sections at times. The fabulous scenery, the remote setting and the wilderness camping opportunities certainly make up for the more challenging nature of the trail. The road climbs steadily towards the Santa Rosa Summit. The route travels through mainly wooded terrain and crosses the historic Dewdney Trail and a few smaller creeks. The Forestry Recreation site at Trout Creek makes a nice resting area and the views from the summit are certainly rewarding.

The Cascade Highway, also called the Santa Rosa Road and the Queen's Highway was completed in 1922. It created the first good road west from Rossland to Christina Lake. The road was built without the use of any machinery except an old Model T Ford to haul supplies. Amazingly, this rough and windy route was really the only road west of Rossland all the way until 1962, when the modern highway was opened up north of Nancy Greene Provincial Park.

As you drop down into the Big Sheep Creek basin, the road becomes quite rough and care should be taken when travelling this section. Several switchbacks later, you will pass by the Santa Rosa Creek Recreation Site. For the purposes of this book, we will use this point as the dividing line between the Boundary and West Kootenay Regions.

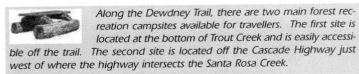

Along the Dewdney Trail, there are two main forest recreation campsites available for travellers. The first site is located at the bottom of Trout Creek and is easily accessible off the trail. The second site is located off the Cascade Highway just west of where the highway intersects the Santa Rosa Creek.

As the Cascade Highway approaches the Santa Rosa Summit, there are several fantastic views of the United States found to the south. When travelling along the route, it is actually somewhat strange to know you are viewing another country to the south.

Old Cascade Highway   J. Klein

BOUNDARY SERVICE PROVIDERS

Accommodations

Christina Lake Chamber of Commerce

A TCT community. Explore the beautiful gorge. Accommodations and food.

Hwy 3 and Kimura Rd
Christina Lake, BC, V0H 1E2
(250) 447-6161
www.christinalake.com

Western Traveller Motel

Accommodations with storage for equiptment. 1 block from TCT.

1591 Central Ave.
Grand Forks, BC
(250) 442-5566

Sunflower Inn B&B

Beautiful log home. Covered deck, dock, canoe, bike, storage. Near marina, private beach.

159 Alpine
Christina Lake, BC, V0H 1E1
(250) 447-6201
suninnbb@sunshinecable.com
www.christinalake.com/suninnbb

Lakeview Motel

Comfortable, clean, quiet accommodation. Close to everything.

1658 Hwy3
Christina Lake, BC, V0H 1E3
(250) 447-9358
lakeview@sunchinecable.com

www.**backroadmapbooks**.com

Motel 99

Brand new 3 storey, house keeping, kitchenette/fridge units, a/c. Beside rec. center, restaurants and Trans-Canada Trail.

7424 Donaldson Drive
Grand Forks, BC, V0H 1H0
(250) 442-8501

Tours and Guides

travel@britishcolumbiatours.com
1-800-797-6335

Supplies & Services

WildWays

Full service repair/ rental shop. Shuttle service, multi-sport trips, and tours.

1925 Hwy 3
Christina Lake, BC, V0H 1E2
(250) 447-6561
1-888-wildway* (945-3929)
www.wildways.com

West Kootenay

The Trans Canada Trail through the West Kootenay Region continues the trend of following historical routes through the province. In this region, the majority of the route follows closely to the historical pack trail known as the Dewdney Trail. The creation of logging road systems and the discontinued use of the original trail has resulted in most of the trail having all but disappeared. For this reason, travellers will only be able to follow short pieces of the original trail. The Trans Canada Trail has been able to piece together the route by following sections of the Dewdney Trail, fabulous local trail systems and various road networks.

As far as individual types of travellers, various trail users will be able to follow most of the West Kootenay section. It is perhaps the most challenging part of the Trans Canada Trail route in B.C. since both the west and east end of the regions travel through mountainous terrain. Hikers and cyclists should have no trouble following the route in its entirety. Although you will gain and lose a lot of elevation, most of the grade is quite gentle. A downfall of the route is that there are sections of highway travel to contend with. This could deter some hikers and especially equestrian riders, cross-country skiers and snowmobilers from following the entire route through the West Kootenays. In general, there are some wonderful stretches of trail in the West Kootenays that will please all trail users.

Currently, the Trans Canada Trail route in the West Kootenay Region is under a state of flux. There are land use problems on several pieces of the proposed trail. For this reason, travellers will find many interim trails that are not signed. Official sections are planned to be signed starting in the summer of 2001. Before heading out be sure to check locally, with Trails BC or visit www.backroadmapbooks.com for updates on the route. It is also important to stay on the trail, to follow proper trail and wilderness etiquette and to avoid trespassing.

Another important point to note is that the West Kootenay portion of the Trans Canada Trail travels through a predominantly wilderness area. Wildlife is common in this area of the province and it is essential to take precautions to avoid encounters with certain animals such as bears and cougars. It is also important to be prepared for wilderness travel. Weather can change abruptly in the mountains and in some sections civilization is a long ways away.

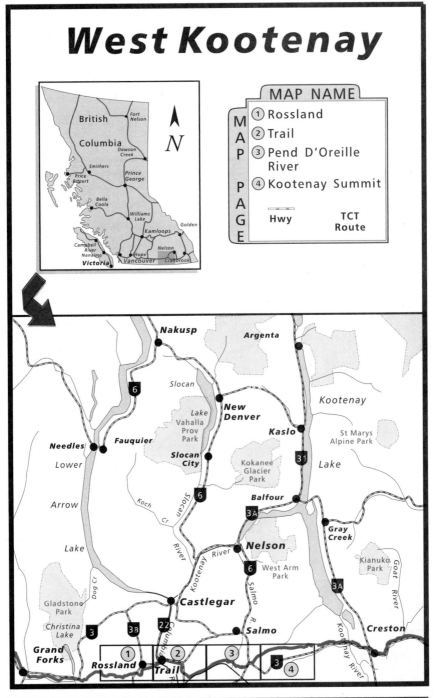

West Kootenay

MAP NAME

MAP PAGE

1. Rossland
2. Trail
3. Pend D'Oreille River
4. Kootenay Summit

— Hwy   TCT Route

British Columbia

Fort Nelson

Dawson Creek

Smithers

Prince George

Prince Rupert

Golden

Bella Coola

Williams Lake

Kamloops

Campbell River
Nanaimo

Nelson

Hope

Cranbrook

Victoria   Vancouver

Nakusp

Argenta

Slocan

Lake Vahalla Prov Park

New Denver

Kaslo

Kootenay

St Marys Alpine Park

Needles   **Fauquier**

Lower

Slocan City

Kokanee Glacier Park

Lake

Arrow

Koch Cr

Slocan River

Balfour

Lake

Kootenay River

Nelson

Gray Creek

Kianuko Park

Goat River

West Arm Park

Gladstone Park

Dog Cr

Castlegar

Salmo R.

Christina Lake

Columbia R.

Creston

Grand Forks

Rossland

Salmo

Kootenay River

Trail

1   2   3   3   4

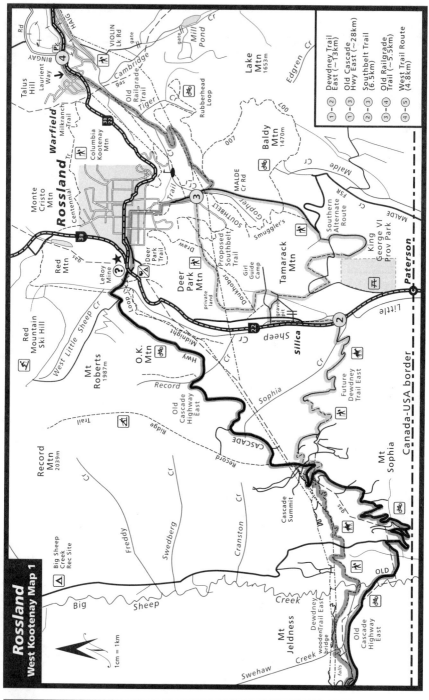

Rossland
West Kootenay Map 1

1cm = 1km

① — ②	Dewdney Trail East (~13km)
① — ③	Old Cascade Hwy East (~28km)
② — ③	Southbelt Trail (6.5km)
③ — ④	Old Railgrade Trail (~5.5km)
④ — ⑤	West Trail Route (4.8km)

West Kootenay Map 1: Rossland

West Kootenay Section 1-2
~ 13 km
Dewdney Trail East

The Trans Canada Trail continues on the Dewdney Trail past the Cascade Summit to a final crossing of the Old Cascade Highway. Due to private landowner concerns, we are asked to re-direct travellers north along the road and down into Rossland. It is hoped that by the summer of 2001 travellers will be able to continue along the Dewdney Trail east.

After the Santa Rosa Creek Recreation Site, the route crosses the Cascade Highway again. The trail is signed and easy to follow despite the network of old logging roads in the area. The route parallels the highway and powerlines for a distance, making it generally easy to maintain your bearings if you end up off the trail.

Trail Horseman Society   R. Mann

The Dewdney Trail descends into a small valley area where there are a few homesteads. The trail dips into the Big Sheep Creek Valley and crosses a bridge, where cyclists are required to detour on the main road. This detour is about 3.5 km, while the hiking route is only 1 km. When the two trails join, the trail begins another 4 km ascent towards the Cascade Summit.

Just west of the summit, the trail once again crosses the Old Cascade Highway. This is where the temporary detour is necessary. In the future, the route should continue down to Highway 22. The trail is quite steep and dynamic as it drops almost 900 m (2,950 ft) over 5 km. Part way down, you will come to a section of logging roads that form the base for the trail. This last section is also well signed.

One of the Sheep Creek Valley landowners, Peaceful Acres, is willing to allow camping onsite. They offer cabins and trailers as well as a basic camping area for travellers looking for a more comfortable overnight stay.

From Big Sheep Creek Valley east to Rossland, the trail crosses several parcels of private property. This is a unique situation that has resulted in generous donations or agreements by landowners to allow travellers to pass through their property. Please respect this privilege by obeying trail rules and do not stray from the marked and signed route.

West Kootenay Section 1-3
~28 km
Old Cascade Highway East

The alternate Trans Canada Trail route continues east on the Old Cascade Highway. The road becomes a little easier to follow as you begin the next big challenge. You will pass by a few homesteads before the relentless climb up to the Cascade Summit. The switchbacks marked on the map should warn you of the elevation you will need

View From Cascade Summit J. Marleau

to gain. Eventually you will skirt the slope of O.K. Mountain as the road drops towards Highway 22 just west of Rossland.

At the junction with Highway 22, travellers will see the signs for the Lions Campground. Just cross the highway and enter the campground. If you are not interested in camping, route signs will direct travellers through town to rejoin the main Trans Canada Trail at the Old Railgrade leading to Warfield. It is rather tricky to find the railgrade so be sure to follow the signs.

Alternatively, the railgrade trailhead is found southeast of town. From Columbia Avenue in downtown Rossland, turn south on Le Roi Avenue and then south on Davis Street. Davis leads to Union Avenue. Continue east on Union past Spokane Street to the start of the Old Railgrade. Another parking area is found further south off Spokane Street, which turns into Southbelt Road. This is not part of the route but rather a temporary alternative if the signs are not up.

While in Rossland be sure to take the time to visit the Information Centre and Museum as Le Roi Mine. In addition to viewing the many old mining artifacts be sure to allow time to take the underground tour of the old mine site.

Rossland was originally established as a mining town in the 1890's. Even from the very early days downhill skiing has always been a popular pastime. Today many skiers revere the relatively unknown, Red Mountain as one of the best ski hills in North America. Rossland also claims to be the Mountain Biking Capital of North America. With hundreds of kilometres of trails ranging from gentle rail grades to extreme single-track trails, one can spend weeks exploring this beautiful mountainous region. All amenities, including bike repairs, accommodation, food and any other needed supplies can be found in this quaint little mountain town. The Information Centre has trail maps for those wishing to explore the area.

West Kootenay Section 2-3

~6.5 km

Southbelt Trail

The proposed Trans Canada Trail route continues north up the hill from the Dewdney Trail next to the pretty Highway 22. Until the private land issue is solved, it is advisable to simply follow the highway up into the mountain town of Rossland. The highway is not very busy and offers a surprisingly peaceful route to follow.

The maps show the proposed off-highway alternatives in this area. It is hoped that in the near future the trails will be open to the public and Trans Canada Trail travellers will enjoy this beautiful area south of town. You can check locally, with Trails B.C. or visit www.backroadmapbooks.com for any current route changes.

The area south of Rossland is riddled with old roads and trails, many of which where used by smugglers during the times of Prohibition. People used to smuggle alcohol across the border using these trails. The mountain area is quite beautiful and it is certainly fun to spend some time exploring the many trails in and around the Trans Canada Trail.

West Kootenay Section 3-4

~5.5 km

Old Railgrade Trail

No matter which way you get there, the Trans Canada Trail continues east to Warfield on the Old Railgrade Trail. The trail to Upper Warfield forms one of the nicest interurban recreational routes you will find in the country. The lush Trail Creek Valley is very scenic and is home to an abundance of wildlife, including a variety of birds, deer and bears.

Although you descend 300 m (985 ft), the gentle grade of the route makes for an easy route. The railgrade drops into the Trail Creek Drainage, where the old railway ties cause a few extra bumps to contend with. Eventually, you pass a pretty horse pasture before coming into the outskirts of Warfield. Here you cross Highway 3B/22 and continue on the paved Laurient Way next to the highway. The short path was named after the former mayor of the village and leads down to Webster Elementary School next to Bingay Road.

The railway was once used to haul gold from the local mine down to the smelter in Trail. Part way down the route you will see the first of a series of spurs known as Rubberheads. The trains used these short spurs in order to negotiate the sharp switchbacks along the railway.

West Kootenay Section 4-5

4.8 km

West Trail Route

Cross Bingay Road and the schoolyard to Highway 3B, where there are a few options. The easiest route is to follow the highway 3.3 km down to East Trail. Watch your speed as the busy highway follows a significant grade but does offer a nice shoulder to ride on. At the bottom of the hill you will enter an area known as the Gulch. This area has seen some recent improvements to restore the character of the buildings. Continue along the highway, which is now called Rossland Avenue, through the lights and past the historic Trail Memorial Arena next to the Columbia River Bridge.

The more scenic route involves following several backroads. Follow the highway downhill for about 500 m to the Warfield Pool. Turn right here and follow Lower Murray Road as it drops down to a pretty suburb found next to Trail Creek. Crossing the creek will take you to Haig Road. Sandwiched between the creek and a grassy hill, this road has a nice a country feel. It takes you past the suburb known as Annable before dropping toward the Gulch on Reservoir Road.

Old Railgrade Sign   R. Mussio

Reservoir turns to Esling and then Binns Street. A left leads down to Rossland Avenue, which is actually the highway. Instead continue along Binns Street to sample the unique street network of West Trail. Binns leads to Austad Lane. Follow Austad to Glover Road. A left here drops down to Rossland Avenue near the Best Western Hotel. Follow Rossland Avenue through the lights to the bridge.

If you have time, it is certainly worthwhile visiting the hills above the Gulch. The tiny streets and terraced hills have a definite European feel. The many Italian workers in the area built the houses before the bridges were built across the Columbia River. The close proximity of the houses, the narrow streets and views are amazing. The Italian flair of the community is still prominent today. From unique products in the grocery stores to the restaurants in the area, Little Italy is alive and well.

 Trail, BC is the home of the world's largest lead-zinc smelter. The smelter owner, Cominco, has just completed a 20 year modernization program, which has resulted in significant reductions in emissions to the air and water. If you look at the once barren canyon walls, you can see that the trees and vegetation are coming back. This is a prime example of how an industrial area can be cleaned up. The Cominco Interpretive Centre, located at the Chamber of Commerce, provides more insight into the past and future of this region.

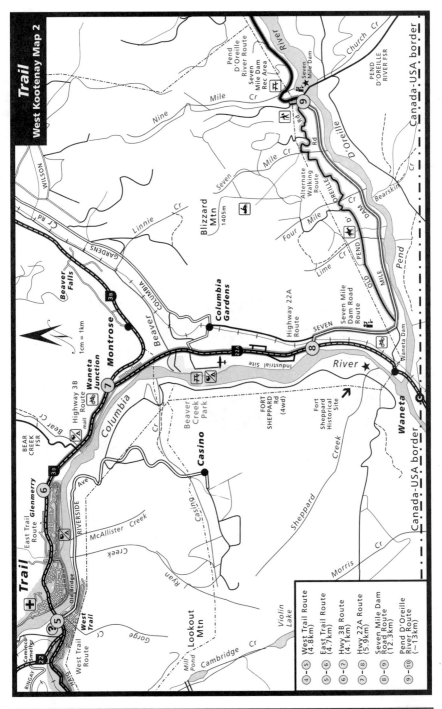

Trail
West Kootenay Map 2

1cm = 1km

Beaver Falls

Montrose

Waneta Junction

Highway 3B Route

BEAR CREEK FSR

Bear Cr

Glenmerry

East Trail Route

Trail

Cominco Smelter

West Trail

West Trail Route

Lookout Mtn

Columbia River

Columbia Gardens

Blizzard Mtn 1405m

Nine Mile Cr

Linnie Cr

Seven Mile Cr

Casino

Beaver Creek Park

FORT SHEPPARD Rd (4wd)

Fort Sheppard Historical Site

McAllister Creek

Ryan Creek

Mill Pond

Gorge Cr

Cambridge Cr

Violin Lake

Sheppard Creek

Morris Cr

Pend D'Oreille River Route

Seven Mile Dam Rec Area

Seven Mile Dam

Pend D'Oreille River

Church Cr

Four Mile Cr

Lime Cr

Highway 22A Route

Seven Mile Dam Road Route

Industrial Site

Waneta Dam

Waneta

Alternate Walking Route

PEND D'OREILLE RIVER FSR

OLD SEVEN MILE DAM Rd

Bearskin Cr

Canada-USA border

4	5	West Trail Route	(4.8km)
5	6	East Trail Route	(4.7km)
6	7	Hwy 3B Route	(4.1km)
7	8	Hwy 22A Route	(5.9km)
8	9	Seven Mile Dam Road Route	(12.3km)
9	10	Pend D'Oreille River Route	(~13km)

West Kootenay Map 2: Trail

West Kootenay Section 5-6

4.7 km

East Trail Route

The Trans Canada Trail route in Trail is not complete yet. The route was to turn south and cross the Old Bridge over the Columbia River. Unfortunately, the bridge is closed. For this reason, we will provide an interim route. It is recommended to contact the local Chamber of Commerce (250) 368-3144 for updates before heading out.

Near Trail BC   R. Mussio

The interim route crosses the Columbia River Bridge. Cyclists will want to turn right at the first light onto Second Avenue. A short hill takes you past Safeway and a four way intersection. Turn right on Bailey Street and left on Columbia Avenue, where you will see the Old Bridge ahead. Walkers should look for the steps at the east end of the bridge. Follow the path to Columbia Avenue and the Old Bridge.

If the Old Bridge has been resurfaced, turn right on Bay Street at the last light before the Columbia River Bridge. This road takes you through the small downtown core of Trail next to the river. Continue straight past a few more lights to where the road narrows into Riverside Avenue. The Trans Canada Trail route follows this interesting road to the Old Bridge and the preferred crossing of the Columbia River.

You may notice the cement retaining walls are found well above the river. It is hard to imagine that before the river was dammed, Trail was the site of several devastating floods.

Follow Columbia Avenue east past a few more homes before it winds its way up and around a small creek draw. The route continues past the Ford car dealership where you have a couple of options. Turning left will bring you back to the busy highway, while continuing straight takes you through the suburb of Glenmerry along Highway Drive. If you continue straight, Highway Drive turns into Rosewood Drive and then Carnation Drive before looping north and back to the highway.

Trail is known as the Home of Champions due to its tremendous sporting past. Most notable are the Trail Smoke Eaters hockey club. The team was made up of local smelter workers who helped the city gain worldwide notoriety by producing two World Hockey Championships back in the days when only amateur athletes were allowed to participate. They won the tournament in 1939 and 1961 with an impressive combined record of fourteen wins and one tie. The Smoke Eaters were so good in 1939 that they outscored their opponents by 42-1 in eight games. The lone goal against was actually scored by mistake by Smoke Eater Tom Johnson during the game with Czechoslovakia.

West Kootenay Section 6-7

4.1 km

Highway 3B Route

From the end of the Trail suburb of Glenmerry, the route follows Highway 3B east. The highway has a wide shoulder but is extremely busy with traffic. Please be very cautious on this section of highway and be sure to stick to the shoulder of the road.

Follow the highway as it drops down to the desert like area on the flats surrounding Wantea Junction. You will pass a few industrial sites, a local shopping mall and a few restaurants before the Highway 22A junction.

On the north side of the highway, just before McDonalds, the municipal campground offers travellers a place to camp. Wantea Plaza and the few restaurants in the area represent your last chance to get food and supplies for quite some time. If you are indeed trying to follow the complete Trans Canada Trail route through B.C., it is recommended to stock up on food and especially water.

West Kootenay Section 7-8

5.9 km

Highway 22A Route

At the junction of Highway 3B and Highway 22A, the route veers south along the much quieter Highway 22A. The upgraded highway does not see much traffic but large transport trucks do frequently barrel along the road.

The route follows the highway along the east side of the Columbia River towards the United States border. Continue past the rural neighbourhood before the road dips into the Beaver Creek Valley and past Beaver Creek Park. A short uphill climb leads to the long open straight stretch next to the airport. Continue along the highway all the way to the junction with the Seven Mile Dam Road, some 5 km north of the U.S. border.

Along the way to the Seven Mile Dam Road, the route passes by Beaver Creek Park, which is found next to a scenic stretch of the Columbia River. There is a picnic area near a popular fishing and swimming hole as well as camping and boat launch facilities. With such amenities as showers, this is one of the best camping options if you plan to camp in the Trail area.

The Columbia River was the focus of the Columbia Basin Treaty signed with United States many years ago. The treaty was desired by the U.S. in order to create hydroelectric dams along the Columbia to feed their increasing power demands. The river was once home to one of the largest salmon runs in the world until the construction of a large series of dams was completed. Today, the only remnants of the once massive salmon run are landlocked sockeye, known as kokanee. Kokanee can be found in a few of the dammed river reservoirs such as the Arrow Lakes to the north of Trail. The river continues to boast a world-class fly fishery. The feisty rainbow trout and walleye are the most prized sport fish taken from this stretch of the Columbia.

West Kootenay Section 8-9
12.3 km
Seven Mile Dam Road Route
At the junction of Highway 22A and Seven Mile Dam Road, the Trans Canada Trail continues its eastward trek towards the Alberta border via the Seven Mile Dam Road. The road begins along a steep ascent along the shoulder of Blizzard Mountain before veering eastward. You will be travelling along an exposed road, which can be very hot during the summer. Be sure to have plenty of water.

7 Mile Dam   *J. Marleau*

The Seven Mile Dam Road traverses high above both the Columbia and Pend D'Oreille Rivers. As the road drops back down toward the smaller river, hikers and horseback riders should look for the Old Pend D'Oreille Road to the north. Although this 10.2 km gravel road is longer, it is not as busy and offers a more dynamic route for travellers. You will skirt by a few farms, past some scenic viewpoints and around some refreshing creek draws. The road spills out on the Pend D'Oreille River Road just north of the Seven Mile Dam.

Cyclists will find the paved Seven Mile Dam Road quite rewarding. Outside of a few short hills, it is an easy cycle. The easy access to the warm river offers plenty of chances to take a break or a refreshing swim. The light traffic and incredible views add to the ambience of this route. This section of the route ends with a short climb to the impressive Seven Mile Dam.

There are some truly spectacular vantage points along this route. The initial uphill climb is rewarded with a number of good views of the Columbia River below. Further along, the scenic Pend D'Oreille River can be found meandering through the tranquil countryside. Finally, the Seven Mile Dam also offers a fantastic view. The massive dam dominates the landscape and offers a nice viewpoint next to the reservoir.

 Just east of the Seven Mile Dam there is a small day-use BC Hydro Recreation Site. Found along the shore of the scenic Pend D'Oreille River, it makes a great picnic or swimming destination.

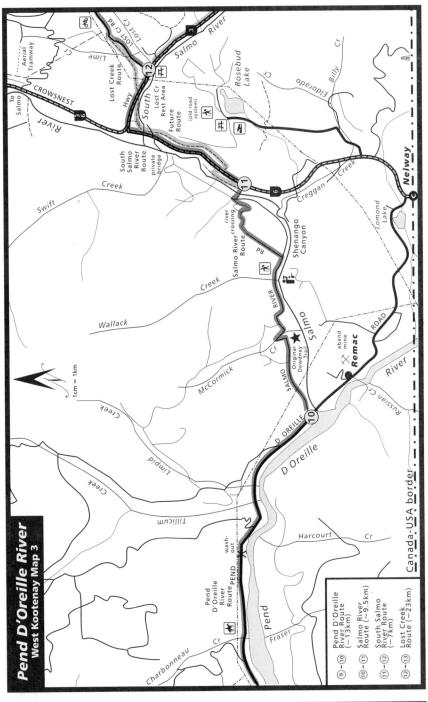

Pend D'Oreille River
West Kootenay Map 3

1cm = 1km

Legend:
- ⑨–⑩ Pend D'Oreille River Route (~13km)
- ⑩–⑪ Salmo River Route (~9.5km)
- ⑪–⑫ South Salmo River Route (~7km)
- ⑫–⑬ Lost Creek Route (~23km)

West Kootenay Map 3: Pend D'Oreille River

West Kootenay Section 9-10

~ 13 km

Pend D'Oreille River Route

From the Seven Mile Dam site, the Trans Canada Trail winds its way down to the Pend D'Oreille River via the Pend D'Oreille Road. The road is made up of hard pack gravel and travels along the north side of the river. Along the route, there are several fantastic views of the river and valley offered. There are also several easy access areas to the river as well as many historical sites to explore.

Pend D'Oreille River Road   J. Klein

Just before Tillicum Creek, a small landslide that only 4wd vehicles can negotiate has blocked the Pend D'Oreille Road. Travellers should have no trouble negotiating the slide. Shortly after, the route meets the Salmo River Road. Before Seven Mile Dam was built, the mouth of the Salmo River was the site of a spectacular canyon and some fantastic fishing.

The Trans Canada Trail route from the mouth of the Pend D'Oreille River through the Lost Creek Summit follows the historical route of the Dewdney Trail. There are a number of highlights to be explored on this section of the route. 15 Mile Creek is the site of rock walls built by Dewdney Trail workers. Ghost Flats is named after the graves of past travellers or settlers along the trail. Below the road at McCormick Creek, a 1 km section of original trail can be followed across the creek. Scenic Shenango Canyon, just east of Wallack Creek, is the site of an old placer miners cabin and cable car crossing. Just north of the West Kootenay Bridge crossing is the former site of the original bridge built by Pete the Packer. Finally, there are two short pieces of original trail between the Salmo River and the Lost Creek Valley.

The Pend D'Oreille Valley was first settled in the 1890's and orchards and homesteads once ran the length of the valley. Placer mining was quite common in the area from the 1850's until the 1930's. In fact, the first gold in B.C. was discovered in 1854 at the mouth of the Pend D'Oreille River. Today, only a few farms are found at the south end of the valley but old orchards are scattered throughout the valley and still make a delicious discovery.

West Kootenay Section 10-11

~9.5 km
Salmo River Route

The Trans Canada Trail continues east on the road on the north side of the scenic Salmo River. Along the way there are signs of the old Dewdney Trail and the fabulous Shenango Canyon is certainly a highlight. Unfortunately, the trail leaves the road and the course of the historic pack trail and requires the traveller to ford the river near the old cable crossing. Due to water levels this river crossing is only recommended during August and September.

Please do not stray from the trail in this area and respect the wishes of private landowners. There are several items such as cabins, cable crossings and bridges that are off limits to Trans Canada Trail travellers. In the near future, it is planned to construct a bridge or another cable crossing for the Trans Canada Trail.

If the river crossing is safe, continue east to the highway.

West Kootenay Section 11-12

~7 km
South Salmo River Route

In the interim, the easiest option is to follow Highway 6 north to the junction with

Highway 3 south of Salmo. The highway traverses a tight valley carved out by the Salmo River making for great scenery and a pleasant journey. Along this section of highway there is ample shoulder area for safe travel. However there are a few sections that can be quite danger ous due to lim ited visibility cre ated by sharp turns in the road. Other than the

Pend D'Oreille River   J. Klein

odd transport truck, the highway is not a busy road.

At the highway junction, continue east for a short jaunt on the much busier Highway 3. Look for the Lost Creek Road to the north. The Lost Creek Rest Area is a bit further east but is certainly worth visiting. In addition to washrooms and picnic tables, you can find delicious huckleberries in August.

> *Plans are well under way to make an off-highway trail in this area. The trail will follow the steps of the historical Dewdney Trail before eventually crossing the South Salmo River southwest of the Lost Creek Road junction. Be sure to check locally, with Trails BC or www.backroadmapbooks.com for updates on the route in this area.*

> *Before venturing up and over the Kootenay Summit, it is a good idea to stock up on supplies. A recommended side trip is to travel up to the town of Salmo about 12 km north of the Highway 3 and Highway 6 junction along Highway 3. Salmo is a charming logging town set along the Salmo River. The town was originally settled as a mining supply town in the early 1900's. Evidence of the early mining period can be found in the mountains that surround Salmo. In particular, the Sheep Creek Forest Service Road takes you past a few former mines. Salmo also offers a tent & trailer park just to the west of town.*

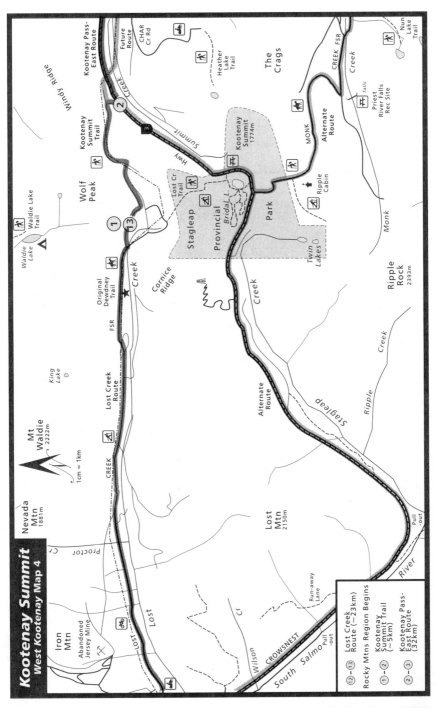

Kootenay Summit
West Kootenay Map 4

Nevada
Mtn
1881m

Mt
Waldie
2222m

1cm = 1km

②-⑬	Lost Creek Route (~23km)
	Rocky Mtns Region Begins
①-②	Kootenay Summit Trail (~5km)
②-③	Kootenay Pass-East Route (32km)

Winnipy Ridge

Kootenay Pass-East Route

Future Route

CHAR Cr Rd

Heather Lake Trail

The Crags

CREEK FSR

Nun Lake Trail

Kootenay Summit Trail

Kootenay Summit 1774m

MONK

Alternate Route

falls

Priest River Falls Rec Site

Wolf Peak

Waldie Lake Trail

Lost Cr Trail

Bridal L.

Stagleap Provincial Park

Ripple Cabin

Waldie Lake

Twin Lakes

Monk

Ripple Rock 2393m

Original Dewdney Trail

Cornice Ridge

Creek

Stagleap

Ripple

Creek

King Lake

Lost Creek Route

CREEK

Alternate Route

Lost Mtn 2150m

Proctor Cr

River

Pull out

Iron Mtn

Abandoned Jersey Mine

LOST

Lost

Run-away Lane

Pull out

Wilson Cr

CROWSNEST

South Salmo Pull-out

West Kootenay Map 4: Kootenay Summit

West Kootenay Section 11-12

~23 km
Lost Creek Route

The Trans Canada Trail continues to follow pieces of the historical Dewdney Trail. This section of the route takes travellers up the Lost Creek Valley to the infamous Kootenay Pass. The gradually rising valley does have a few steep hills but is generally easy to negotiate. Due to snow accumulation, the route has a limited season for cyclists, walkers and equestrian riders. It is recommended to limit summer travel to between July and September.

Lost Creek Road in June   J. Klein

You can find the Lost Creek Road off the north side of Highway 3 about 2 km east of the Highway 3/ Highway 6 junction. Lost Creek Road is a rarely used forest access road that traverses the small valley between Mount Waldie and Lost Mountain. Unfortunately, there a few parcels of private property to cross on the way up the valley. Please pay attention to any signage in the area. It may be necessary to follow the alternate highway route described below.

After about 6 km, the road gradually begins to degrade becoming quite rough as it climbs towards Wolf Peak. As the road reaches the section between Wolf Peak and Cornice Ridge, it becomes steeper but the sub-alpine scenery is very rewarding. Near the top of the road, the route intersects the original Dewdney Trail. Small sections of the original rock wall can be seen in the area. The summit is marked by a small meadow. In addition to fabulous view of the Windy Ridge and Wolf Peak, the meadows make a fine overnight stop for weary travellers. The summit marks the end of the West Kootenay section of the Trans Canada Trail.

Between the Wolf Peak and Cornice Ridge, an established side road veers south off the main road. This road leads to a trail that eventually traverses over to Stagleap Provincial Park and back to Highway 3.

The Lost Creek Valley has a storied history. Most noteworthy for modern day travellers was the 1860 expedition. Arthur Sullivan from the Palliser Expedition spent five days travelling the length of this valley. Bad weather and difficult conditions hampered travel. Today's travellers should be prepared for sudden weather changes, fog and even snow.

23.8 km
Kootenay Pass Alternate Route

During the shoulder seasons (spring and fall), cyclists are recommended to follow Highway 3 up and over the Kootenay Pass. The route to the summit follows a well-maintained highway offering spectacular views surrounding one of the highest and most treacherous highway passes in British Columbia. The trek is a consistent uphill climb to the summit and although the grade is gradual, it will take a toll on bikers.

The route begins its climb by crossing Lost Creek as it starts to follow the shoulder of Lost Mountain. All along the route, there are nice views of the South Salmo River found below the highway. Travellers will also have plenty of time to catch a glimpse of the rugged mountainous wilderness area surrounding the highway. Just when you think the climb will never end, the summit seems to creep within reach. As you round the corner to the summit, you reach the heart of Stagleap Provincial Park marked by the small Bridal Lake, a few snow removal buildings and a cabin. The Kootenay Summit sits an amazing 1,774 m (5,820 ft) above sea level.

Be sure to stay alert for oncoming traffic and stay well off the highway. Many vehicles, especially transport trucks, cannot make sudden direction changes and/or stops along the steep grade.

 Stagleap Provincial Park is a small provincial park that was established to protect a portion of the magnificent Kootenay Summit. The park is home to a few small alpine lakes and a wide variety of wildlife, including mountain goats, caribou and elk. In addition to a short cross-country skiing and hiking trail system, there is a warm-up hut, washrooms and picnic tables available for day visitors.

Lost Creek Road   J. Klein

WEST KOOTENAYS SERVICE PROVIDERS

Tours and Guides

Peaceful Acres

We host horse trail rides in September.
Camping and cabins available.
Found along the Dewdney Trail by Big
Sheep Creek.

1132 Findley Rd.
Kelowna, BC, V1X 5A8
(250) 765-3010
or (250) 362-5532

Rossland Historical Museum

Guided underground mine tours.
Museum, goldpanning & more.

Hwy Junction 22 & 3B
Rossland, BC, V0G 1Y0
(250) 362-7722
1-888-448-7444

To find out more about HI-Hostels in BC
visit:

www.hihostels.bc.ca

1 - 8 0 0 - 6 6 1 - 0 0 2 0

travel@britishcolumbiatours.com
1-800-797-6335

HI-Rossland

Located in Downtown Rossland. Great
golf and Lakes nearby.

2125 Columbia Ave.
Rossland, BC
(250) 362-7160
www.hihostels.bc.ca

1 - 8 8 8 - 3 9 3 - 7 1 6 0

Rocky Mountains

The Rocky Mountain section of the Trans Canada Trail is the longest stretch of trail in Southern British Columbia and due to many factors, it was initially the least developed region of the Trans Canada Trail in BC. The route was literally a mere idea as of the fall of 2000. With the immense planning and volunteer work of the local Trails BC members, the Rocky Mountains region is happy to boast the longest section of the trail, complete from the Kootenay Pass all the way to the Elk Pass. Due to the sheer mountain terrain and wilderness sections along the route, the Rocky Mountain volunteers had to be very ingenious in developing the route. From old forest access roads to rail beds to historic trails, the Rocky Mountain region is truly a magnificent and unique part of the Trans Canada Trail in British Columbia.

Info for different travellers

Throughout the Rocky Mountain region, many alternate routes have been proposed or are in development. Portions of the trail travel along highway and road shoulders, making for difficult travel for hikers and especially for horseback riders. Wherever possible, we have suggested some unofficial and official alternate routes to help accommodate all travellers. Urban areas such as Creston, Cranbrook, Fernie and Sparwood have only recently considered the Trans Canada Trail, hence alternates for horseback riders may not always be available. For bikers, Highway 3 is actually a very rewarding and fun ride in several section, most notably the portion from Creston to Cranbrook.

There are several proposed route changes for the Rocky Mountain Trans Canada Trail region. The most notable proposed changes are the route from the Moira Lake area north to Cranbrook and the route north of Fernie to Sparwood. Due to mainly geographical challenges in these sections, volunteers have been hard pressed to find a viable alternative other than Highway and urban road travel. In the coming years, the hard work and dedication of Trails BC is sure to shine through in the development of more rural trail routes. When planning your trip through the Rocky Mountains, be sure to check with Trails BC or www.backroadmapbooks.com for up to date information on changes on the Rocky Mountain section of the Trans Canada Trail.

Since large stretches of the main Trans Canada Trail route through the Rocky Mountains follow close to Highway 3, help is usually always nearby. There are a few areas, however, that you should be prepared for wilderness travel. One such area is the Lost Creek alternate over the Kootenay Pass. This alternate traverses through rugged terrain, and travels up into a sub-alpine environment, making conditions very unpredictable. Another remote stretch of the route is the large trek north of Elkford. Essentially, the further away from Elkford that you travel, the more remote the terrain becomes. Loggers and outdoor enthusiasts throughout the summer months frequent the Elk Valley north of Elkford, however you may be hard pressed to find anyone at times. Although the valley is remote, it is one of the most spectacular sections of the Rocky Mountains and perhaps British Columbia.

Rocky Mountains

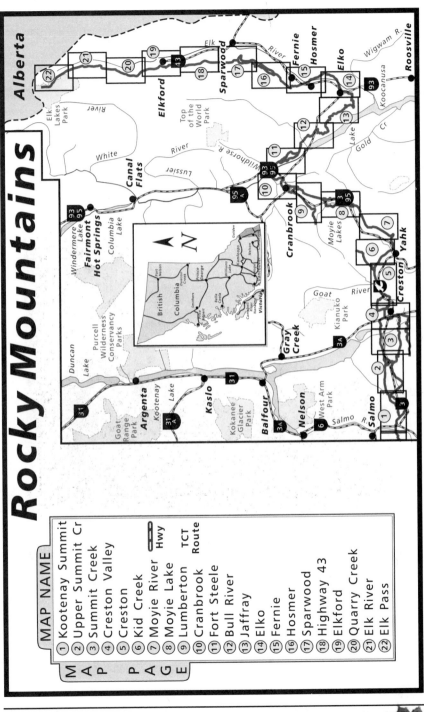

MAP NAME

M 1 Kootenay Summit
A 2 Upper Summit Cr
P 3 Summit Creek
  4 Creston Valley
  5 Creston
P 6 Kid Creek
A 7 Moyie River
G 8 Moyie Lake
E 9 Lumberton
  10 Cranbrook
  11 Fort Steele
  12 Bull River
  13 Jaffray
  14 Elko
  15 Fernie
  16 Hosmer
  17 Sparwood
  18 Highway 43
  19 Elkford
  20 Quarry Creek
  21 Elk River
  22 Elk Pass

Hwy
TCT Route

Rocky Mountains Map 1: Kootenay Summit

Rocky Mountains Section 1-2
~5 km
Kootenay Summit Trail

From the Kootenay Summit, the rough road continues east by winding down the mountainside back to Highway 3. The fabulous alpine scenery continues to dominate the landscape. To the east, there are fabulous views offered of the jagged mountain formation named 'The Crags', while to the north lie Wolf Peak and the Windy Ridge.

Mountain View   J. Marleau

In the future, plans may be developed to follow the Monk Creek Forest Service Road from the Kootenay Summit to the Creston Valley, enabling a bypass of a large portion of Highway 3 over the Kootenay Summit. To do this, travellers will have to backtrack on Highway 3 past the rest area and lake that forms the hub of Stagleap Provincial Park. Currently, the Monk Creek Forest Service Road is in good shape much of the way to the valley, except for a rough portion encountered on the eastern shoulder of Mount Huscroft about 2/3 of the way along the route. You would exit the mountains on the Dodge Creek Forest Service Road south of Creston.

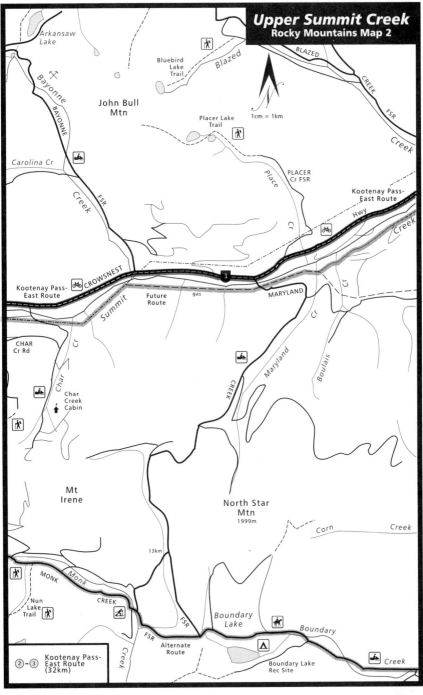

Upper Summit Creek
Rocky Mountains Map 2

1cm = 1km

N

Arkansaw Lake

Bluebird Lake Trail

Blazed

BLAZED

CREEK FSR

John Bull Mtn

Bayonne

BAYONNE

Placer Lake Trail

Placer

Cr

PLACER Cr FSR

Creek

Carolina Cr

Creek

FSR

Kootenay Pass-East Route

Hwy

Creek

Kootenay Pass-East Route

CROWSNEST

3

Summit

Cr

Future Route

gas

MARYLAND

Cr

Maryland

Cr

Boulais

CHAR Cr Rd

Char Cr

Char Creek Cabin

CREEK

Mt Irene

North Star Mtn
1999m

Corn   Creek

13km

MONK   Monk

CREEK

Nun Lake Trail

FSR

FSR

Boundary Lake

Boundary

Creek

Alternate Route

Boundary Lake Rec Site

② - ③ Kootenay Pass-East Route (32km)

Rocky Mountains Maps 2/3: Upper Summit Creek/Summit Creek

Rocky Mountains Section 2-3

32 km

Kootenay Pass East Route

The Trans Canada Trail begins its downward trek towards the Creston Valley by following the Crowsnest Highway on a steady descent into the valley. The highway parallels Summit Creek all the way to the valley and is actually quite a scenic trip. Along the way you will pass a number of forest access roads, which travel north into the high country above the highway, as well as the pretty Blazed Creek Rest Area. As the route settles into the valley, the grade decreases and the scenery changes. The large valley is dominated by the wetlands surrounding the Kootenay River where you can see the town of Creston nestled below Mount Thompson and the Iron Range. Just before the route meets the valley bottom, look for the Summit Creek Campsite off the north side of the highway.

In the future, a trail may be developed to follow the south side of Summit Creek. The off-highway alternative would be much more enjoyable, especially to hikers and equestrian riders. Unfortunately, the steep terrain next to the creek may prove to be too difficult to maintain such a trail.

If you are looking for outdoor accommodation in the Creston area, the Summit Creek Campsite is a good choice. It is a nice campground that offers plenty to see and do. Be sure to bring your bug repellent. There are a few more campgrounds found in and around the city of Creston.

For an added adventure along this stretch of the trail, it is quite easy to venture north along one of the forest service roads up into the sub-alpine environment. Along the Bayonne Creek Forest Service Road, you will find the beautiful Arkansaw Lake along with a rustic campsite area. The Placer Lake Trail and the Bluebird Lake Trail also can be accessed off of forest service roads and provide exciting hikes into the rugged sub-alpine environment. Please practice no-trace camping if you do visit Placer and Bluebird Lakes.

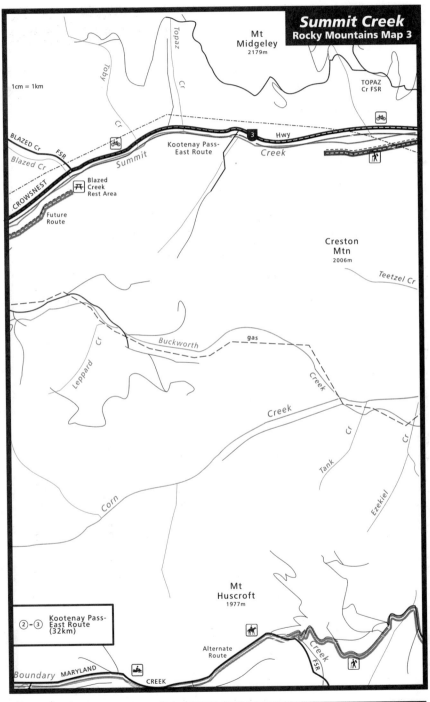

Summit Creek
Rocky Mountains Map 3

Mt Midgeley
2179m

TOPAZ Cr FSR

1cm = 1km

BLAZED Cr FSR

Blazed Cr

CROWSNEST

Summit

Kootenay Pass-East Route

3 Hwy

Creek

Blazed Creek Rest Area

Future Route

Creston Mtn
2006m

Teetzel Cr

Buckworth

gas

Creek

Leppard Cr

Creek

Tank Cr

Ezekiel Cr

Corn

Mt Huscroft
1977m

Kootenay Pass-East Route
②-③ (32km)

Alternate Route

Creek FSR

Boundary MARYLAND CREEK

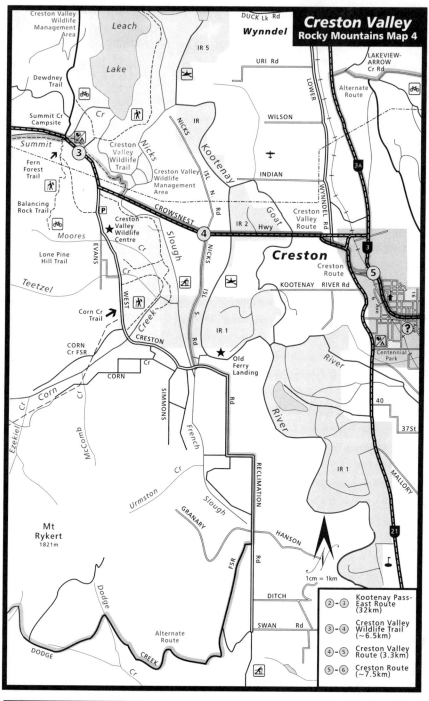

Creston Valley
Rocky Mountains Map 4

Wynndel

Creston

Region markers and labels:
- Creston Valley Wildlife Management Area
- Leach Lake
- Dewdney Trail
- Summit Cr Campsite
- Summit
- Fern Forest Trail
- Balancing Rock Trail
- Moores Cr
- Lone Pine Hill Trail
- Teetzel
- Corn Cr Trail
- CORN Cr FSR
- CORN Cr
- Ezekiel Cr
- Corn Cr
- McComb Cr
- SIMMONS Cr
- French Cr
- GRANARY Slough
- Urmston Cr
- Mt Rykert 1821m
- Dodge Cr
- DODGE CREEK
- Alternate Route
- RECLAMATION Rd
- HANSON Rd
- DITCH Rd
- SWAN Rd
- FSR
- Creston Valley Wildlife Centre
- Creston Valley Wildlife Trail
- Creston Valley Wildlife Management Area
- EVANS
- WEST CREEK
- CRESTON
- CROWSNEST Rd
- NICKS ISL N Rd
- NICKS ISL S Rd
- Nicks Cr
- Slough
- IR
- IR 2
- IR 1
- Old Ferry Landing
- KOOTENAY RIVER Rd
- Kootenay Rd
- Goat River
- Creston Route
- Creston Valley Route
- DUCK Lk Rd
- IR 5
- URI Rd
- WILSON
- INDIAN
- Kootenay River
- LOWER
- WYNNDEL Rd
- LAKEVIEW-ARROW Cr Rd
- Alternate Route
- Creston River
- Centennial Park
- KOOTENAY RIVER Rd
- 6 Ave
- 16
- 40
- 37 St
- MALLORY
- IR 1
- Goat Hwy

Highway markers: 3, 4, 3A, 3, 5, 6, 21

1cm = 1km

N

②-③	Kootenay Pass-East Route (32km)
③-④	Creston Valley Wildlife Trail (~6.5km)
④-⑤	Creston Valley Route (3.3km)
⑤-⑥	Creston Route (~7.5km)

Rocky Mountains Map 4: Creston Valley

Rocky Mountains Section 3-4

~6.5 km
Creston Valley Wildlife Trail

From Highway 3, the Trans Canada Trail turns north onto the Summit Creek Campsite Road. The trail travels through the campsite area and onto a maintained trail through the Creston Valley Wildlife Management Area. This section of trail is actually part of the historic Dewdney Trail.

Creston Valley   J. Marleau

The trail travels through the lowlands south of Leach Lake. The terrain is part of lush wetlands surrounding the Kootenay River and the trail can be muddy at times, especially in spring. The trail crosses Nicks Slough before reaching Nicks Island North Road. The Trans Canada Trail route follows Nicks Island North Road south all the way to the intersection with Highway 3. The route is a popular spot for bird lovers and is a relatively easy trek.

Waterfowl abound in the Creston Valley Wildlife Management Area. Bird lovers will find the route through the refuge a real treat as over two hundred nesting bird species can be viewed throughout the year. Along with the superb bird viewing opportunities at the wildlife area, there are also several kilometres of trails around Leach Lake and Duck Lake to the north. The trail systems are well used and are ideal for hiking or easy biking.

Rocky Mountains Section 4-5

3.3 km

Creston Valley Route

After the scenic route through the Creston Valley Wildlife Management Area, the Trans Canada Trail links back up with Highway 3. Along this portion of the route, the trail passes next to several farms. If you time it right, you can take advantage of the seasonal crops.

There is ample room for travellers along the side of the highway, although traffic can be busy at times. The highway traverses the flat valley bottom offering fine views of this agricultural area. Once you reach the junction area with Highway 21, follow the cut off to Highway 21 south. This is the beginning of the route into Creston.

L. Timbs

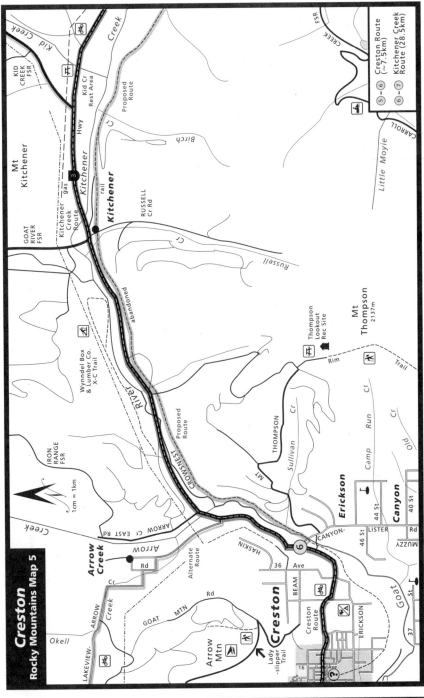

Creston
Rocky Mountains Map 5

Mt Kitchener

KID CREEK FSR

Kid Creek

Kid Cr Rest Area

Proposed Route

Birch Cr

CREEK FSR

Little Moyie

CARROLL

Creston Route (~7.5km) ⑤–⑥

Kitchener Creek Route (28.5km) ⑥–⑦

Kitchener Hwy

Kitchener gas

Kitchener Creek Route

rail

GOAT RIVER FSR

Kitchener

RUSSELL Cr Rd

Russell Cr

Thompson Lookout Rec Site

Mt Thompson 2137m

Rim

Trail

Wynndel Box & Lumber Co. X-C Trail

abandoned

River

Proposed Route

CROWSNEST

THOMPSON Cr

Sullivan Cr

Camp Run Cr

Old Cr

MT THOMPSON

Erickson

Canyon

44 St

46 St

40 St

LISTER Rd

MUZZY

CANYON

IRON RANGE FSR

1cm = 1km

Creek

ARROW CR EAST RD

Arrow Creek Rd

Alternate Route

HASKIN

36 Ave

BEAM

Creston

Creston Route

ERICKSON

Goat St

GOAT MTN Rd

Arrow Mtn

Lady-slipper Trail

ARROW Creek Cr

LAKEVIEW

Okell

16

⑥

37

283

Rocky Mountains Map 5: Creston

Rocky Mountains Section 5-6
~7.5 km
Creston Route

The Trans Canada Trail veers south along Highway 21 for about a kilometre before reaching the hiway by-pass road. This road links back up with Highway 3 in the town of Creston. The route follows the highway through the heart of this peaceful valley town. The small downtown area includes a strip mall and several other retail shops that can help you stock up on supplies.

As you head east, the trail begins a marginal climb as it leaves town. There are several fruit stands in this rural area. The highway eventually veers north along the Goat River and begins it's slow climb out of the Creston Valley.

European settlement of the Creston area started in the late 1800's. By the early 1900's, Creston had grown to include a sawmill, a few marginal mining operations and promising agricultural prospects. With the construction of dikes along the Kootenay and Goat River systems, land was claimed from the normally flooded rivers creating a fertile base for agriculture. Today, the town is known best for its agriculture; however, forestry continues to employ many in the region.

An interesting side route is the trip up to the Mount Thompson Lookout. As the Trans Canada Trail route leaves town, look for Mount Thompson Road off the south side of the highway. The gravel road climbs to near the top of Mount Thompson at 2,137 m (7,011 ft). The view at the lookout is spectacular and you will be rewarded with a panoramic sight of the entire Creston Valley.

An alternate route around Creston is available by first following Highway 3A north at the junction of Highway 3 and Highway 21. Follow Plasco Road east to Lakeview-Arrow Road, which bypasses Creston and reconnects with Highway 3 east of the town. The route offers fantastic views of the valley as it climbs up the highway to Plasco Road. The rest of the trek is generally easy, traversing along semi-paved roads through rural areas back to the highway.

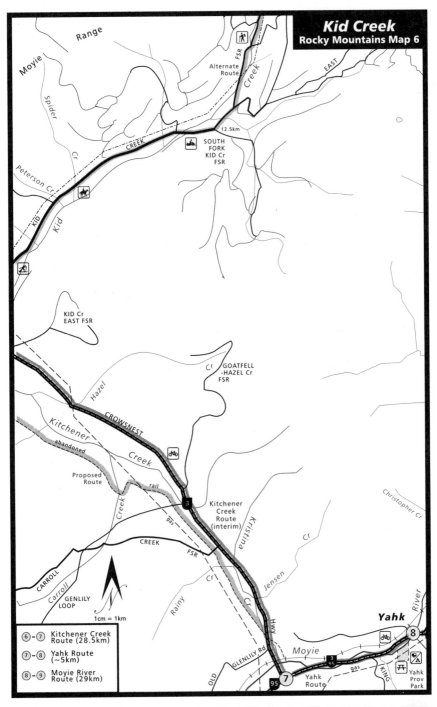

Kid Creek
Rocky Mountains Map 6

Range

Moyie

Range

Spider

Cr

Peterson Cr

KID

CREEK

Kid

Kid

Alternate Route

FSR

Creek

EAST

12.5km

SOUTH FORK KID Cr FSR

KID Cr EAST FSR

Cr

GOATFELL -HAZEL Cr FSR

Hazel

Kitchener

CROWSNEST

abandoned

Creek

Proposed Route

rail

CREEK

gas

Creek

FSR

CARROLL

Carroll

GENLILY LOOP

Kristina

Cr

Jensen

Cr

Christopher Cr

River

Yahk

Kitchener Creek Route (interim)

Cr

Rainy

Cr

Hwy

Moyie

GLENLILY Rd

OLD

Yahk Route

gas

KING

Yahk Prov Park

N

1cm = 1km

⑥-⑦ Kitchener Creek Route (28.5km)

⑦-⑧ Yahk Route (~5km)

⑧-⑨ Moyie River Route (29km)

Rocky Mountains Map 6: Kid Creek

Rocky Mountains Section 6-7

28.5 km

Kitchener Creek Route

The interim Trans Canada Trail follows Highway 3 east along the Goat River as the route heads towards Cranbrook. The highway can be busy at times, although there is usually ample shoulder available off the side of the highway for safe travel. Although this section of the Trans Canada Trail travels along the highway, the route is quite pleasant and very scenic. Although you will be gaining elevation for much of the route, the gentle grade makes for a great cycling route. Hikers, on the other hand, may not enjoy this section due strictly to the highway traffic.

Mountain Biking   *R. Mussio*

As the route follows Highway 3, it begins to follow Kitchener Creek south. Forested slopes and mountainous terrain dominate the landscape interrupted by the occasional creek or roadside pond. The route passes the Kid Creek Forest Service Road and Rest Area before the summit of this section of highway is reached near the Carroll Creek Forest Service Road. The highway drops back to the scenic Moyie River Valley and crosses the river just before reaching the junction with Highway 95.

In the future, there are plans in place to use the abandoned rail line to the south of the highway from Creston to Highway 95. This would make a beautiful off-highway alternative that all trail users could enjoy. A current alternative is to follow the Kid Creek Forest Service Road north off Highway 3. This road eventually leads up and over the pass to the Moyie River Forest Service Road. The route ends up back at Highway 3 south of Cranbrook. Currently, this is a rough wilderness route that is only feasible by looking at maps. The route has not yet been officially scouted as a viable alternative.

Rocky Mountains Section 7-8

~5 km

Yahk Route

At the junction with Highway 3 and Highway 95, the Trans Canada Trail heads east along Highway 3/95. The highway parallels the Moyie River almost all the way to Cranbrook and is quite scenic as it travels through the forested Moyie River valley. After about 5 km along the route, the trail passes the small settlement of Yahk. Just past Yahk, the highway veers northward as it proceeds up the valley.

Yahk offers a gas station and a small provincial park, which provides overnight tenting options from May 1 to September 15. The roadside park is found next to the rushing Moyie River and is a surprisingly peaceful place to stay. For a more wilderness camping option, look for the Yahk Meadow Road off the south side of the highway. About 4 km down the road, you will find the first of a series of Forest Service recreation campsites. Most of the sites are set just off the lovely Hawkins Creek and all make fantastic overnight spots or a base camp for further adventures into the surrounding area.

Yahk is another small East Kootenay town that can trace its roots to the mining industry. In the hills above the town you will find old mine sites and a few mining artifacts. Not much remains of the town today but if you look hard enough you may be able to dig up one of the popular shirts with the slogan, "I've been to Yakh and back!"

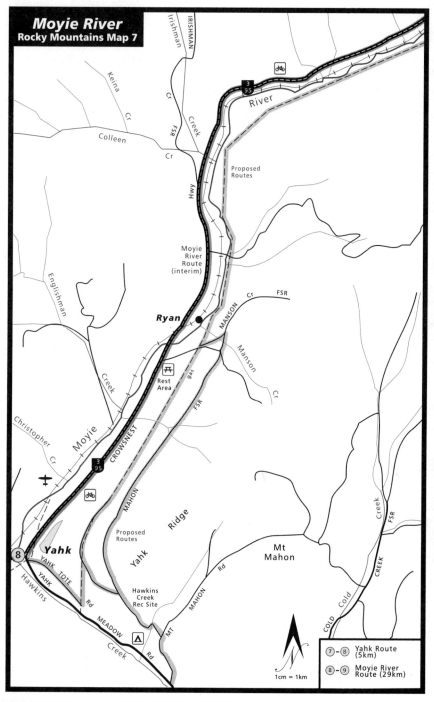

Moyie River
Rocky Mountains Map 7

Irishman

IRISHMAN

Keina Cr

Colleen Cr

FSR

Creek

Cr

3 95

River

Proposed Routes

Hwy

Moyie River Route (interim)

Ryan

MANSON Cr

FSR

Manson Cr

Rest Area

Englishman

FSR

Creek

Christopher Cr

Moyie

CROWSNEST

3 95

MAHON

Yahk Ridge

Proposed Routes

Mt Mahon

MANSON Cr

Cold Creek

FSR

Yahk

8

YAHK TOTE Rd

YAHK

Hawkins

MEADOW

Creek Rd

Hawkins Creek Rec Site

MT MAHON Rd

COLD CREEK

Cold

N

1cm = 1km

⑦ - ⑧ Yahk Route (5km)

⑧ - ⑨ Moyie River Route (29km)

288

Rocky Mountains Map 7: Moyie River

Rocky Mountains Section 8-9

29 km
Moyie River Route

The scenic valley dominates the scenery, as the route continues to follow the highway north to Moyie Lake. Despite the traffic, this interim route is quite pleasant. There is a small rest area before the highway crosses the river. From this point to the lake the river is a meandering stream that teams with wildlife. Beavers, waterfowl, osprey and many other creatures can be seen along the river. If you are fortunate, you may even spot a passing train.

West on Moyie River   A. Skucas

Currently, there are plans in place to create an off-highway trail option from Yahk to the Hidden Valley Road. The routes are shown on our maps but may take some time before they are completed. Before planning your trip, be sure to visit www.backroadmapbooks.com or www.trailsbc.ca for updates.

The town of Moyie Lake hosts a small gas station and a popular roadside pub. The town was once a booming mining community that had a few notorious saloons. In the early 20th century the St. Eugene Mine was Canada's largest lead silver mine. It employed over 400 people in it's heyday. It reopened briefly in the 1930's but has been closed ever since. Today, tourism is the mainstay of the economy with the popular recreational lake being the main attraction.

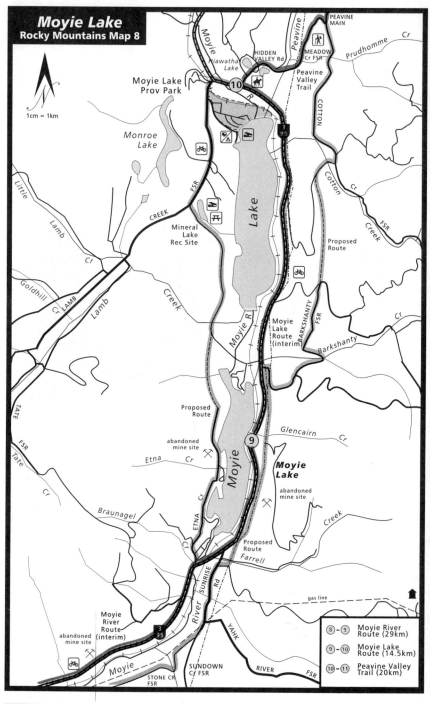

Moyie Lake
Rocky Mountains Map 8

1cm = 1km

Moyie Lake
Prov Park

Monroe
Lake

Mineral
Lake
Rec Site

Lake

HIDDEN
VALLEY Rd

Hiawatha
Lake

10

95

Little
Lamb

Cr

Goldhill
Cr

LAMB

CREEK

FSR

Lamb

Creek

TATE

Tate

FSR

Cr

Braunagel

Moyie R

Moyie

Proposed
Route

abandoned
mine site

Etna   Cr

ETNA Cr

PEAVINE
MAIN

MEADOW
Cr FSR

Peavine
Valley
Trail

Prudhomme   Cr

COTTON

Cotton

Cr

FSR

Cotton
Creek

Proposed
Route

Moyie
Lake
Route
(interim)

BARKSHANTY

FSR

Barkshanty

Cr

Barkshanty

9

Glencairn   Cr

Moyie
Lake

abandoned
mine site

Creek

Moyie
River
Route
(interim)

abandoned
mine site

3
95

River

SUNRISE

Rd

YAHK

Proposed
Route
Farrell

gas line

RIVER

FSR

Moyie

SUNDOWN
Cj FSR

STONE CR
FSR

⑧-⑨	Moyie River Route (29km)
⑨-⑩	Moyie Lake Route (14.5km)
⑩-⑪	Peavine Valley Trail (20km)

Rocky Mountains Map 8: Moyie Lake

Rocky Mountains Section 9-10

14.5 km
Moyie Lake Route

If you blink you might miss the town of Moyie Lake. Continue past the tailing piles from past lead-silver mining operations and enjoy the views of the lake. The highway skirts along the cliff side above the picturesque interior lake providing superb views along the way.

Above Moyie Lake   A. Skucas

The interim Trans Canada Trail route continues along the east side of the lake, eventually meeting the Hidden Valley Road. Moyie Lake is a large interior lake that is a popular outdoor recreation spot during the summer. The lake is home to a number of cabins as well as a popular provincial park.

 Moyie Lake Provincial Park is a full service park offering basic camping amenities such as running water, flush toilets and showers. The park is open from April through October and is busiest during the summer when people flock to the popular beach area. If you plan to stay at the park, it is recommended to make reservations in advance. Call Discover Camping at 1-800-689-9025.

Moyie Lake is actually made up of two separate water bodies. The lower lake is somewhat smaller at 316 ha in size while the upper lake is 583 ha. Both lakes host a variety of recreational opportunities from fantastic fishing to every conceivable water sport. Resorts, private cabins and campgrounds line the lake.

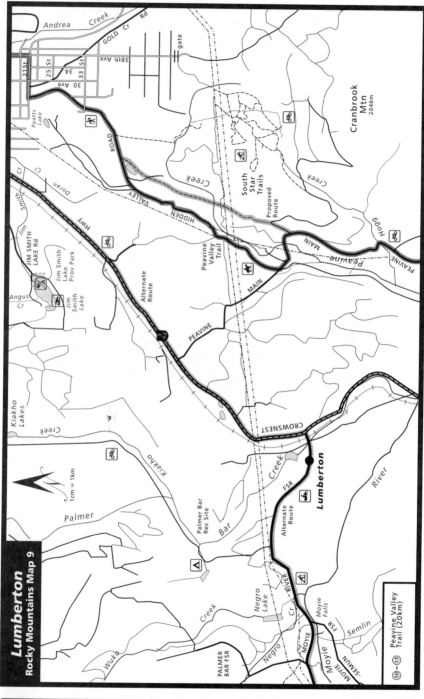

Lumberton
Rocky Mountains Map 9

1cm = 1km

Peavine Valley Trail (20km)

Rocky Mountains Map 9: Lumberton

Rocky Mountains Section 10-11

20 km
Peavine Valley Route

The Trans Canada Trail finally begins to follow an off-highway section as it follows the Hidden Valley Road off Highway 3/95. The Peavine Valley Route follows close to the original Dewdney Trail although remnants of the historical trail are all but gone. The gentle grade up the valley only ascends about 90 m (300 feet) in elevation.

Peavine Valley   A. Skucas

Railway surveyors originally planned to route the CP Crowsnest Railway through the Peavine Valley in the 1890's but opted for the route to the west along the Moyie Valley instead. At the meadows at the south end of the route a booming railway camp came into existence for a brief time during railway construction. It was named Sifton City after the then Minister of the Interior, Clifford Sifton.

Beginning along the Hidden Valley Road, this section of the route follows various logging roads as it gains elevation in a mostly forested setting. After crossing over the Peavine Creek the route then travels north along the Meadow Creek Forest Service Road. A moderate 1 km climb leads to Peavine Main, another forestry road. Essentially, the Hidden Valley Road travels along the west side of Peavine Creek and the Peavine Main Road follows the east side of the creek. The route travels north before veering west to cross the creek again.

Shortly after the creek crossing look for the Hidden Valley Road again off the northeast side of the road. Once on the Hidden Valley Road, the road will stop climbing and will start to descend gently towards the city. In the rural Gold Creek area, to the south of the city of Cranbrook, the Trans Canada Trail meets up with 21st Street. The route follows 21st Street east to 38th Avenue, where the route then heads north into Idlewild Park.

 An easy alternative to Cranbrook from Moyie Lake is to simply follow highway 3/95 north all the way to the city. The route is easy, although not as gratifying, due to the significant traffic flow that you are sure to experience along the way. One advantage of this route; however, is that you will pass by the Elizabeth Lake Bird Sanctuary. Found just before you enter the city, the pretty sanctuary lies off the east side of the highway and is home to hundreds of various bird species, including the nesting site to many provincially significant waterfowl.

A good nearby camping option around Cranbrook is Jim Smith Lake Park. Just before you enter Cranbrook, the park is found via Jim Smith Lake Road off the west side of Highway 3/95. The park is open from May 1 to the end of October and offers camping along with running water and a popular beach area.

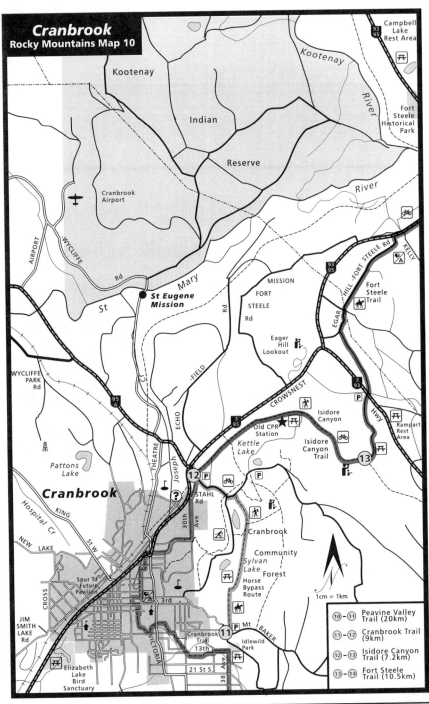

Cranbrook
Rocky Mountains Map 10

Kootenay

Indian

Reserve

Kootenay

River

River

Campbell
Lake
Rest Area

Fort
Steele
Historical
Park

Cranbrook
Airport

AIRPORT

WYCLIFFE

Rd

St

Mary

**St Eugene
Mission**

MISSION

FORT

STEELE

Rd

FIELD

Rd

Eager
Hill
Lookout

Fort
Steele
Trail

EGAR HILL–FORT STEELE Rd

KELLY

93
95

93
93

Fort
Steele
Trail

CROWSNEST

Old CPR
Station

Isidore
Canyon

Rampart
Rest
Area

WYCLIFFE
PARK Rd

49
A

THEATRE

Joseph

ECHO

3
95

*Kettle
Lake*

Isidore
Canyon Trail

HWY

13

Pattons
Lake

Cranbrook

Hospital Cr

KING

St W

NEW   LAKE

CROSS

JIM
SMITH
LAKE Rd

Spur To
Future
Pavilion

30th   Ave

12   P

?

STAHL
Rd

3rd

P

Cranbrook
Community
*Sylvan
Lake*   Forest
Horse
Bypass
Route

VICTORIA

Cranbrook
Trail
13th

21 St S.

38   Ave.

11

P

Mt   BAKER

Idlewild
Park

Elizabeth
Lake
Bird
Sanctuary

1cm = 1km

N

⑩–⑪	Peavine Valley Trail (20km)	
⑪–⑫	Cranbrook Trail (9km)	
⑫–⑬	Isidore Canyon Trail (7.2km)	
⑬–⑭	Fort Steele Trail (10.5km)	

Rocky Mountains Map 10: Cranbrook

Rocky Mountains Section 11-12

9 km
Cranbrook Trail

The route from Idlewild Park is quite varied as it travels along a newly established paved trail all the way to 8th Street North. From the end of the path, city roads avoid the highway. The dynamic trail should be completed and signed by the fall of 2001.

Cranbrook Trail

A. Skucas

From the park proceed north past 9th Street South, where the trail traverses northwest to 15th Avenue and 3rd Street South. Pass by the municipal campground and follow the paved path to it's end at 8th Street North.

From here the route intercepts 10th Street North and continues east to Kootenay Avenue. Kootenay veers northeast to 30th Avenue, where the route continues

The route passes by the centre of the City of Cranbook, but still provides easy access to retail stores for supplies or repairs. If desired, there is plenty of first class accommodations found next to the main strip (Highway 3). The Trans Canada Trail also passes by the Cranbrook Muncipal Campground, where tenters are always welcome.

north towards Highway 3. A right onto Stahl Avenue helps avoid the busy highway. A short 300 m jaunt brings you to the Isidore Canyon Trailhead.

In the late 1800's, the construction of the CPR railway through the area was vital to the establishment of the community of Cranbrook. Cranbrook was a major divisional point along the railway with rail lines stretching south towards the American border. Shortly after the completion of the railway, Cranbrook was established in 1905. The region quickly grew other economic interests, including a diverse natural resources industry based on mining and later forestry operations. Today, Cranbrook can add another growing natural resource industry to its forte, outdoor recreation. Nestled between the Purcell Mountains to the west and the Rocky Mountains to the east, Cranbrook is poised to become a major outdoor recreation centre.

Cranbrook Horseback alternate

Since horses are not permitted within the city trail system of Cranbrook, Trails BC has derived an alternate route around the city. The route begins at the south entrance to Idlewild Park at 13th Street South. Follow 13th Street east for approximately 400 m to Mount Baker Road. The trail follows Mount Baker Road north until the road veers west. At this point, there is a small parking area for horse trailers and vehicles, which borders the Cranbrook Community Forest. From the parking area, several interconnected trails can be followed north eventually meeting the gravel forest access road about 4 km later. A safe bet would be to follow the trail along the west side of the boundary fence for the entire length. Once you reach the gravel road, follow the road west down a slope to the valley floor and the parking area for the Isidore Canyon Trail.

Rocky Mountains Section 12-13

7.2 km
Isidore Canyon Trail

From the Cranbrook Visitor Centre, on Highway 3/95, you can easily link up with the Isidore Canyon Trail. Follow the highway north for a few hundred metres and take the last road east before the Highway 3/ Highway 95A junc

Rock Ovens A. Ridge

tion (the overpass). Shortly down this road and past Sandor Rental, you will find the Isidore Canyon Trailhead and parking area.

> *Several points of interest are found on the Isidore Canyon Trail. At the 4 km marker, there are the remains of an old CPR Station as well as the first picnic site. Other picnic tables are found at 7 km and 9 km markers where one gets a panoramic view of the Rocky Mountains. In addition to the scenic canyonn, one-hundred-year-old rock ovens, used for baking bread during the railway construction, are found at the 6 km mark.*

The Trans Canada Trail/Isidore Canyon Trail is a century old CPR railbed that was abandoned during the 1970's. The trail is well signed and easy to follow as it travels east along the old railbed. At about the 8 km marker along the route, the Trans Canada Trail heads north off the railbed marking the beginning of the route to the historic site of Fort Steele.

Rocky Mountains Section 13-14

10.5 km

Fort Steele Trail

From the Isidore Canyon Trail, the Trans Canada Trail winds northward through forest and grasslands with breathtaking views of the Steeples Range, part of the Rocky Mountains to the east. The trail is well signed and easy to follow. A good access point to this section is found at the rest area on Highway 3/93. From the rest area, where washrooms and picnic tables are found, it is a short 1 km jog north to the Trans Canada Trail.

Table With the View   A. Ridge

After crossing Highway 3, the trail continues north through a mix of forest cover and fields to the junction with the old paved Eager Hill –Fort Steele Road. On this section of trail you get a view of the highest mountain in the region, Mount Fisher. At 2,846 m (9,337 ft) the peak is quite a sight.

Follow the road for about 4 km until it joins Highway 93/95 just 500 metres west of the Kootenay River Bridge at Fort Steele. From here cyclists and hikers can follow the highway across the Kootenay River. The Historical Provincial Heritage Town of Fort Steele is located on the east end of the bridge.

The first humans to inhabit the Fort Steele area were the Kootenay (Ktunaxa) natives, whose presence can be dated back to the postglacial period. European settlers arrived in significant numbers in the area by the 1860's when gold was discovered in the nearby Wildhorse Creek. The influx of Europeans to the area strained what was until then good relations between the natives and European settlers. The Mounted Police were assigned to the area to retain peace in the region guided by their superintendent Samuel B. Steele, who the fort named after. Today, the old town site has been preserved and created into a historic park for visitors to enjoy.

Besides visiting Fort Steele, a few short side trips are suggested. You can travel the last few kilometres of the Dewdney Trail to the original diggings of the Wild Horse Gold Rush and the former site of the town of Fisherville. Here you can view the Chinese Graveyard, the few remaining buildings and the large water cannons used in last century for mining gold. Another option is to hike the relatively easy Lakit Mountain Trail. This hike offers a great view with a small climb. Finally, hikers looking for a more rugged mountain experience, can try a day hike up to the summit of Fisher Peak. Directions for each of the above can be obtained at the Information Centre in Fort Steele.

A variety of accommodation is found around Fort Steele. The options include two campgrounds, one Bed & Breakfast and a Dude Guest Ranch.

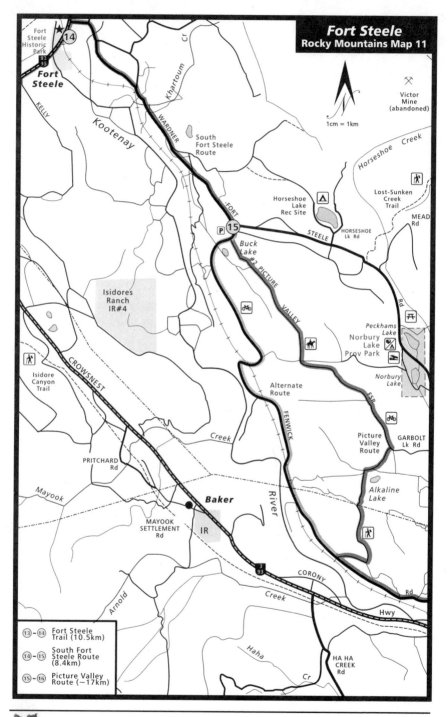

Fort Steele
Rocky Mountains Map 11

1cm = 1km

Fort Steele Historic Park

Fort Steele

Victor Mine (abandoned)

Horseshoe Creek

Kootenay

Khartoum Cr

WARDNER

South Fort Steele Route

Horseshoe Lake Rec Site

Lost-Sunken Creek Trail

MEAD Rd

KELLY

FORT — STEELE

HORSESHOE Lk Rd

Buck Lake

PICTURE VALLEY

Isidores Ranch IR#4

Peckhams Lake

Norbury Lake Prov Park

Norbury Lake

Rd

Isidore Canyon Trail

CROWSNEST

Alternate Route

FENWICK

FSR

Creek

Picture Valley Route

GARBOLT Lk Rd

PRITCHARD Rd

Mayook

Baker

MAYOOK SETTLEMENT Rd

IR

River

Alkaline Lake

Arnold

3 93

CORONY

Creek

Hwy

Rd

Haha Cr

HA HA CREEK Rd

(13)-(14) Fort Steele Trail (10.5km)

(14)-(15) South Fort Steele Route (8.4km)

(15)-(16) Picture Valley Route (~17km)

Rocky Mountains Map 11: Fort Steele

Rocky Mountains Section 14-15

8.4 km

Fort Steele South Route

The Trans Canada Trail begins another scenic stretch as it turns southeast to follow the Wardner-Fort Steele Road. The rough paved road is marked by the general store perched on the corner of Highway 3. Be sure to stock up on supplies if need be, as the next supply stop is a significant distance away.

The route crossed Wild Horse Creek and follows the road as it winds its way through the Kootenay River Valley. To the east of the road, you will be presented with several fantastic views of the Rocky Mountains, while to the west the majestic Kootenay River winds its way southward. The terrain in this valley is reminiscent of the Okanagan as stands of second growth coniferous trees can be found between cleared ranch lands. Once at Fenwick the Trans Canada Trail continues its journey southward.

Forst Steele   J. Marleau

If you remain on the Wardner-Fort Steele Road, you will pass near the Horseshoe Lake Forest Recreation site and through Norbury Lake Provincial Park. The recreation site offers basic campsites along the shore of the small Horseshoe Lake, while the tranquil Norbury Lake Provincial Park offers a nice picnic area and a separate campsite. The recreation site can be utilized year round but the provincial park campground is only open from May 15 to the Labour Day long weekend in September.

Rocky Mountains Section 15-16

~17 km

Picture Valley Route

Off Fenwick Road, there are a couple different options to choose from. The preferred route follows # 2 Picture Valley Forest Service Road. The Picture Valley Road runs between Fenwick Road to the west and the Wardner-Fort Steele Road to the east. This route follows the original line of the Southern Kootenay Railway built in 1901.

To find the forest road, watch for the big yellow sign near the gravel pit on Fenwick Road about 100 m from the junction with the paved Wardner-Fort Steele Road. The scenic route winds through wooded country and rejoins Fenwick Road about 5 km from the fish hatchery.

If you choose to remain on Fenwick Road, expect a little more traffic. The 16.3 km route continues to offer some stunning views of the mountains to the east and the Kootenay River to the west. If you are lucky, you may be able to spot a mule deer along the route as the species is quite abundant in this region.

The road starts off as a gravel surface road. You will pass Buck Lake, several nice viewpoints of the Kootenay River and some active ranching areas. Be sure to be aware of cattle that can venture onto the route. The road becomes paved just before the route passes the trout hatchery and meets the junction with the Wardner-Fort Steele Road. There is not much vehicular traffic to contend with on this section of the Trans Canada Trail.

The Kootenay Trout Hatchery is found about a kilometre north of Bull River just off the Wardner-Fort Steele Road. The hatchery raises young trout for transplant into lakes throughout the Kootenays. Here you can see fish eggs hatching and various sizes of trout waiting to be sent to lakes, helping make the region one of the finest trout fishing spots in the country. The hatchery also serves as a trailhead for the Trans Canada Trail.

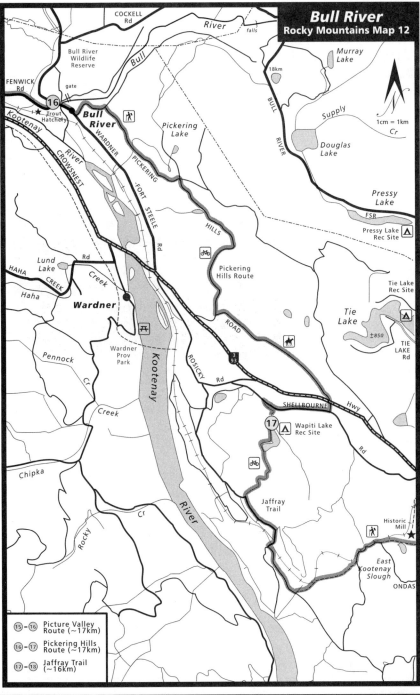

Bull River
Rocky Mountains Map 12

COCKELL Rd

River

falls

Bull River Wildlife Reserve

Bull

18km

Murray Lake

FENWICK Rd

gate

16

BULL RIVER

Supply Cr

Trout Hatchery

Bull River

Pickering Lake

Douglas Lake

1cm = 1km

Kootenay

WARDNER

PICKERING

Pickering

River

CROWSNEST

FORT STEELE

Pressy Lake

FSR

Pressy Lake Rec Site

Rd

Lund Lake

Rd

HILLS

HAHA

CREEK

Creek

Pickering Hills Route

Tie Lake Rec Site

Haha

Wardner

Tie Lake

±850

Pennock

Wardner Prov Park

Kootenay

ROAD

TIE LAKE Rd

Cr

ROSICKY Rd

3 93

Creek

SHELLBOURNE

Hwy

Rd

Chipka

17

Wapiti Lake Rec Site

Cr

Jaffray Trail

Historic Mill

Rocky

River

East Kootenay Slough

ONDAS

15 – 16 Picture Valley Route (~17km)

16 – 17 Pickering Hills Route (~17km)

17 – 18 Jaffray Trail (~16km)

303

Rocky Mountains Map 12: Bull River

Rocky Mountains Section 16-17
9 km
Pickering Hills Route

The trail continues east by following the Wardner-Fort Steele Road past the small settlement of Bull River. Here travellers will find a charming little pub, which has long been a favourite of people exploring this popular recreational area.

Shortly past Bull River, the Trans Canada Trail meets the Pickering Hills Road. There is a new sign for the Mill Pond Ranch and an old sign marking the road at this junction. The Pickering Hills Road leads up to a confusing network of forestry roads. For this reason and the fact the route dissects the

Hay Field   *J. Klein*

Pickering Hills Wildlife Sanctuary, it is important to stay on the main trail and watch for trail signs and markers. Regardless, this old road network makes an ideal route for all Trans Canada Trail travellers.

The route continues east up and over an undulating path through generally loose forest cover eventually meeting Highway 3/93. Cross the highway to the short path leading to Shellbourne Road. Shellbourne Road is a gravel road that somewhat parallels the highway and leads 4 km east to the village of Jaffray. Trans Canada Trail travellers are encouraged to follow the road west for about 1 km to the Wapiti Lake Forest Service Road. The beautiful valley lake is found about 500 m further south.

For campers, there are a number of easily accessible options through this region. The most notable is the Wapiti Lake Forest Recreation Site. The lake offers rustic campsites next to a picturesque lake. Another camping alternative is Tie Lake. It is found north of Jaffray on the Tie Lake Road. The lake offers several fantastic lakeside campsites in a relaxing atmosphere.

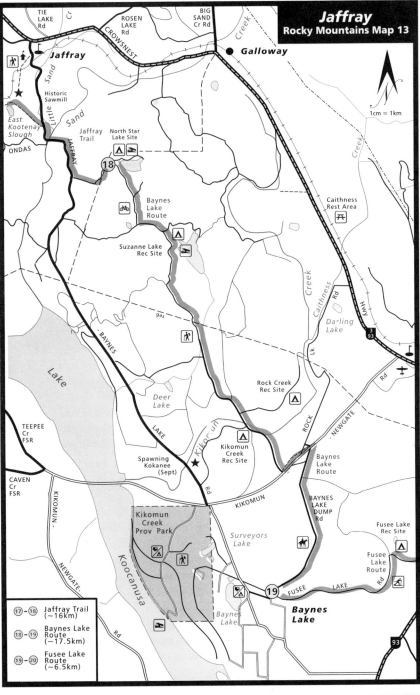

Jaffray
Rocky Mountains Map 13

N

1cm = 1km

TIE LAKE Rd

Cr

ROSEN LAKE Rd

BIG SAND Cr Rd

CROWSNEST

Creek

Galloway

Jaffray

Historic Sawmill

Little Sand

Sand

East Kootenay Slough

ONDAS

JAFFRAY

Jaffray Trail

North Star Lake Site

18

Baynes Lake Route

Suzanne Lake Rec Site

Caithness Rest Area

Creek

gas

BAYNES

Caithness

Creek

Darling Lake

Caithness Rd

Hwy

3 93

Lk

Rock Creek Rec Site

Lake

Deer Lake

LAKE

Kikomun Rd

Spawning Kokanee (Sept)

Kikomun Creek Rec Site

ROCK

NEWGATE

Baynes Lake Route

Rd

TEEPEE Cr FSR

CAVEN Cr FSR

KIKOMUN - NEWGATE

Koocanusa

Kikomun Creek Prov Park

KIKOMUN

BAYNES LAKE DUMP Rd

Surveyors Lake

Fusee Lake Rec Site

Fusee Lake Route

Rd

19

FUSEE LAKE

Baynes Lake

Baynes Lake

Rd

93

17 - 18 Jaffray Trail (~16km)

18 - 19 Baynes Lake Route (~17.5km)

19 - 20 Fusee Lake Route (~6.5km)

Rocky Mountains Map 13: Jaffray

Rocky Mountains Section 17-18
4 km
Jaffray Trail

The Trans Canada Trail continues to explore an area rich in history. Follow the trail markers, which lead along the forest roads south of Wapiti Lake. You will cross the Canadian Pacific Railway (CPR) tracks before reaching the East Kootenay Slough. The concrete remains of a historic sawmill, which was once the largest in the area, can still be seen. From the slough, the Trans Canada Trail winds southeast to the junction with

The Dewdney Trail   *A. Ridge*

the paved Jaffray-Baynes Lake Road at Ondas Road.

The Trans Canada Trail is easily reached from Jaffray. An access trail is found by crossing the railway tracks at the local school. Follow the road along the tracks a short distance until it veers into the countryside and reaches the East Kootenay Slough less that 1 km away.

Jaffray has a long tradition as a forestry-based community. A number of mills began popping up in the area in the late 1800's, creating an economic base for the growth of the community. However, in the early 1900's many of these mills closed as the distances the logs had to be transported made it uneconomical to run the mills. Today, the community is quite small, relying on forestry and the growing tourism industry.

A few kilometres south of Ondas Road, the Jaffray-Baynes Lake Road intersects with the North Star Lake Forest Service Road. The forest access road is a rougher dirt road that quickly takes the traveller into a more remote setting from the main road. The open countryside can get quite hot during the summer. Not far down the forest access road, the trail meets North Star Lake.

> North Star Lake is a small lake that offers a great spot for overnight camping. The lake is home to a forest recreation site, complete with picnic tables and a boat access area. The site is quite popular during the summer months with anglers.

Rocky Mountains Section 18-19

~ 17.5 km

Baynes Lake Route

From North Star Lake, the Trans Canada Trail heads south along the edge of the lake on the forestry road. The road is relatively flat and easy to follow. You will traverse past another great recreation lake, Suzanne Lake before passing over a small creek and later Kikomun Creek before reaching the paved Kikomun-Newgate Road.

> During September and early October, the Kikomun Creek becomes alive with spawning kokanee. Kokanee are landlocked sockeye salmon and literally fill the creek during spawning season as they complete their life cycle. The red coloured spawning salmon are quite an amazing site to see.

At the Kikomun-Newgate Road, follow the trail to the northeast that parallels the fence line along the Kikomun-Newgate Road. This fence line turns into an abandoned railbed of the historic Great Northern Railway. Follow the old railway for less than a kilometre to the junction with the Baynes Lake Dump Road. Despite the unappealing name, the route is quite enjoyable as you traverse the open flat lands east of Lake Koocanusa. The trail then travels south along the Baynes Lake Dump Road, eventually curving west into the small settlement of Baynes Lake.

> Camping enthusiasts will be delighted with this stretch of the trail, as there are several fantastic camping locations found in the Baynes Lake area. The most popular camping area is probably Kikomun Creek Provincial Park, which lies along the eastern shore of Lake Koocanusa. The park offers full service campsites including flush toilets, picnic tables and showers. The park is also home to a number of day-use trail systems that are ideal for exploring. The park can be found by heading west from Baynes Lake to the Jaffray-Baynes Lake Road and then by travelling north to the Kikomun-Newgate Road. There are signs at the junction that direct you to the park entrance. This park is open from the beginning of May to the end of October and can be busy during the summer months. Call 1-800-689-9025 for park reservations.

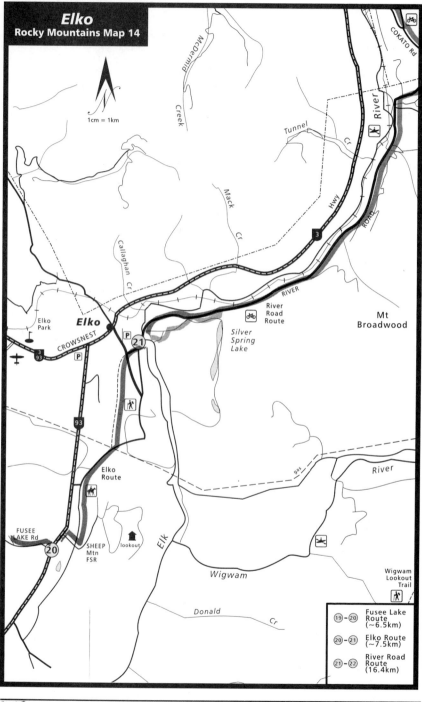

Elko
Rocky Mountains Map 14

1cm = 1km

McDermid Creek

Tunnel Cr

River

COKATO Rd

Hwy

3

ROAD

RIVER

River Road Route

Mt Broadwood

Mack Cr

Callaghan Cr

Elko Park

Elko

CROWSNEST

3 93

P

P 21

Silver Spring Lake

93

Elko Route

FUSEE LAKE Rd

20

SHEEP Mtn FSR

lookout

Elk

Wigwam

Donald Cr

gas

River

Wigwam Lookout Trail

19–20 Fusee Lake Route (~6.5km)

20–21 Elko Route (~7.5km)

21–22 River Road Route (16.4km)

Rocky Mountains Map 14: Elko

Rocky Mountains Section 19-20

?? km

Fusee Lake Route

East of the settlement of Baynes Lake, travellers will find a horse corral on the Palmer Ranch property. If this is your mode of travel, you may want to stop here. The route follows the Fusee Lake Road. The dirt road can be a little rough in sections, although makes for an easy hike or bike. The road veers north for about 1 km before heading east again and soon passes Fusee Lake. Fusee Lake is a very small lake that is also home to a small Forest Recreation campsite.

Smelling the Flowers   *J. Klein*

East past the lake, the Trans Canada Trail eventually meets up with Highway 93 south of the town of Elko. Most of this section travels through the exposed flat lands. Excellent views of the Rocky Mountains to the east are offered on occasion.

Baynes Lake and the surrounding community are named after an original landowner in the area. When the railway came through the area they purchased a large tract of his land and soon brought extensive settlement around the area. At one time, there were a number of established operations in the community, including a sawmill, a number of retail operations, two schools, a hotel and even a small hospital. With the removal of the railway tracks in early 1909, the growth of the community slowed. When the mill closed in 1939, large emigration from the community began. Today, Baynes Lake is a quiet community that is one of the focal points for visitors to the area.

Rocky Mountains Section 20-21

~7.5 km
Elko Route

The Trans Canada Trail route continues on the east side of the highway and follows the Sheep Mountain Forest Service Road north to Elko. The road is flat and parallels both Highway 93 and the abandoned railbed of the historic U.S. Great Northern Railway. It was used to haul coal from the Elk Valley to feed the rising industrial economy of the Pacific northwest of the United States.

Most of this section travels through the exposed flat lands. The route travels north past the sensitive Sheep Mountain Wildlife Sanctuary eventually crossing the gravel log haul road a few kilometres south of Elko. Excellent views of the Rocky Mountains to the east are offered on occasion.

The route follows the swath below the powerline and through a portion of the Mt. Broadwood-Wigwam River Wildlife Conservation Area before meeting up with River Road south of Elko.

Both the Wildlife Sanctuary and Conservation Area offer a unique opportunity to view wildlife. Sheep can often be spotted on the rocky bluffs of Sheep Mountain. Look for the small white figurines, especially around dawn or dusk.

At the turn of the century, the Canadian National and Kootenay Central Railways planned Elko to be a major traffic junction for rail traffic in the valley. With the construction of the CN Railway, Elko quickly began to fulfil its promise, eventually supporting up to two churches, five hotels and several other retail operations. The promise of the town soon turned dismal as several disastrous fires in the late 1920's and 1930's reduced much of the town to a memory.

Today, Elko is a small stop along the Trans Canada Trail offering a convenience store providing basic supplies such as water and various snack items. The town is home to one of the region's largest sawmill operations owned by Tembec Industries. It is also site of a small dam on the Elk River that supplies electrical power into the provincial power grid. River waters that parallel the Trans Canada Trail upstream are placid and navigable while waters downstream are dangerous white water rapids that requires expert skill to navigate.

Rocky Mountains Section 21-22

16.4 km
River Road Route

The Trans Canada Trail heads eastward towards the mountain town of Fernie by first following River Road. River Road is found just to the south of the settlement of Elko and is easily accessed by the hydro dam road that crosses the Elk River. River Road is a main forestry access road and can be busy with logging traffic at times. A large loaded truck can be quite an imposing site barrelling down this dusty gravel road. An off-road alternative is currently being constructed next to River Road.

About half way along this stretch of the trail, you will be rewarded with several superb sights of the valley and the surrounding mountainsides. At one point along this section you can actually look across the river to the highway and one of the tunnels through the mountain. It was quite an engineering feat to cut the highway between the cliffs and the Elk River.

The route veers east somewhat and meets a junction with the Morrisey Forest Service Road. About 1.5 km from the Morrisey Forest Service Road junction, you travel a very short section of the Lodgepole Forest Service Road before the route meets up with the Cokato Road. Be sure not to get confused and stay on River Road.

Shortly there after you will see the turn-off to the highway at the Morrissey-Cokato Road junction. A nice riverside picnic area is found here if you cross the small bridge over the Elk River. If you wish to continue on the Trans Canada Trail route stay on Cokato Road.

A trail off River Road is currently under construction. If you are planning on visiting this section of the Trans Canada Trail, portions of the trail may be passable. Keep your eyes open for signs. In the meantime, horseback riding is not recommended.

Named after early explorer Jim Morrissey, the remains of the original townsite are found a short distance down Morrissey Road from the junction with Lodgepole Road. This short spur goes past a long line of historic brick coke ovens active when the coal mines operated at Morrissey during the early 1900's. Morrissey was also site of a World War I detention camp for people of Austrian and German descent. These miners were detained while the war raged in Europe. After being released many of these people returned to work in the nearby mines.

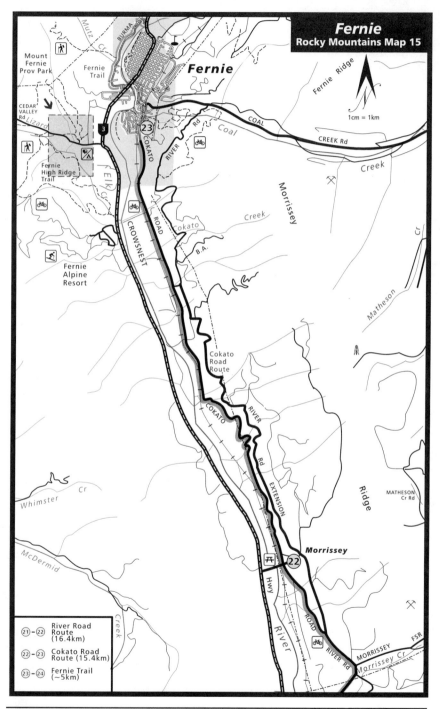

Fernie
Rocky Mountains Map 15

1cm = 1km

Mount
Fernie
Prov Park

Fernie
Trail

Fernie
Ridge

CEDAR
VALLEY
Rd

Fernie

Fernie
High Ridge
Trail

COAL
CREEK Rd

Coal
Creek

Fernie
Alpine
Resort

Morrissey
Creek

CROWSNEST ROAD

Cokato

B.A.

Matheson

Cokato
Road
Route

COKATO RIVER Rd

Whimster
Cr

McDermid

Ridge

MATHESON
Cr Rd

HWY EXTENSION

Morrissey

Creek

MORRISSEY
ROAD RIVER Rd

Morrissey Cr

FSR

Hwy
River

21 – 22	River Road Route (16.4km)
22 – 23	Cokato Road Route (15.4km)
23 – 24	Fernie Trail (~5km)

Rocky Mountains Map 15: Fernie

Rocky Mountains Section 22-23

15.4 km

Cokato Road Route

The interim Trans Canada Trail route follows Cokato Road to begin the last leg of the journey to the town of Fernie. The route follows this gravel road through a mainly treed area next to the Elk River. There are ample areas where a clear view of the river can be found. The traffic may deter hikers and horseback riders but it is quite a peaceful and enjoyable route to cycle.

The route begins with a modest climb and travels high above the river valley bottom. As the road descends towards Fernie, it crosses over several small feeder streams and creeks that are definitely more noticeable in the spring during the run-off period. The turn-off to Morrissey provides access to a nice riverside picnic area. As the route gets closer to town, homes

Cycling in the Rockies   J. Klein

can be spotted along the river to the west. Eventually the route opens up as you cross between field areas.

Near the end of this section Cokato Road changes to Pine Avenue before meeting

Ridgemont Drive. Unless you really pay attention to all the road signs you would never notice the change in street names. The Trans Canada Trail ends at the junction of Ridgemont Drive in the east side of Fernie.

Rocky Mountains Section 23-24
~5 km
Fernie Trail
Fernie is a beautiful mountain town that is just beginning to experience the growth and excitement similar to the mountain towns like Banff and Whistler. The town lies in the middle of the Elk Valley set along the shore of the Elk River.

The Trans Canada Trail through Fernie runs from Cokato Road on the south end to the Fernie Travel Information Centre at the north end. A quick detour takes you into the heart of historic dowtown Fernie.

> The City of Fernie is named after William Fernie, a gold commissioner of the late 1800's. William Fernie discovered coal nearby, which eventually led to the creation of the Crowsnest Pass Coal Company, the economic basis for the community. The City of Fernie was founded in 1898 and soon became a thriving coal mining town. The mining operations near the community sustained Fernie well into the 20th Century. In recent years, the growing demand for outdoor recreation has created a surge in tourism related businesses. Set amid the heart of the Canadian Rockies, many feel Fernie has the potential to become the next resort phenomenon similar to Whistler and Banff.

The Fernie Aquatic Centre, which is found off Cokoto Road, acts as the southern trailhead for the city. Parking and washrooms are available here. The actual Trans Canada Trail is found about half a kilometre south of the Aquatic Centre at the small black railway bridge across Coal Creek.

The Trail through the city begins at the railway bridge and leads to the Elk River. Follow the trail along the edge of the river and cross Highway 3 at the West Fernie bridge. Continue along the river in the Annex area to the North Fernie bridge where the route rejoins Highway 3. A short jaunt north takes you to the trailhead at the Fernie Visitor Centre.

The Fernie Alpine Resort ski area has grown significantly over the years with nearby resorts and development popping up annually to help meet the demand for winter recreationists. During the summer months, the area boasts a seemingly endless network of trails for mountain bikers and hikers to explore. Other activities such as fishing and rafting are also very popular in the area. Fernie also offers all the creature comforts of a full service community, including ample accommodation, retail shops and outfitters to help service any need you may have when visiting this "last hidden gem" of the Rockies. For more information, be sure to stop by the friendly Travel Information Centre north of town.

An optional route is available at the West Fernie bridge. Follow the highway south over the river to Riverside West Road, which is the first road encountered after the river crossing. Take Riverside West Road west to Beach Road and follow Beach Road west to Burma Road. Burma Road travels north along the west side of the Elk River essentially bypassing the main commercial strip of Fernie but providing a more scenic route for the traveller.

Along Burma Road, the magnificence of the Rockies can be taken in with ample views to the east and north of Fernie. From Burma Road, the route eventually meets up with Aspen Crescent. Follow Aspen Crescent north to Cedar Avenue, then follow Cedar Avenue down to Highway 3. The route then traverses along the west side of the highway north to the Fernie Visitor Centre.

Mount Fernie Provincial Park is found southwest of Fernie next to the cascading Lizard Creek. The provincial park offers camping in a semi-remote and scenic setting, complete with amenities such as flush toilets and running water. There is plenty to do at the park, including several fantastic hiking and biking trails as well as fishing opportunities and even wildlife viewing (the park seems to attract an uncanny amount of black bears, deer and elk). The park is open from the beginning of June to October 15 for camping. Reservations are recommended before arrival, as the park can be quite busy throughout the season.
Call 1-800-689-9025 for park reservations.

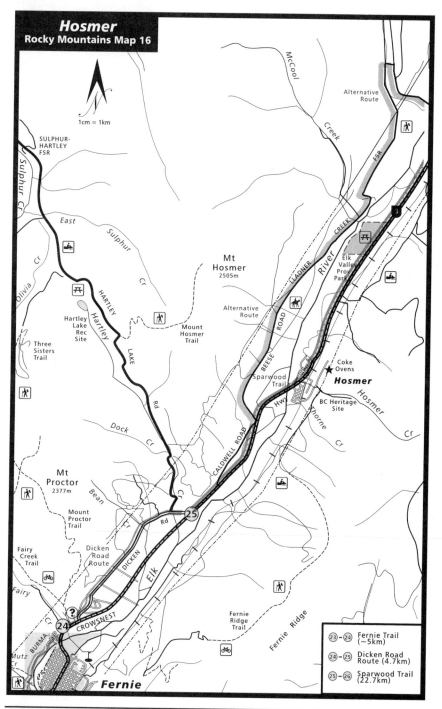

Hosmer
Rocky Mountains Map 16

1cm = 1km

SULPHUR-
HARTLEY FSR

Sulphur Cr

East
Sulphur
Cr

Olivia Cr

Sulphur Cr

HARTLEY

HARTLEY LAKE Rd

Hartley
Lake Rec
Site

Three
Sisters
Trail

Dock Cr

Mt
Proctor
2377m

Mount
Proctor
Trail

Bean Cr

Fairy
Creek
Trail

Fairy Cr

Mutz Cr

BURMA Rd

DICKEN Rd

Fernie

CROWSNEST

Dicken
Road
Route

ELK Rd

McCool Creek

Alternative
Route

FSR

3

Elk
Valley
Prov
Park

Mt
Hosmer
2505m

Mount
Hosmer
Trail

Alternative
Route

LADNER CREEK

ELK RIVER

BEESE ROAD

Sparwood
Trail

Coke
Ovens
★

Hosmer

BC Heritage
Site

Hosmer Cr

CALDWELL ROAD

Thorne Cr

Hwy

25

Fernie
Ridge
Trail

Fernie Ridge

	Fernie Trail (~5km)
23–24	Fernie Trail (~5km)
24–25	Dicken Road Route (4.7km)
25–26	Sparwood Trail (22.7km)

Rocky Mountains Map 16: Hosmer

Rocky Mountains Section 24-25

4.7 km
Dicken Road Route
From the Fernie Visitor Centre, the Trans Canada Trail continues its northern trek along Dicken Road. The road is a paved route that traverses a mainly rural area dotted with the odd home. Dicken Road is a brief detour of Highway 3 and is recommended, especially for hikers. Along the way, the vistas of the surrounding mountains dominate the backdrop scenery. Mount Proctor, at 2,377 m (7,798 ft) sits to the north of the route, while the Fernie Ridge can be seen in the distance to the south. The route intersects Hartley Lake Road where an off-road alternative heads northeast. Cyclists should continue onto the highway.

Overlooking the Elk River　　　*J. Klein*

From the junction with Dicken Road, about 8 km north along the Hartley Lake Road will lead you to the Hartley Lake Forest Recreation site. Be prepared for a steep ascent and vehicle traffic on the winding road. If you are looking for a picturesque mountain camping location with good fishing, this is it. The campsite is also the ideal base camp location to further explore the surrounding mountains including the Mount Hosmer Trail. The road continues north to the Bull River where you can take the Bull River Road downstream to the community of Bull River and the junction with the Trans Canada Trail.

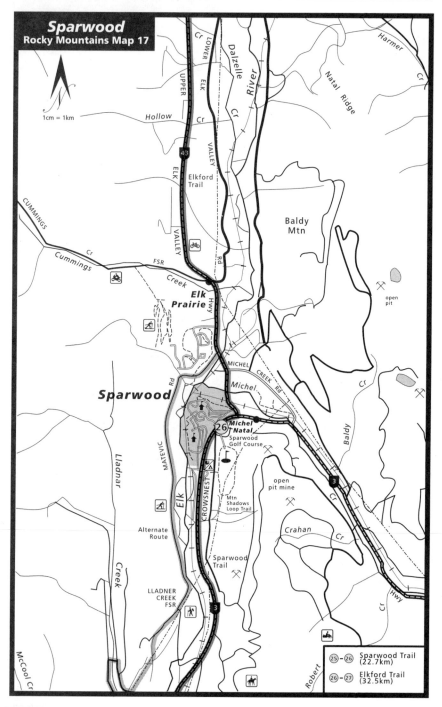

Sparwood
Rocky Mountains Map 17

1cm = 1km

LOWER ELK Cr

UPPER ELK

Hollow Cr

Dalzelle Cr

River

Harmer Cr

Natal Ridge

43

ELK VALLEY

Elkford Trail

Baldy Mtn

CUMMINGS

Cummings Cr

Cummings Creek FSR

ELK VALLEY

Elk Hwy

open pit

Elk Prairie

Sparwood

MICHEL CREEK Rd

Michel

Baldy Cr

Rd

MATEVIC

Lladnar

26 Michel Natal
Sparwood Golf Course

open pit mine

Baldy Cr

3

CROWSNESS

ELK

Mtn Shadows Loop Trail

Crahan Cr

Alternate Route

Sparwood Trail

McCool Cr

LLADNER CREEK FSR

3

Robert

Cr Hwy

| 25 – 26 | Sparwood Trail (22.7km) |
| 26 – 27 | Elkford Trail (32.5km) |

Rocky Mountains Map 17: Sparwood

Rocky Mountains Section 25-26

22.7 km
Sparwood Trail

At the junction of Dicken Road and Highway 3, the route turns north along Highway 3 for the trek towards the mining town of Sparwood. There is ample shoulder space along the highway for bikers, although the highway can be busy at times. The first main site the route passes by is the historical village of Hosmer. Hosmer is located on the east side of the Elk River and is the home of the B.C. Heritage site of the Crowsnest Pass Coke Ovens.

West Side of the Rockies   *J. Marleau*

 The Hosmer Coke ovens can be found just to the north of town and are remnants of an era long gone. In the early 1900's, these ovens were used to purify coal into what was known as 'coke'. Coke was used in heavy industry to create the temperatures required for smelting iron ore and refining other metals. Coal was cooked at around 1,000 degrees Celsius for almost two days to burn off impurities and create coke.

The route continues north past Hosmer and past a splendid picnic area at Elk Valley Provincial Park before reaching Sparwood. The route follows the Elk River along the valley floor and offers splendid views of the surrounding mountains along the way. As you travel into Sparwood, you will pass a number of businesses, a few motels and a small strip mall, which is home to the "largest truck in the world". Past the mall, the Trans Canada Trail meets the junction of Highway 3 and Highway 43. Heading east along Highway 3 will take you to the Crowsnest Pass and the Province of Alberta. North of Sparwood, the Trans Canada Trail begins one of the last legs in its B.C. route as it travels along Highway 43 towards Elkford.

Sparwood is truly a mountain mining town. "The largest truck in the world" displayed at the Information Centre is a sample of the massive vehicles used to remove mining deposits from the many mines in the area. An amazing sight is the way the open pit mining activities on Baldy Mountain are literally taking down the mountain. Sparwood also offers an interesting loop trail through town. In addition to picking up any supplies needed, one can enjoy viewing the murals throughout the downtown core.

In the future, there are plans in place to create a more remote route to bypass the highway north to Sparwood. In the meantime, the best off-highway alternative is to follow Beese Road to Lladner Creek Forest Service Road. The road system follows a historic railway right-of-way high above the Elk River. Following the powerline the road links up with Matevic Road. Matevic Road will bring you out to Highway 43 north of Sparwood. Although, this section is not official Trans Canada Trail routing, it can be a decent alternative to travelling along the busy Highway 3.

To the east of Sparwood, one can find the former community of Michel-Natal. Other than a widening of the area surrounding the highway, only the large pink Michel Hotel remains as a ghostly reminder of the glory days. Michel, named after Chief Michel of the Flathead Indians from the south, was the first community established in the early days of tunnel coal mining. Natal, named after the area in South Africa, arose with further expansion of the mining operations in the area in the late 1920's. The community that eventually developed between the two communities became known as Middletown. Once the centre of coal mining, the towns became covered with coal dust and services were in need of repair. Consequently, people were relocated to Sparwood in 1966 and the old buildings were bulldozed or burned down.

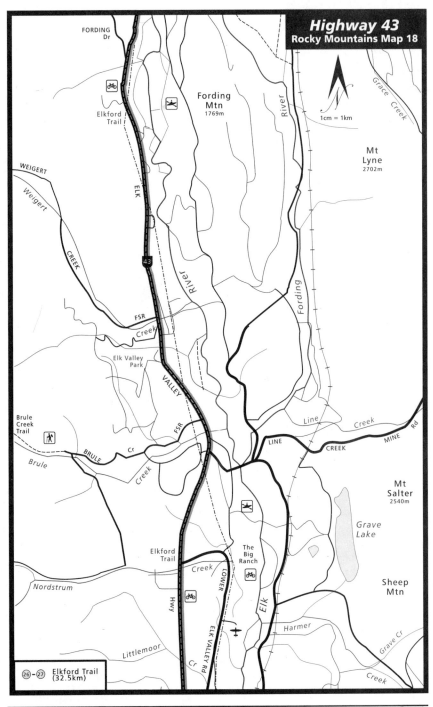

Highway 43
Rocky Mountains Map 18

1cm = 1km

FORDING
Dr

Fording
Mtn
1769m

Mt
Lyne
2702m

Grace Creek

River

Elkford
Trail

ELK

WEIGERT

Weigert

CREEK

43

River

Fording

FSR

Creek

Elk Valley
Park

VALLEY

Line

Creek

MINE Rd

Brule
Creek
Trail

FSR

LINE

CREEK

BRULE

Cr

Brule

Creek

Mt
Salter
2540m

Grave
Lake

Elkford
Trail

Creek

LOWER

The
Big
Ranch

Nordstrum

Hwy

Sheep
Mtn

ELK VALLEY Rd

Elk

Harmer

Cr

Grave Cr

Littlemoor

Creek

㉖–㉗   Elkford Trail
(32.5km)

Rocky Mountains Maps 18/19: Highway 43/Elkford

Rocky Mountains Section 26-27

32.5 km

Elkford Trail

From Sparwood, the Trans Canada Trail heads north towards the town of Elkford and into the wilds of the Upper Elk Valley. Despite the highway travel it is actually provides an enjoyable route, especially for bikers. The quiet highway is not very busy and is quite scenic. There is also plenty of room on the highway shoulder for travellers.

Near the Rockies   *J. Klein*

The highway follows the west side of the Elk River passing several forest service roads and some refreshing creek draws. On warm days, you can feel the cool air as you pass by these streams. Much of the terrain along the valley bottom is made up of a mix of forests and farms. Even more notable is the relatively little elevation gain. To the east and west of the valley bottom, the massive undulating mountains of the Rockies tower over the valley.

 Elkford is a small mining community that was essentially created for the Fording Coal Mines. The mainstay of the Fording operation is located on the Greenhills Range, which can be seen from the Trans Canada Trail as you travel further north. The town of Elkford is found literally at the end of the highway and is the last civilized stop along the trail before Elk Pass. All the basic supplies can be found in the small town.

 If you plan to spend some time in Elkford, there is plenty to do in the area. In and around the town there are over 40 km of hiking and biking trails found in the surrounding mountainsides. A few of the more popular trails are the Lost-Lily Lakes Trails, the Bare Hill Trail and the River Walk. It is best to inquire at the local Travel Information Centre for detailed directions to these loop trails.

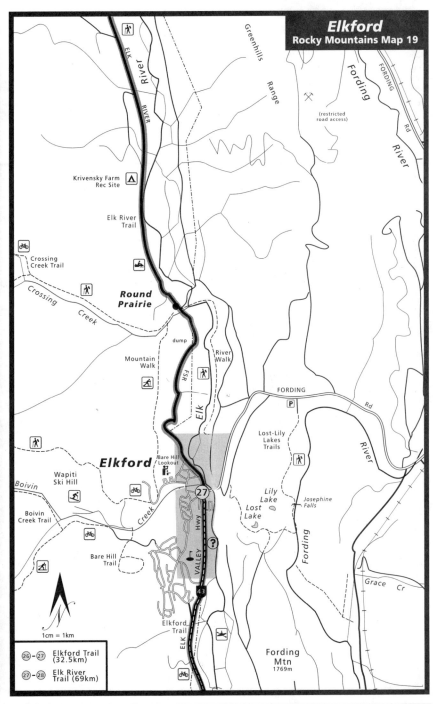

Elkford
Rocky Mountains Map 19

Greenhills Range

Fording River

FORDING Rd

(restricted road access)

ELK RIVER

Krivensky Farm Rec Site

Elk River Trail

Crossing Creek Trail

Crossing Creek

Round Prairie

dump

FSR

River Walk

FORDING

Rd

Mountain Walk

Elk

P

Lost-Lily Lakes Trails

Elkford

Bare Hill Lookout

Fording River

Wapiti Ski Hill

Boivin

Lily Lake

Lost Lake

Josephine Falls

Boivin Creek Trail

Creek

27

Bare Hill Trail

HWY

?

Fording

Grace Cr

VALLEY

43

N

Elkford Trail

1cm = 1km

ELK

Fording Mtn
1769m

26–27 Elkford Trail (32.5km)

27–28 Elk River Trail (69km)

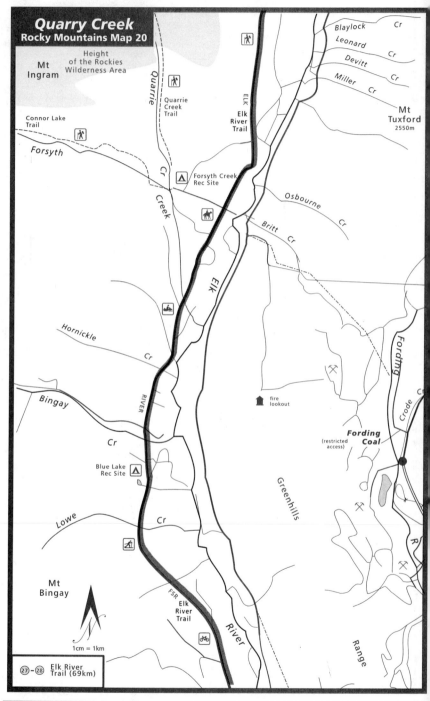

Quarry Creek
Rocky Mountains Map 20

Mt Ingram

Height of the Rockies Wilderness Area

Quarrie Creek Trail

Elk River Trail

Blaylock Cr

Leonard Cr

Devitt Cr

Miller Cr

Mt Tuxford
2550m

Connor Lake Trail

Forsyth

Forsyth Creek Rec Site

Osbourne Cr

Britt Cr

Creek

Elk

Hornickle Cr

Bingay

RIVER

Cr

Fording

Crode Cr

fire lookout

Fording Coal
(restricted access)

Blue Lake Rec Site

Lowe Cr

Greenhills

Mt Bingay

FSR
Elk River Trail

River

Range

1cm = 1km

27 – 28 Elk River Trail (69km)

Rocky Mountains Maps 20-22 Quarry Creek/ Elk River/Elk Pass

Rocky Mountains Section 27-28

69 km

Elk River Trail

The Elk River Trail portion of the route is the last leg of the route in eastern British Columbia. This section of the trail is also one of the most fascinating and magnificent portions of the route, a perfect way to finish or begin your Trans Canada Trail adventure. The route travels along the valley bottom of what remains wilderness terrain. Along with the spectacular scenery, chances are that you may even catch a glimpse of a wild animal such as a moose, Rocky Mountain bighorn sheep, deer, black bear or perhaps even a grizzly bear!

Park Cabin   J. Marleau

From Elkford, the Trans Canada Trail follows the Elk River Forest Service Road north into the Upper Elk Valley. Essentially, Highway 43 stops just north of town and becomes a gravel road. The route winds its way through the valley bottom following the Elk River and crossing the river in several locations. Along the way, most of the terrain is dominated by forest cover, interrupted by the odd forest access road or cut block. As you trek further up the valley, the scenery simply gets better as the jagged mountains to the east and west of the valley dominate the landscape.

The road is generally in good shape throughout its entirety except for a few spots that may get muddy during runoff periods. Although there are a few dips and hills, you will generally be gaining elevation on a steady but easy grade. Vehicular traffic exists but is rarely a concern.

The many creeks provide a refreshing place to stop while the ample Forest Recreation sites provide good reference points. They are located about 10 km apart and provide ideal camping or picnic locations. The first real building the route encounters in the valley is a small cabin off the east side of the road about 5 km south of the park headquarters. The cabin is user-maintained complete with a wood stove and bunks, making a great overnight location if available.

Other than the main trail up the valley, there are also countless other trails that can be easily accessed off the main route. Most trails lead deep into the mountains either to the east or west of the Trans Canada Trail.

Not far north of the cabin, lies the Elk Lakes Provincial Park Headquarters tucked at the end of a short trail from the road. The park headquarters is a nice log structure building, which is staffed throughout the summer season. Unfortunately, the building is locked during the off-season. From the headquarters, the Trans Canada Trail continues north along an old road that leads over the Elk Pass and to Alberta.

> *Grizzly bears often frequent the upper reaches of the Elk Valley, especially around the Cadorna Creek basin south to Aldridge Creek. Although grizzlies are very reclusive by nature, which is good for both humans and the bears, in this section grizzly tracks can sometimes be spotted along the Elk River just metres away from the Trans Canada Trail. Please take appropriate precautions when travelling this section of the route. Above all, stay on the trail and exercise responsible camping practices for the safety and enjoyment of yourself and other travellers on the Trans Canada Trail.*

> *The only accommodation along the stretch of trail north of Elkford is backcountry camping. No trace camping is permitted outside of park land, although it is recommended to camp at one of the many Forest Recreation campsites that are found along this 69 km stretch of trail. There are eight established Forestry Recreation camping areas along the route with no more than about 10 km distance between each area. Most of these camping areas are well established with fire rings and/or even pit toilets at some sites. Please ensure you leave your campsite clean or even cleaner than when you arrived.*

The terrain to the north of Elkford is largely wild and rugged. A round trip from Elkford to the park headquarters in a vehicle can easily take over 12 hours and help is not readily available. Be prepared for wilderness conditions with unpredictable mountain weather conditions.

Rocky Mountains Section 28-29

5 km

Elk Pass Trail

The Elk Lakes Provincial Park Headquarters is a unique site set amid such rugged terrain in literally the middle of nowhere. The Trans Canada Trail heads north over the Elk Pass and to Alberta along an old powerline access road that was built some time ago. The road is no longer used by vehicles and provides the ideal base for Trans Canada Trail travellers wishing to access the Great Divide between Alberta and British Columbia.

At Elk Pass, the road meets up with the Elk Pass Trail in Peter Lougheed Provincial Park in Alberta. This trail will take you down to the parking area off Kananaskis Lakes Trail, which is actually a road, where the Trans Canada Trail

Approaching Elk Pass   J. Klein

The Elk Lakes Provincial Park encompasses some 17,325 hectares of fragile mountain terrain. In addition to the impressive mountain peaks another park highlight are the Elk Lakes. The infamous alpine lakes can be found via a hiking trail from the park headquarters and are well worth the visit. Other popular mountain hikes in the area include a viewpoint trail on the Lower Elk Lake, the Petain Falls and Glacier Trail and Cadorna Lake Trail. Camping is permitted within the park at designated camping areas found near the Upper and Lower Elk Lakes as well as near the headwaters of the Petain Creek.

The terrain over the Elk Pass is easily accessible with only a moderate elevation gain. Waters on the B.C. side of the Great Divide flow to the Pacific Ocean while those on the Alberta side flow to the Atlantic Ocean. There is a hiking trail over the pass in Elk Lakes Provincial Park (no cycling is allowed in the park) or cyclists can continue on the powerline service road. The powerline brings power from Alberta to supply the needs of the coal mines on the B.C. side of the boundary.

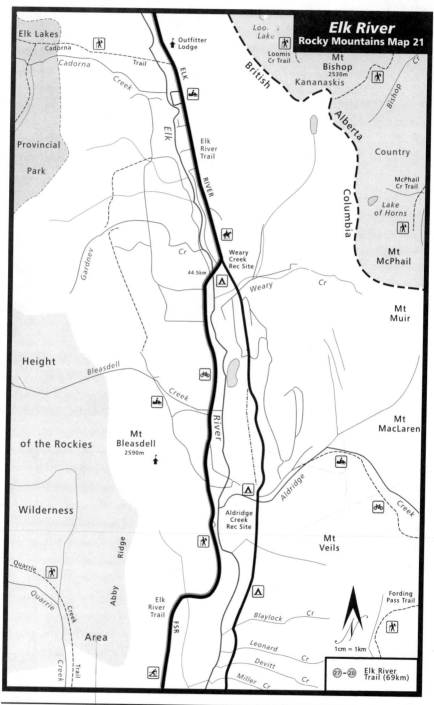

Elk River
Rocky Mountains Map 21

Elk Lakes

Cadorna

Cadorna   Trail

Creek

Outfitter
Lodge

Loomis
Lake

Loomis
Cr Trail

British

Mt
Bishop
2530m
Kananaskis

Alberta

Bishop
Cr

ELK

Elk
River
Trail

Provincial

Park

Country

ELK

McPhail
Cr Trail

RIVER

Columbia

Lake
of Horns

Mt
McPhail

Gardney

Cr

44.5km

Weary
Creek
Rec Site

Weary

Cr

Mt
Muir

Height

Bleasdell

Creek

River

Weary

Mt
MacLaren

of the Rockies

Mt
Bleasdell
2590m

Aldridge

Creek

Wilderness

River

Aldridge
Creek
Rec Site

Mt
Veils

Abby

Ridge

Quarrie

Quarrie

Creek

Elk
River
Trail

FSR

Fording
Pass Trail

N

Area

Creek

Trail

Blaylock   Cr

Leonard   Cr

Devitt   Cr

Miller   Cr

1cm = 1km

27 – 28   Elk River
Trail (69km)

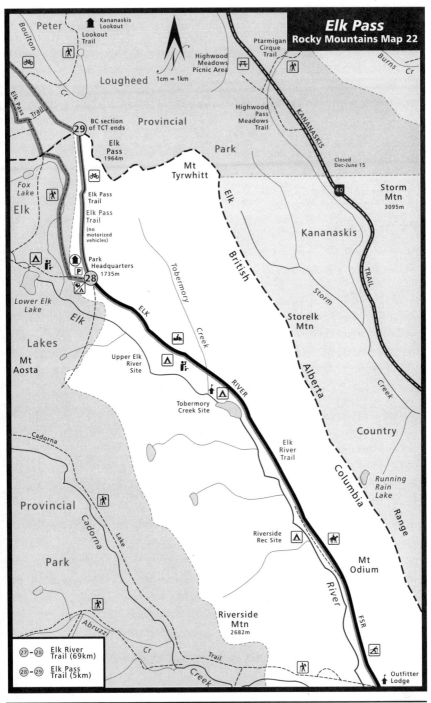

Elk Pass
Rocky Mountains Map 22

1cm = 1km

Peter

Kananaskis Lookout
Lookout Trail

Boulton Cr

Lougheed

Highwood Meadows Picnic Area

Ptarmigan Cirque Trail

Burns Cr

Elk Pass Trail

BC section of TCT ends

Elk Pass 1964m

Provincial

Park

Highwood Pass Meadows Trail

KANANASKIS

Closed Dec-June 15

Fox Lake

Mt Tyrwhitt

Storm Mtn 3095m

Elk

Elk Pass Trail

Elk Pass Trail (no motorized vehicles)

Kananaskis

British

40

Park Headquarters 1735m

Lower Elk Lake

Elk

Tobermory Creek

Storm

Storelk Mtn

Lakes

Mt Aosta

Upper Elk River Site

ELK

RIVER

Alberta

TRAIL

Creek

Tobermory Creek Site

Elk River Trail

Country

Cadorna

Columbia

Running Rain Lake

Provincial

Cadorna Lake

Riverside Rec Site

Range

Park

Mt Odium

River

Riverside Mtn 2682m

Abruzzi Cr

Trail

FSR

Creek

Outfitter Lodge

	Elk River Trail (69km)
27 - 28	
28 - 29	Elk Pass Trail (5km)

ROCKY MOUNTAINS SERVICE PROVIDERS

Accommodations

HI-Fernie

Friendly and relaxed atmosphere.
Whitewater rafting.

892 6th Avenue
Fernie, BC, V0B 1M0
(250) 423-6811

www.hihostels.bc.ca

HI-Cranbrook

Summer Hostel close to
Parks, Trails, and Lakes.

Bag 9000, 2700 College Way
Cranbrook, BC, V1C 5L7
(250) 489-8282

www.hihostels.bc.ca

Emery's Mountain View B&B

Located on TCT. Friendly atmosphere.

183 Wardner- Fort Steele Rd.
Fort Steele, BC, V0B 1N0
(250) 426-4756
www.bbcanada.com/3207.html

Bull River Guest Ranch

Guest Ranch with horseback riding,
fishing, canoeing, hiking and
much more...

P.O. BOX 133
Cranbrook, BC, V1C 4H7
(250) 429-3760
bullriverranch@cyberlink.bc.ca

Lizard Creek Lodge

Luxury Accommodation. Complimentary
shuttle service to and from Fernie.

5346 Highline Drive
Fernie Alpine Resort
Fernie, BC, V0B 1M1
(250) 423-2057
info@lizardcreek.com

Supplies & Services

Fernie Tourism Association

Four-season information and
resevation service: events, accommodations, restaurants & outdoor
advantures.

1-888-754-7325
info@fernietourism.com
www.fernietourism.com

Attractions

Creston Valley Wildlife Centre

Waterfowl, viewing plantations,
nature trails and interpretive centre
P.O. Box 640
Creston, BC, V0B 1G0
(250) 428-3260

Fort Steele Heritage Town

Over 60 Heritage shops, homes, and
display buildings.

Fort Steele, BC, V0B 1N0
(250) 426-7352
www.heritage.gov.bc.ca

WHITE SHIPS. BLUE SEAS.

WHAT OUR *most* BEAUTIFUL PLACES

HAVE IN COMMON.

British Columbia's coastline is blessed with an abundance of breathtaking natural wonders. With over 40 passenger and vehicle carrying vessels serving up to 46 ports of call, BC Ferries can show you them all: Victoria and Vancouver Island, the Gulf Islands, the Sunshine Coast, the Inside Passage, Discovery Coast Passage, and Queen Charlotte Islands. Set sail with us and experience the immense beauty of British Columbia first-hand. You'll find each trip more than memorable. In fact, if it wasn't for the water, you'd feel the earth move.

Toll-free in B.C. 1-888-BC FERRY (250)386-3431 1112 Fort Street, Victoria, B.C. Canada V8V 4V2 **www.bcferries.com**

BC FERRIES

Map Index

A

Abbotsford 120
Adra Station 197
Albion Trail 110
Anaconda Station 226
Arawana Station 197
Arawana Station Trail 192
Arbutus Ridge 70
Ardmore 70
Arlington Lakes Trail 208, 211
Arrow Creek 283
Atchelitz 126
Aurum Station 148

B

Backier 182
Baker 300
Bald Range Trail 189
Bamberton 70
Barrowtown 120
Baynes Lake Route 305
Beacon Hill Park 25
Beacon Hill Trail 25
Beaver Falls 259
Beaver Lake 65
Beaverdell Trail 214
Belcarra Regional Park 100
Belfort Trail 174
Boundary Falle Station 226
Bowen Park Route 61
Bradner 116
Braeloch 202
Brentwood Bay 65
British Properties 83
Brodie Trail 154, 158
Brookmere Trail 154, 158
Bull River 303
Burnaby Heights Trail 95
Burnaby Mountain Park 95, 100
Burnaby Park Trail 95, 100
Burnaby 95, 100
Burrard Inlet 76, 83, 88, 95

C

Canyon Heights 83
Canyon 283
Capilano Park Trail 83
Carmi Station Detour 214
Casino 259
Cassidy Route 55, 58
Cedar 58
Center Creek Trail 135
Chain Lake Trail 182
Chase River 58
Chemainus 50
Chemainus Route 50, 55
Chilliwack Lake Prov Park 140
Chilliwack Lake Trail 135
Chinatown & Portside Trail 88, 95
Christina Lake Trail 243
Chute Lake Trail 197
Cinnabar Valley 58
Clayburn Creek Trail 120
Clayburn Trail 120
Coal Harbour Trail 88
Coalmount Trail 170
Cokato Road Route 312
Coldwater River Prov Park 154
Colquitz 25, 65
Columbia Gardens 259

Colwood 30, 65
Cooksen Station 208, 211
Coquihalla Station 153
Coquihalla Summit Rec Area 150, 153
Coquihalla Summit Trail 148, 150, 153
Coquitlam River Trial 104
Coquitlam 100, 104
Cordova Bay 65
Coulfeid 76
Cowichan River Provincial Park 43
Cowichan River Railgrade Trail 40, 43
Cowichan Valley Demonstration Forest 43
Cowichan Valley Trail 40, 43
Cranbrook Trail 295
Crescent Beach 189
Creston Route 280, 283
Creston Valley Route 280
Creston Valley Wildlife Management Area ... 280
Creston Valley Wildlife Trail 280
Crofton Route 50
Crump Trail 186, 189
Cultus Connector 126
Cultus Lake Prov Park 126
Cultus Lake 126
Cultus Trail 126
Cypress Provincial Park 76

D

Deep Cove 70
Dellwye Station 214
Demuth Station Trail 182, 186
Departure Bay 61
Dewdney Trail East 243, 252
Dewdney Trail 243
Dicken Road Route 316
Duncan 40

E

Eagle Creek Trail 76
East Cypress Creek Trail 76
East Trail Route 259
Edgemont Trail 83
Eholt Station 234
Eholt Station Trail 226
Elk Lakes Provincail Park 328, 329
Elk Pass Trail 329
Elk Prairie 318
Elk River Trail 323, 324, 328, 329
Elkford Trail 318, 321, 323
Elko Route 308
Erickson 283
Erris Station Trail 174, 179
Esquimalt Harbor 30
Esquimalt 25, 65
Extension 58

F

Faulder Trail 186, 189
Fenwich Road Route 303
Fernie Trail 312, 316
Fisherman Station Trail 234, 238
Fording Coal 324
Forest Knolls 110
Fort Langley Heritage Trail 110
Fort Steele Trail 295, 300
Fraser River 110, 116, 120
Fusee Lake Route 305, 308

G

Galloping Goose Trail 25, 30, 65
Galloway 305
Gifford Matsqui 116

Gilpin 238
Glen Valley 116
Gleneagles 76
Glenfir Station 197
Glenmerry 259
Glenora 40
Goat Mountain Trail 234, 238
Golden Ears Prov Park 110
Goldstream Provincial Park 30
Granby Station 238
Grand Forks Trail 238
Granite City 170
Greendale 120, 126
Greenwood Trail 226, 234
Guildford Way Trail 100, 104

H
Haney Heritage Trail 110
Harmac 58
Hastings Trail 95
Hatzic 120
Height of the Rockies Wilderness Area 328
Hillcrest 40
Hodges Station Trail 234
Hope Heritage Trial 143
Hope 143
Horseshoe Bay 76
Hosmer 316
Howe Sound 76
Hwy 22A Route 259
Hwy 3B Route 259
Hydraulic Lake Trail 208, 211

I
Iago Station 150
Interim Connector Trail 120
Interim Trail – Abbotsford 116
Interim Trail – Langley 116
International Ridge Prov Park 126
Isidore Canyon Trail 295

J
Jaffray Trail 303, 305
Jellicoe Station Trail 179, 182
Jersey 269
Jessica Trail 148, 150
Juliet Trail 153, 154
Jura Station 174, 179

K
Kananaskis Country 328, 329
Keating 65
Kettle River Park Trail 221
Kettle River Trail 238, 243
Kettle Valley 221
Kikomun Creek Prov Park 305
Kilgard 120
Kinsol Trail 40
Kirton Station 186
Kitchener Creek Route 283, 285
Kitchener 283
Kootenay Pass – East Route 269, 277, 279, 280
Kootenay River 303
Kootenay Summit Trail 269
Kulleet Bay 55
Kuper Island 50

L
Ladysmith Harbour 55
Ladysmith Route 55
Lake Cowichan 43
Lake Koocanusa 305
Lakevale Station 211
Langford 30, 65
Langford Lake 30

Langford Trial 30
Larson Bench Trail 131
Leach Lake 280
Lear Station 148
Liumchen Trail 126
Lochside Trail – Side Route 65, 70
Lois Station 214
Lois Station Trail 211, 214
Lorna Station 202
Lorna Station Trail 197, 202
Lost Creek Route 265, 269
Lumberton 292

M
Malahat Alternate Route 65, 70
Malahat Route 30, 36
Manning Station 166
Maple Ridge Dike Trial 110
Maple Ridge 110
Matsqui Island 116
Matsqui Trail 116, 120
Mcculloch 208
McCulloch Trail 202, 208
Michel Natal Route 318
Midway Trail 221, 226
Milford Station Trail 182
Mill Bay 70
Millstream 65
Mission 116, 120
Montrose 259
Moody Center Trail 100
Moody Inlet Trail 100
Morrissey 312
Mosquito Creek Trail 83
Mount Lehman 116
Moyie Lake Route 290
Moyie River Route 285, 288, 290
Myra Canyon Trail 202, 208
Myra Station 202, 208

N
Nanaimo Harbour 61
Nanaimo 61
Nanaimo Waterfront Trail 61
Naramata 197
Nelson Creek Trail 76
Nelway 265
Nesakwatch Valley Trail 131, 135
Newcastle Island 61
Newcastle Provincial Park 61
Niagara 234, 238
North Duncan Route 50
North Duncan Trail 40
North PoCo Trail 104
North Vancouver 83, 95

O
Odlum 143
Okanagan Lake 192
Okanagan Lake 189, 197
Okanagan Mission (Kelowna) 202
Okanagan Mountain Prov Park 197
Okangan Lakeview Trail 197
Old Cascade Hwy East 243, 252
Old Cascade Hwy West Trail 243
Old Railgrade Trail 252
Osprey Lake Trail 182
Othello Canyon Trail 143, 148
Otter Lake 166, 170
Otter Valley Trail 158, 166

P
Paldi Trail 40, 43
Paleface pass Trail 135

Parr Tail 170, 174
Peavine Valley Trail 290, 292
Pend D'Oreille River Route 259, 265
Penticton Trail 192
Peravine Valley Trail 295
Peter Lougheed Provincail Park 329
Pickering Hills Route 303, 305
Picture Valley Route 300
Pitt Meadows Dike Trail 104, 110
Pitt Meadows 104
Pitt River 104
Poplar Grove 192
Port Coquitlam 104
Port Moody Arm 100
Port Moody 100
Portage Inlet 25
Portia Station 148, 150
Prairie Valley Station 189
Princeton Trail 174
Promontory 126

R

Remac 265
Rhone Trail 218
Ridgedale 120
River Road Route 308, 312
River Trail 110, 116
Roaneys Station 174
Rock Creek 221
Rock Ovens Trail 197
Romeo Station 153
Rossland 252
Rotary Vedder River Trail 120, 126
Round Prairie 323
Ruth Station Trail 202
Ryan 288
Ryder Lake 126

S

Saanich Inlet 70
Saanichton 65, 70
Sahtlam 40
Salmo River Route 265
Saltair 50, 55
Sardis 126
Scenic Park Trail 95
Seabus 88
Seaview Walk Trail 76
Separation Lakes Trail 174, 179
Seven Mile Dam Road Route 259
Shawnigan Lake 36, 70
Shawnigan Lake Route 36
Shoreline Trail 100
Shylock Station 148, 150
Sidney 70
Silica 252
Silver Creek 143
Silver Lake Trail 143
Silver Skagit Trail 140, 143
Silver Valley 110
Silverdale 116
Silverhill 116
Silverhope – Hicks Trail 140
Skyline Trail 76, 83
Sleese Trail 131
Slesse Park 126, 131
Somenos 40, 50
Sooke Hills Wilderness Regional Park 30, 36
Sooke Lake 36
South False Creek Trail 88
South Fort Steele Route 300
South Salmo River Route 265
South Wellington 58

Southbelt Trail 252
Sparwood Trail 316, 318
Spearing Station Trail 158
St Eugene Mission 295
Stagleap Provincial Park 269
Stanley Park Trail 88
Starks 58, 61
Straition 120
Stuart Channel 50
Sumas Mountain Trail 120
Sumas River Trail 120
Sumas Vedder Trail 120
Summerland – Penticton Trail 192
Summerland 189, 197
Summerland Trail 189, 192
Swartz Bay 70

T

Tamihi Trail 126, 131
Taurus Station Trail 218
Thalia Station Trail 158
The Abyss Trail 58, 61
The Parkway Trail 61
The West Gorge Trail 25
Thetis Lake 30
Thetis Lake Reg Park 30
Thirsk Lake Trail 182, 186
Thirsk Station 182, 186
Thurstion Trail 131
Tillicum Park 25
Town Center Trail 104
Trail 259
Trout Creek 189, 197
Tulameen Trail 166, 170

U

UBC Research Forest 110
Upper Silverhope Trail 135, 140

V

Vancouver 88, 95
Vedder Crossing 126
Victoria Harbour 25
Victoria 25
View Royal 25, 65

W

Walnut Grove 110
Waneta Junction 259
Waneta 259
Wardner 303
Warfield 252
Waterfront Trail 83, 88
West Cypress Creek Trail 76
West End Trail 88
West Hieghts 116
West Kettle River Trail 218, 221
West Shawnigan Lake Route 36, 40
West Trail Route 252, 259
West Vancouver Bike Route 76, 83
West Vancouver 76, 83
Westbench 192
Westbridge 221
Westholme 50
White Rapids Interim Route 58
White Rapids Interim Trail 61
Whonnocle 116
Winslow Station 189, 192
Wynndel 280

Y

Yahk Route 285, 288
Yarrow 126

Z

Zamora Station Trail 221